DEDICATION

For Helen, Rose and Lucy . . .
With Love

TABLE OF CONTENTS

Praise for . . .

The Writer's Guide to Everyday Life in Regency and Victorian England

"Extremely useful for authors, an admirable browsing companion for readers; packed with little nuggets of information, the fruit obviously of wide reading and research."

—Anthony Lejeune, author of *The Gentlemen's Club of London*

"*The Writer's Guide to Everyday Life in Regency and Victorian England* is just what the writer needs to begin that Regency or British historical they have always wanted to write. From the proper time to mourn one's mother-in-law to the dicey problems of how to address a duke, author Kristine Hughes offers up just the right amount of information in an interesting and informative style that is definitely user-friendly. Any writer from the novice to the multi-published will want this one on their bookshelves. The year-by-year account at the end of the book is particularly helpful. Thank you, Ms. Hughes!"

—Joan Overfield, author of more than fifteen books, including *A Rose in Scotland* and *Exquisite*

"This is an extremely informative and entertaining tool for historical writers, filled with fascinating and illuminating facts about high life and low life, country and city, agriculture and industry. Subject bibliographies and timelines make this an easy-to-use reference. Ms. Hughes, through painstaking research, presents a detailed portrait of this century of rapid change and innovation. Society, politics, transportation, food and drink, the arts, and more—it's all here. Even Victoria would be amused—and impressed!"

—Margaret Evans Porter, best-selling and award-winning author of *Road to Ruin* and *Dangerous Diversions*

"*The Writer's Guide to Everyday Life to Regency and Victorian England* is a superb resource for writers of the nineteenth-century British historicals. I wish it had been available when I started writing. Much time and pain would have been saved!"

—Mary Jo Putney

"A fabulous resource. No writer who sets work in nineteenth-century England should ever be without this book. The very accessible format of the volume is a rare delight and Ms. Hughes's attention to consise detail will thrill you."

—Stella Cameron, best-selling author of *The Best Revenge* and *Wait for Me*

A book writers will find enormously helpful . . . I find it jolly useful."

—Dr. David Parker, Curator, The Dickens House Museum, London

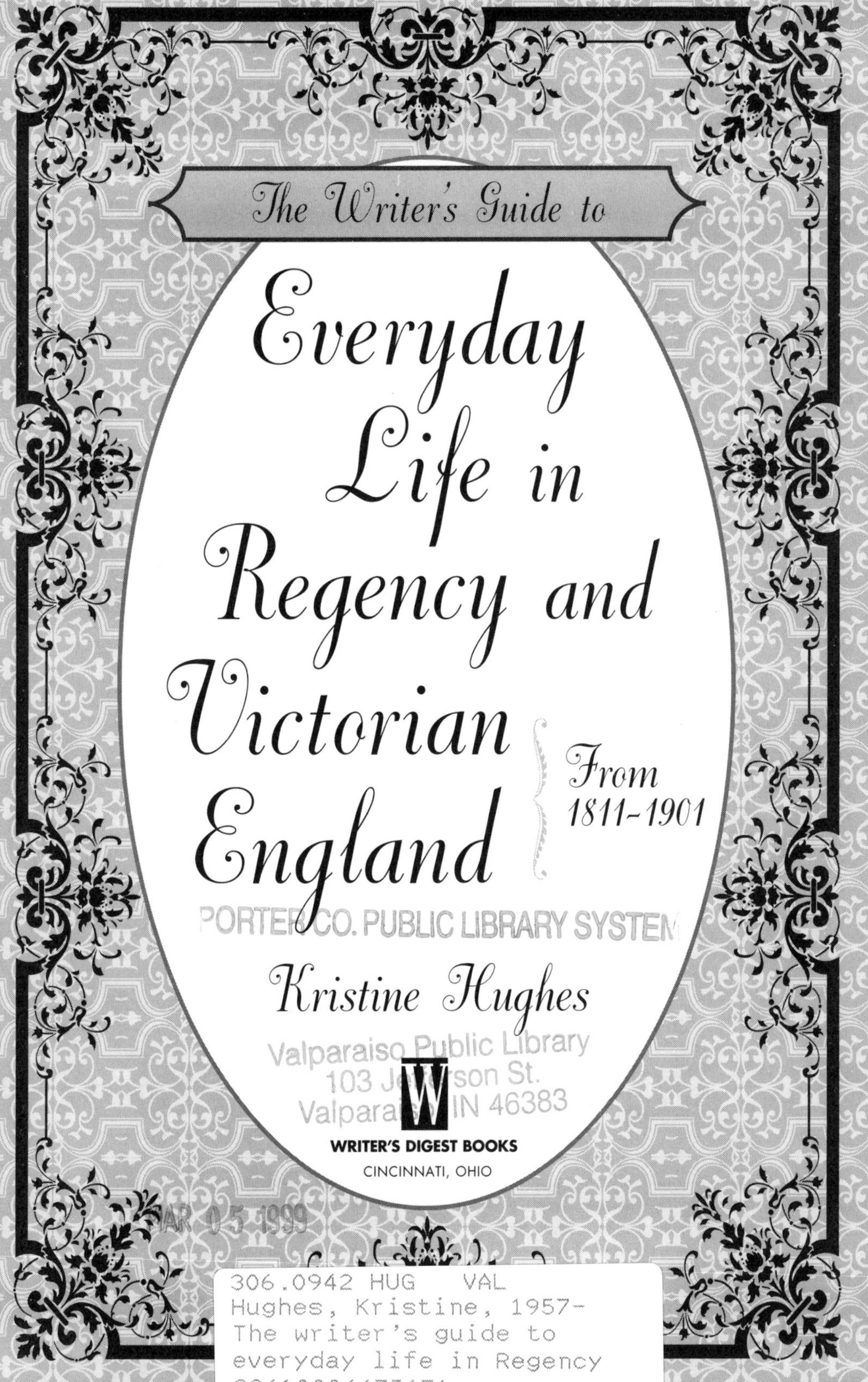

The Writer's Guide to

Everyday Life in Regency and Victorian England

From 1811–1901

Kristine Hughes

WRITER'S DIGEST BOOKS
CINCINNATI, OHIO

ABOUT THE AUTHOR

Kristine Hughes has self-published books on various aspects of British history and is a regular contributor to a number of publications, including *Romantic Times, Regency Plume, The Common Reader Literary Quarterly* and *The Medieval Times.* She also reviews books for *Publishers Weekly, Romantic Times* and *Lady's Gallery Magazine.* She is a frequent speaker and writer's conferences and historic seminars, and conducts biannual research tours to Great Britain. She lives in Naples, Florida.

 Published by Writer's Digest Books, an imprint of F&W Publications, Inc., 1507 Dana Avenue, Cincinnati, Ohio 45207. (800) 289-0963. First edition.

Other fine Writer's Digest Books are available from your local bookstore or direct from the publisher.

02 01 00 99 98 5 4 3 2 1

Library of Congress Cataloging-in-Publication Data

Hughes, Kristine.
The writer's guide to everyday life in Regency and Victorian England / Kristine Hughes
p. cm.
Includes bibliographical references and index.
ISBN 0-89879-812-4 (alk. paper)
1. England—Social life and customs—19th century—Handbooks, manuals, etc. 2. Great Britain—History—Victoria, 1837–1901—Handbooks, manuals, etc. 3. Historical fiction—Authorship—Handbooks, manuals, etc. 4. Regency—England—Handbooks, manuals, etc. I. Title.
Drawing—Technique. I. Title.
DA533.H93 1998
306′.0942′09034—dc21 97-48716
CIP

Content edited by Roseann S. Biederman
Production edited by Patrick G. Souhan
Interior designed by Sandy Kent
Cover designed by Angela Lennert Wilcox

PART THREE:

Society

INTRODUCTION

The nineteenth century was an era of great transition. Technological, industrial and manufacturing advancements altered every aspect of daily life, including transportation, commerce and law. Between the regency of King George III and the reign of Queen Victoria, a person might have witnessed the advent of steam locomotives, photography, refrigeration or the telegraph. This progress heralded a wealth of new employment opportunities, speculative plans for financial gain and a general sense of well-being as overall living conditions improved.

The nineteenth century was also a time of paradox, for while the people embraced most of these advancements, they adhered more rigidly than ever to time-honored social values and rules of behavior. Each person, at whatever level in society, was aware of his or her place in that society and the social restrictions or obligations thereof. And, should anyone have been in doubt as to how to proceed, he or she might have read one of the hundreds of etiquette books published during the period.

Just as the nineteenth century was a blend of technology and social niceties, so too does this book present a well-balanced mix of both elements. The necessary information, facts and figures are represented in this book through its text, numerous time lines, illustrations, charts and in-depth bibliographies, saving the reader hours of valuable research time. In addition, this book presents the personal side of nineteenth-century history through excerpts from contemporary diaries and letters. Providing insight into the social life of the era, these firsthand accounts will prove invaluable to the student of history. Authors, researchers and period enthusiasts will find the book's content to be concise, while at the same time offering details that would be difficult to uncover elsewhere. Though similar books have attempted to scratch the surface of many areas of daily life, *The Writer's Guide to Everyday Life in Regency and Victorian England* provides those substantial details necessary to solid story construction.

FREQUENTLY CITED SOURCES

Creevey, Thomas—Member of Parliament born March 1768. Married a wealthy widow, upon whose death Creevey was reduced to living on about two hundred pounds per year. Apparently, Creevey had no home or property of his own and lived as a guest, staying at the homes of various friends. He died in 1838.

Maxwell, Sir Herbert, ed. *The Creevey Papers.* 2 vols. New York: E.P. Dutton & Co., 1903.

Farington, Joseph—His diary dates from July 13, 1793, to December 30, 1821. Farington, a member of the Royal Academy, was an artist and left behind many topographical drawings. In London, the diary was first published in installments in the *Morning Post,* beginning January 23, 1922.

Greig, James, ed. *The Farington Diary.* 2 vols. New York: George H. Doran Co., 1923.

Greville, Charles Cavendish Fulke—Born April 2, 1794, grandson of the fifth Lord Warwick; educated Eton and Oxford. First held secretaryship of Jamaica, and in 1821 became Clerk of the Council in Ordinary. Greville went on to hold a permanent office in the Privy Council for the next forty years. During the last twenty years of his life, Greville occupied a suite of rooms in the house of Earl Granville in Bruton Street, where he died January 18, 1865.

Reeve, Henry, ed. *The Greville Memoirs: A Journal of the Reigns of King George IV and King William IV.* 2 vols. New York: D. Appleton & Co., 1875.

Gronow, Captain Rees Howell—Born 1794, Gronow's reminiscences were first published in 1862 and cover the Regency to early Victorian periods. Gronow spent six years in the army, retiring in October 1821. In 1831, Gronow moved into a house in Chesterfield Street, Mayfair, which had belonged to Beau Brummell. Gronow was elected a member of Parliament in 1832.

Hibbert, Christopher, ed. *Captain Gronow: His Reminiscences of Regency and Victorian Life 1810–60.* London: Kyle Cathie Ltd., 1991.

The Habits of Good Society—The book was published, with the identity of its author being a mystery. The first line of its preface reads, "I am the Man in the Club-Window. Which club and which window? you ask, and is it in Pall Mall or St. James' Street? I regret that I must decline to satisfy your very laudable curiosity." Regardless of who the author really was, the book, a guide to manners and etiquette, contains detailed insight into the workings of nineteenth-century society.

The Habits of Good Society. New York: Carleton, 1864.

Puckler-Muskau, Prince Hermann—The prince was a German noble upon whom Count Smorltork, of Dickens's *Pickwick Papers,* was based. After finding himself in debt, he and his princess decided to divorce so that Puckler-Muskau might go to England in search of a rich wife. He returned to Germany with neither a new wife nor a fortune, but, philosophically, saw his stay as an interesting experience. The letters were first published in 1832.

Butler, E.M., ed. *A Regency Visitor: The English Tour of Prince Puckler-Muskau Described in His Letters 1826–1828.* London: Collins, 1957.

Spencer, Lady Sarah—Born July 29, 1787, the eldest daughter of the second earl of Spencer went on to marry Lord Lyttleton at the age of twenty-six. In 1838, a year after her husband's death, Lady Sarah became a lady in waiting to Queen Victoria and in 1842 was made governess to the royal children, a post she held for nine years. She died on April 13, 1870, at the age of eighty-two.

Wyndham, Mrs. Hugh, ed. *Correspondence of Sarah Spencer Lady Lyttelton.* London: John Murray, Ltd., 1912.

Part One

Everyday Life

Chapter One

Lighting, Heating and Plumbing

LIGHTING

During the nineteenth century, modes of lighting underwent drastic changes. At the beginning of the century, primitive means of lighting, rush lights and tallow candles, were the norm, while by the century's end, electricity was available to all. These innovations affected all walks and aspects of daily life: shopping, theaters, home life and the workplace. With the advent of oil lamps, labor hours could be extended, and with gaslight, social evenings were no longer confined to those nights on which a full moon could be depended upon to light the way home.

Rush Lights

As only the nobility could afford wax candles, and even tallow candles were beyond the means of most of the population, rush lights were the most common form of illumination for most country people early in the nineteenth century. They could be made at home when the cut rushes were still green. After being soaked, the hard outer skin of the rushes was peeled away, leaving the pith exposed, which made an excellent wick. The rush was then dipped into warm animal fat, mutton fat being the best for this purpose. Depending to an extent upon what type of fat was used and also the length of the rush, these lights could smoke and emit an unpleasant odor. While a fifteen-inch rush only burned for about half an hour, one that was twenty-eight inches in length could burn for an hour.

When the rush was being used as a night light, it was usually placed beneath a perforated metal shade. A person could control the burning time of the rush by placing two pins into the pith, which would extinguish the rush light once it had burned down to the pins. These lights were also used by servants and tradesmen and could be placed in a holder, which kept the rush at an angle via a notch or spring. This way, the rush never required snuffing, as it only had to be moved up in the holder as it burned. In some cities and towns, rushes were still being used and sold as late as the mid-nineteenth century.

Candles

Candles were first made by repeatedly dipping the wicks in wax or tallow until achieving the desired circumference. Candle molds were invented in the fifteenth century, and the candle-making machine in the nineteenth century. Tallow candles were taxed at one pence per pound (see chapter nine for further explanation of monetary units) from 1709 to 1831 and, officially, could only be purchased from licensed chandlers. However, this tax had no impact on candles made in the home. Likewise, wax candles were also taxed, at three and a half pence per pound, and so remained a commodity only the wealthy could afford. Wax candles were made from either beeswax or spermaceti, the wax found in a cavity within the head of the sperm whale.

Stearine, wax or spermaceti candles could be kept a long time if covered with paper when still in their boxes to prevent discoloration. Tallow candles were best used within six months, for once they turned old they were likely to sputter. Wax candles were expensive, and so were rationed. According to an instruction book called *The Servants Guide,* "Wax candles, four in the pound, will last about eleven hours and should be used only when the evening is expected to be five hours as, in that case, each candle will serve for two nights. Shorter candles, of six to the pound, are preferable when required to burn six or seven hours."

Cheaper tallow candles were used when no visitors were present and by servants. However, these candles gave off an unpleasant odor, prompting some people to burn pastilles to dispel the odor. Pastilles were round balls made of gunpowder, and while their smell masked that of the tallow, the resulting minor explosion caused when the pastille was lit often startled any unwary females who were present. The stubs of wax candles were the perquisite of the housekeepers, who sold them to peddlers and tradesmen who made a cheap form of candle from these ends, bits and pieces.

Candlewicks

Candlewicks were made from rushes or cotton. Cotton was first bleached and then twisted to form a wick, a method that made constant clipping of the wick necessary. In time, cotton wicks were instead braided and did not require clipping as they were consumed by fire. A wick measure was used when making candles so that all wicks would be uniform in length. The wick measure was a flat board with an upright wooden arm at one end and a bent piece of wire at the other. The wick was wound twice around the rod and then extended to the wire before being cut.

Candle Advancements

While candlelight had long been the most common form of illumination, its drawbacks were sputtering flames and acrid smoking of the wicks. In the 1820s, candlewicks were doused with boric acid, and this did away with faltering flames. In the early 1830s, the invention of the snuffless plaited cotton wick meant that candles no longer smoked or required their wicks to be trimmed. By 1847, the least expensive candles were sold for sixpence per pound, while the more costly spermaceti candles sold for one shilling, eleven pence per pound. In 1834, candles no longer needed to be hand dipped and rolled during production, as Joseph Morgan had invented the first machine for the continuous wicking and ejection of candles.

Flambeaux and Carriage Lamps

The links and flambeaux used by runners and footmen when lighting the way for sedan chairs and carriages were made of rope that had been dipped in fat or resin. Later, the candles in carriage lamps were converted to oil use by the introduction of metal "candles," which were fitted with a wick and burned paraffin. The majority of vehicle lamps, such as those on omnibuses, burned colza oil, which burned brightly and did not easily extinguish in a wind. When motor cars appeared at the end of the nineteenth century, their lamps burned oil in large brass lamps fitted with reflectors and lenses. Later, acetylene replaced oil, as it gave off a more powerful light.

A lamplighter and his assistant (1805) make their nightly rounds. The assistant refuels the glass container with oil from his jug.

Oil Lamps

The earliest oil lamps were called floating lamps, as a wick was floated atop the oil in a bowl and set alight. Variations during manufacture of the floating lamp enabled it to be set into a stand or bracket, or carried in the hand. By the early 1780s, a glass chimney for the oil lamp resulted in its draft being drawn upward from the wick, causing the flame to burn a bright yellow instead of the prior smoky red color. Whale oil had also been used for illumination in homes until it became both scarce and expensive. Afterward, lard was substituted by the lower classes. One half pound of lard would burn for sixteen hours.

Another oil used in lamps was rapeseed oil, until the 1840s when mineral oil was developed for lighting purposes. Paraffin lamps were first used in the 1840s, but their filling and cleaning took much work and time. At Belvoir, the duke of Rutland's estate, "no less than six men were kept constantly employed at nothing else but looking after the lamps."

To Prevent the Smoking of a Lamp: Soak the wick in strong vinegar, and dry it well before you use it; it will then burn both sweet and pleasant and give much satisfaction for the trifling trouble in preparing it.

Gas Lighting

Gas, a by-product of coal manufacture, made its first appearance in the early nineteenth century. According to author John Ashton in his book *Social England Under the Regency* (1890), "Gas lighting in the streets of London was first introduced in August 1807, when Golden Lane Brewery and a portion of Beech and Whitecross Streets were illuminated by its means. The Gas-Light and Coke Company got their charter in 1810, and lamps outside their offices in Pall Mall; but progress in this direction was very slow, and the old oil lamps died hard." Ashton also tells us that in 1816, "In August the town of Preston, in Lancashire, was partially lit by gas, and this daring feat is thus recorded: The length of the main pipes already laid is one thousand yards; and in this space it is estimated that more than nine hundred lights, emitting flame equal to four thousand mould candles of six to the pound, will be attached to the main pipes in the ensuing winter. The plan of lighting a considerable space by means of a single burner, placed at an elevated situation, has been carried into effect at Preston."

By 1817, London theaters were being illuminated by gaslight, and in 1834, London had over six hundred miles of gas lines laid in order to feed the street lamps. Money to lay the pipes and erect street lamps was raised through rates, or taxes, levied upon homeowners. Tradesmen, shopkeepers and office workers all benefited from gaslight, but it was not widely used until the mid-Victorian period, due both to public mistrust of it and its high cost. Victoria, the Princess Royal, noted: "The Queen [her mother, Victoria] has a great objection to gas [lighting], and thinks it causes great smells and is unsafe."

Gas Companies

As gas meters were not used until the 1850s for gauging how much gas an individual house used, gas charges were determined instead by the number of gas burners in each house. Gas was first supplied to London by the Gas-Light and Coke Company in 1813, with the first seven customers being located in the Westminster area. These contracts stated that gas was to be used only between dusk and 11 P.M. No gas was to be used on Sundays, unless an additional fee of six shillings was paid. In order to prevent customers from using too much gas, the companies turned off the underground mains during the day.

In the 1830s, gas cooking stoves became available and necessitated the gas supply being made available during the day. Streets were dug up and new "day" mains, complete with meters, had to be laid. By the 1830s, competition between various London gas companies lowered the price of gas from sixteen shillings per thousand cubic feet in the beginning of the century to four shillings. Competition also led to each of the companies laying their own mains and network of pipes.

Without meters, unscrupulous gas companies were known to hook up their new customers to the existing pipes of rival gas firms. Inspectors from the various gas companies made occasional spot checks in order to combat this thievery. The inspector entered the house of a paying customer and blew into the gas supply pipe, which in turn created a surge of pressure in the main outside. The inspector's partner waited in the street outside, watching the house thought to be receiving pirated gas. If, when the inspector blew into the pipes of the first house, the lights in the suspected house surged or "jumped," they had their proof.

At first, gas companies kept their product in brewers' vats, many of which were gotten secondhand from the Golden Lane Brewery Group. By 1815, treacle barrels, rum casks and other ready-made containers were also being used to store gas. The first purpose-built gas holders were erected at Horseferry Road, Curtain Road, Peter Street and Brick Lane, London. The largest holder built was opened in 1868 in Beckton on Thames, while the oldest surviving holder is the No. 2 at Fulham, built in 1830.

Gas Burners

By the Victorian period, gas pipes had been laid in many cities and towns, and gas was being used to light the principal rooms of private houses. However, the round globe-type gas chandeliers that hung from the ceiling gave off only a flickering, insufficient light. Also, the iron gas pipes rusted quickly and grew clogged, making it necessary to burn candles and oil lamps. Another drawback to gas was that the first burners used by customers inside their homes were nothing more than simple holes in the pipes that carried gas into the houses. From 1820 on, the Argand burner was substituted, this being fashioned in the shape of a ring. It was not until 1858 that William Sugg devised a means of regulating gas pressure by introducing a governor-burner, which kept the gas burning at a constant pressure.

While Queen Victoria might have been slow to embrace gas lighting, she finally agreed to its use in 1854, when it was used to light the new ballroom at Buckingham Palace. So delighted with the results were the queen and Prince Albert that gas lighting was soon installed at Windsor Castle.

Matches

For centuries, the only "matches" available were faggots. These were made from a plant called furze, which was harvested in early summer. From these rough cuttings, a skilled hand could make fifty faggots per day. As soon as the faggots had dried sufficiently, they were set into racks located just outside the front door. When needed, seven or eight faggots were used at the same time. After setting them alight at the fire, the faggots were used to light lamps and candles.

Aside from using a faggot, flints and tinder was the most common way to light a fire. When using a tinderbox, a piece of steel was struck against a flint until a spark was made. The spark in turn lit the tinder, which was usually a piece of linen or cotton that had been wet with accelerator. Paper saturated with saltpeter, known as a touchstone, was also used. Once a flame was achieved, a brimstone match was set alight, and this was used to light a fire or candle.

Brimstone matches, in use since the fourteenth century, were made of either deal spills, thin slips of fir or pine, or sticks of juniper that had been dipped in sulphur. The brimstone match was snuffed out as soon as possible, to be used again. These matches were made at home or could be purchased from traveling peddlers or gypsies. It could take up to three minutes to obtain light using a flint and tinder, longer if the tinder was damp. Not surprisingly, the invention of various types of friction matches in the 1820s and 1830s was considered a boon, as these tiny miracles could be lit with a single stroke. Lucifer matches, which were lit by striking them along sandpaper, were invented in the 1820s, and the first safety match was invented by Bryant and May in 1855.

Electricity

Though electricity had been used in various forms since the 1870s, it had no impact on daily life until Thomas Edison and Englishman Joseph Swann each independently invented the carbon filament incandescent lamp in 1878–79. Lighting systems were then installed in such public buildings as St. Enochs Station, Glasgow, and the first public power stations were opened in London in January 1882. British industry was slow to adopt this new innovation, preferring steam and gas for lighting, and it wasn't until Charles Parsons invented the steam turbine in 1897 that Britain caught up with the rest of the world in electrical use.

HEATING

Wood had ceased to be a viable heating source long before the dawn of the nineteenth century. Forests throughout the United Kingdom had been depleted and, in any case, could not have met all the heating needs of a growing population. Therefore, coal became the primary source of fuel, although, in the country, workmen had certain rights to the surrounding woods. While they could no longer cut down trees for their own use, they were allowed to take out all the deadwood they could find "by hook or by crook"; that is a shepherd's hook or a laborer's weeding crook. This ensured that only those who were gainfully employed, and not vagrants, could haul wood.

Coal Fires

Coal was burned on an iron grate, with a portion called "small coal" being burnt initially in order to light the whole. Once this small coal began to fire, a bellows was used to fan the flames, and additional coal was added. Coal was purchased from private companies who made home deliveries. Houses were provided with coal vaults in their basements, and these were filled through a pipe that led from the street to the vault. In the street or pavement (sidewalk), these pipes were covered by round iron plates, much like the manhole covers of today. London's main supply of coal was of the bituminous type, originating in Northumberland and Durham and delivered to the city by barge at Billingsgate. Unless broken up frequently with a poker, this type of coal fire tended to go out frequently. In large houses, with fires set in many rooms, chimneys needed to be swept every three months.

Peat Fires

An alternate form of fuel in the countryside was peat. There are many varieties, ranging from that consisting of light surface fibers resembling dried moss to a thick, dark peat, which more resembles coal. Light, loosely packed peat burns very brightly and very fast, while the denser peat tends to smolder and burn more slowly—perfect for heating foods. By using many varieties of peat, it was possible to keep the fire burning at all times, even when a cottage was empty, as it could be left to smolder safely for days at a time. Peat-cutting season ran from March to July, necessitating the use of alternative fuels. In the country, peat fires are still used.

PLUMBING

Domestic Water Supply

Kitchens were supplied with water from nearby wells or streams. Since shallow wells were likely to become contaminated by the drain-off from the scullery or privy, water had to be boiled and filtered before use. To do this, one filled a wooden bucket with fuller's earth or sand and poured the water in, draining the filtered water out through a spigot near the bottom of the bucket. By mid-nineteenth century, a supply of fresh water was being piped into almost every English town, but not every house was equipped with the plumbing necessary to access this. Some smaller towns made do with a single pump located in the main street, from which residents drew their water. Likewise, many large estates had an additional pump in the stable or courtyard that could supply larger quantities of water.

London Water Supply

Since 1613, the supply of water in the city has been undertaken by private companies. In 1851, these totaled seven, with five north and two south of the river. Although mains had been installed throughout the city, at this time it was calculated that 80,000 houses, inhabited by 640,000 persons, were without a supply of water. Here, too, residents made do with a single pump or standpipe; these were located at street corners and were turned on for a few hours per day, though not on every day and not on Sundays. Wealthier homes had their own wells dug or had water storage tanks in the kitchen.

Lord Frederick Hamilton, whose memoirs, *The Days Before Yesterday*, were published in 1920, recorded a vivid picture of the perils of nineteenth-century water supplies: "We lived then in London at Chesterfield House, South Audley Street, which covered three times the amount of ground it does at present, for at the back it had a very large garden, on which Chesterfield Gardens are now built. . . . The left hand wing was used as our stable and contained a well which enjoyed immense local reputation in Mayfair. Never was there such drinking-water! My father allowed anyone in the neighborhood to fetch their drinking water from our well, and one of my earliest recollections is watching the long daily procession of men-servants in the curious yellow-jean jackets of the 'sixties,' each with two large cans in his hands, fetching the day's supply of our matchless water. No inhabitants of Curzon Street, Great Stanhope Street, or South Audley Street would dream of touching any water but that from the famous Chesterfield House spring. In 1867 there was a serious outbreak of Asiatic cholera in London, and my father determined to have the water of the celebrated spring analyzed. . . . The analyst reported that fifteen per cent of the water must be pure sewage. My father had the spring sealed and bricked up at once, but it is a marvel that we had not poisoned every single inhabitant of the Mayfair district years before."

Bathtubs/Sinks

For centuries, bathing was undertaken in the traditional hip bath or portable bathing tub, made of wood, tin or cast iron. Portable showers had existed since the Tudor period, at least, and resembled a shoulder-height wooden tub, with an apparatus for delivering water through overhead sprays fitted atop the edge. Needless to say, not many homes possessed these, as they were awkward to use and labor-intensive.

By the mid-nineteenth century, Great Britain experienced a much needed overhaul of its water delivery and sewage disposal systems, the most ambitious of these projects taking place in London. Once gas lines had been laid, the water that could now be delivered directly to private homes could also be heated. Water was stored in the home in tanks kept in the attic or on the roof. Once the water no longer had to be fetched and carried, nor heated before being hauled upstairs for use, fitted bathrooms could be built into the home. The bathroom was

A nineteenth-century innovation, a shower ring that fit over the neck

usually set up in what had once been a bedroom. Ceramic sinks were set atop pedestals and attached to bathroom walls, and the sinks boasted brass- or nickel-plated taps, which delivered either hot or cold water. By the 1870s, enameled, cast-iron bathtubs were a common fixture in most bathrooms. In wealthier homes, these were already being fitted out with overhead showers.

In his book, *Old Days and New,* Lord Ernest Hamilton relates the following anecdote about period bathtubs: "Every big country house boasted one or more large iron tanks encased in mahogany, evidently designed to do duty as baths and—judging from their size—designed to accommodate several people at once. At one end of these tanks was a brass dial on which were inscribed the words 'hot,' 'cold' and 'waste,' and a revolving handle manoeuvred an indicator into position opposite such of these inscriptions as a prospective bather might be attracted to. . . . A call on the hot water supply, however, did not meet with an effusive or even warm response. A succession of sepulchral rumblings was succeeded by the appearance of a small geyser of rust-coloured water, heavily charged with dead earwigs and bluebottles. This continued for a couple of minutes or so and then entirely ceased. The only perceptible difference between the hot water and the cold lay in its colour and in the cargo of defunct life which the former bore on its bosom. Both were stone cold."

And in a letter dated August 19, 1822, Charles Cavendish Fulke Greville, Esquire, recalls the details of George IV's bath: "I went to Brighton on Saturday. . . . The Pavilion is finished. The King has had a subterranean passage made from the house to the stables, which is said to have cost three thousand pounds or five thousand pounds. . . . There is also a bath in his apartment, with pipes to conduct water from the sea; these pipes cost six hundred pounds. The King has not taken a sea bath for sixteen years."

Kitchen sinks were fashioned from wood until large pottery firms began to produce them on a wider scale at the beginning of the century. Waste water was drained into a bucket beneath or, in larger, wealthier houses, sinks were fitted with pipes that carried waste outside.

The Privy

Self-contained and flushing toilets had been in existence since before 1777, when Joseph Bramah introduced his innovative model. Previously, a U-shaped pipe system was used, which not only let out waste, but let noxious fumes in. Bramah's toilet incorporated a closed valve that fell back into place after flushing and helped to keep a small amount of water in the pan. By the 1860s, the washout toilet had been developed and replaced Bramah's design. This new system relied on gravity and provided a rush of water from an overhead cistern when flushed, the U-bend being replaced by an S-bend trap.

While Victorians welcomed these new devices into their homes, toilets were most often hidden away. In 1875, Thomas Twyford patented a water closet called the National, which had all its parts enclosed in a wooden box. Over 100,000 were sold between 1881 and 1889. Indoor bathrooms were treated as luxuries and were decorated accordingly. Having taken over a spare bedroom, or been set up in a room especially built to house it, the bathroom was just that—a room. Much larger than our present-day counterparts, Victorian bathrooms were furnished with upholstered chairs, vanities and linen cupboards, as well as mirrors, lighting fixtures and pictures on the walls.

TIME LINE

1800 London's Lyceum Theatre is lit by gas.

1813 The Gas-Light and Coke Company supplies its first seven customers in Westminster with gas in their homes.

1814 Pall Mall and Westminster Bridge are lit by gas.

1817 London theaters are lit by gas.

1820s Stearic acid is used as hardener in candle manufacture. Lucifer matches are invented.

1827 London clock faces are lit by gas.

1830s Snuffless plaited cotton candlewick is invented.

1834 London street lights are fueled by over six hundred miles of gas lines.

Joseph Morgan invents a machine for continuous wicking and ejection of candles.

1840 Mineral oil is used in lamps.

1847 Tallow candles sell for sixpence per pound, spermaceti candles one shilling, eleven pence per pound.

1855 Safety matches are invented.

1870s Enameled, cast-iron bathtubs are common fixtures in most bathrooms.

1875 Thomas Twyford patents the National water closet, having all its parts enclosed in a wooden box.

BIBLIOGRAPHY

Bacot, H. *Nineteenth-Century Lighting.* Atglen, Penn.: Schiffer Publishing Co., 1987.

Cunningham, Colin. *Building for the Victorians.* Cambridge, Mass.: Cambridge University Press, 1985.

Dickinson, H.W. *Water Supply of Greater London.* London: Newcomer Society at the Courier Press, 1954.

Elmes, James. *Metropolitan Improvements; or, London in the Nineteenth Century.* North Stratford: Ayer Company Publishers, Inc., 1978.

Gledhill, David. *Gas Lighting.* Aylesbury, England: Shire Publications, 1981.

Meadows, Cecil A. *Discovering Oil Lamps.* Aylesbury, England: Shire Publications, 1972.

O'Dea, W.T. *The Social History of Lighting.* London: Routledge & Kegan, 1960.

Chapter Two

Cooking

By the seventeenth century, wall fireplaces had come into general use, and these usually had a cupboard fitted with an iron door in one of the three walls, near enough to the main fire to use its heat for slow cooking and to keep foods warm. Small cakes, biscuits and even pies could be baked here. Many of these fireplaces remained in use well into the nineteenth century. Enclosed ranges, the huge, black stoves associated with Victorian kitchens, were patented circa 1815 but not perfected or in wide use until the 1840s. These boasted an oven for roasting meats and baking, and burners atop for simmering and boiling foods. Some ovens additionally offered a separate compartment in which water could be heated for use in washing and housecleaning. Black lead, sold in sticks and made of iron and carbon, was applied to the iron ranges. It was mixed with a drop of turpentine and brushed on using two brushes: one to apply and one to polish.

TENDING THE FIRE

Each evening, ovens and stoves fired by coal had to be swept out, black leaded and then relit by 6 A.M., in time for the day's baking. This routine involved raking out the ashes and cleaning the flues. Grease was then removed from the stove with newspaper, and all steel parts were polished with emery paper, bath brick and paraffin. All iron surfaces were then black leaded, this substance being applied with a soft brush, rubbed vigorously with a stiffer brush and given a final polish with a clean cloth.

A typical stove top/oven combination. The ornate iron grillwork required daily polishing.

CHANGES IN MENU

The Victorian innovations in cooking ranges coincided with changes in meal content and preparation. Toward midcentury, the middle classes employed fewer servants, due to financial restrictions. This meant the lady of the house had some hand in the preparation and cooking of food. Self-contained ranges, offering ovens and stove tops, meant fewer people were required to maintain a kitchen.

In addition, the centuries-old tradition of cooking an entire meal in a single pot was done away with. Many country housewives had hung their huge cooking pots on a hob within their fireplaces. The meat went into the boiling water, and any number of pudding cloths could be hung in the same pot. One cloth might contain a pease pudding to accompany the meat, another a bread pudding for dessert. With the invention of the kitchen range, more sophisticated side dishes, desserts, sauces and gravies might be produced with less work and within a smaller space. This advance was welcomed by the middle-class lady who aspired to produce the more sophisticated meals served by the upper classes.

FISH AND GAME

Fish was scarce and expensive due to there being no way to preserve a perishable commodity. Those people who lived inland never knew the taste of saltwater fish, unless someone sent them a cod or turbot packed in straw within a basket as a gift. Likewise, Londoners didn't have access to freshwater lake fish, such as salmon.

From the mid-eighteenth century on, enormous green sea turtles from the West Indies were transported to England in freshwater tanks fitted into the holds of ships. These turtles were prized by gourmets, who ate the boiled belly and roasted back meat, along with such corner dishes as fins and guts in rich sauces. To host a turtle dinner became a sign of wealth and prestige. For those who could not find or afford these delicacies, mock turtle soup was substituted. The large turtle shells were placed in the center of the dining tables and used as serving dishes.

Isabella Beeton on the cost of turtle soup (1860): "This is the most expensive soup brought to table. It is sold by the quart, one guinea being the standard price for that quantity. The price of live turtle ranges from 8d. to 2s. [8 pence to 2 shillings] per pound, according to the supply and demand. When live turtle is dear, many cooks use the tinned turtle, which is killed when caught, and preserved by being put in hermetically sealed canisters, and so sent over to England. The cost of a tin; containing two quarts or four pounds, is about two pounds for a small tin; containing the green fat, 7s. 6d. [7 shillings 6 pence].

From these about six quarts of good soup may be made.''

Mock Turtle Soup: [From Margaretta Acworth's Georgian recipe] Make a mutton stock using 2 pounds of mutton or lamb on the bone. Cover with water and boil for 2 hours, after this strain the stock and skim off the fat. Put a boned calf's head or 2 pounds of veal knuckle in a saucepan, add juice and rind of 1 lemon, 1 carrot, 1 onion, 3 bay leaves and parsley to taste. Cover with mutton stock, bring to a boil, then simmer for 2 to 3 hours. Strain your stock then trim and dice the gelatinous meat of the calf's head and set it aside. Replace the stock in a saucepan, whisk in 2 egg whites and bring to a boil. Let this boil until the egg whites form a thick scum. Line your sieve with a thick cloth and strain the stock through this into a bowl, and then return the strained liquid to a saucepan. Add 1 cup Madeira or dry sherry, diced meat, some diced parsley, and return to a boil. Serve piping hot.

Game also was scarce and dear. A country gentleman would not have sold his game, although poachers did a good trade. At Christmas, landowners might send hare and other game to friends and relatives in various parts of the country. Buying game off of arriving coaches, however, was risky business, as illustrated in this account from *The Times,* dated January 20, 1803: ''Saturday night last, an epicure from Fish Street Hill anxiously watched for the arrival of a Kentish coach at the King's Head, in the Borough, in order to purchase a Hare from the coachman, for his Sunday's dinner; an outside passenger, having learned his errand, brought him under the gateway and sold him a very large one, as he thought, for nine shillings, which, however, upon his return home proved to be a badger.''

Pigeons and squab, or young pigeons, were always popular table birds and by the eighteenth century were being braised, fricasseed or boiled with bacon. Pigeons and sparrows were rolled in paste and boiled as dumplings. Hot pies made with chicken or pigeon and fruits were well spiced, moistened with butter or marrow. By the seventeenth century, oysters, morels and artichoke hearts were being added to the pies. Birds used for pie during this period also included doves, quails, bustards, cranes and spines, all of which were seasoned with nutmeg, cloves, pepper and salt and sealed in butter. They were kept cold and could keep several days before cooking. When baked in pies that were to be eaten cold, the birds were first given a dose of spices and plenty of butter. Upon cooling, the pie was then filled up with clarified butter.

The Dovecote

These birds were raised by the gamekeeper, who erected a dovecote, a birdhouse used for either doves or pigeons, on the property. This was not a quaint birdhouse perched atop a pole, but a proper building sometimes housing hundreds of birds. The houses could have been constructed from stone, brick, wattle and daub or wood, and were either square, circular or octagonal in shape. The birds could leave the dovecote during the day to feed on growing crops and the like, returning to roost each night, via small openings cut into the dovecote. The ground floor of the dovecote was given over to storing grain, such as corn, during the winter, and the nesting boxes were located under the roof; this level was reached by ladder. During the seventeenth century, there were thought to have been about twenty-five thousand dovecotes in England.

Small Game Receipts

Pigeon Pie: Cut 1½ lbs. of rump steak into pieces and use these to line the bottom of a baking dish, flavoring with salt and pepper. After cleaning your pigeons, pour about ½ oz. of butter into each and lay upon the steak, placing a piece of ham atop each bird. Beat the yolks of 4 eggs and pour over birds, adding stock until the dish is half full. Place puff pastry around the sides of the dish and use it to cover the whole pie. Cut 3, 4 or 6 pigeon feet and stick into the top of the crust, depending on the size of your dish. Brush the top with egg yolk and bake in a hot oven for 1½ hours.

An Old English Jelly Wine Sauce for Game: Slowly melt 1 cup of black or red currant jelly in a saucepan, add 1 cup red wine, mix together and gently simmer, adding a pinch of powdered ginger, the same of clove and 1 tablespoon of lemon juice. Thicken with equal parts of strained game gravy and flour, working until smooth. Just before serving, add 1 tablespoon cognac brandy.

English Stuffing for Small Game (1829): Chop all the tender giblets the birds may yield and ⅓ as much chopped lean smoked bacon. Add 1 teaspoon chopped parsley per cup, 1 pinch nutmeg per cup, 1 pinch thyme per cup, enough bread crumbs to bind and moisten with lemon juice and egg white. Add salt and pepper to taste. Shape the mix into forcemeat balls, which may be placed inside game or ranged around it whilst baking.

TIMETABLE FOR HANGING GAME
(Based on Fall Weather)

Wild Duck	4 to 5 days
Wild Goose	About 6 days
Grouse	8 to 10 days
Partridge	4 to 6 days
Pheasant	8 to 10 days

Apparently game birds were in such high demand that foreigners went to extraordinary lengths to import them into England, as the following passage from John Ashton's *The Dawn of the 19th Century in England* shows:

> February 1816—To such a pitch is mercantile speculation for the luxurious now arrived, that we understand three poor Laplanders have come over in the last packet from Gottenburg, and are on their way to London with five sledges, laden with Lapland Game. (In February) our unfortunate Northern guests had landed on a somewhat inhospitable shore, for they had to pay over fifty pounds duty for imported game, and ten pounds freight from Harwich to London.
>
> But this frozen game was quite novel, and it deserves a contemporary account of what they thought of it at the time. "The state of preservation in which these birds are, is really surprising, after travelling upwards of one thousand miles. They were preserved by being hung up to freeze as soon as killed, and, afterwards, being packed in cases, lined with skin to keep the air out. This process so effectually preserved them, that when the packages are opened, the birds are frozen quite hard; and those packages which are not opened will continue in this state for some weeks. The mode in which the small birds are dressed in Sweden is by

stewing them in cream, with a little butter in it, after being larded, which it is said, gives them an exquisite flavour."

PUDDINGS

For a long time, puddings were made in sausage skins. When sausages began to be made into links in the 1630s, puddings were made skinless; that is, instead of being encased in the sausage casing, they were pressed into pots, where they kept up to a fortnight. The pudding cloth came into use shortly thereafter, and puddings were no longer associated with sausages. The great advantage to the pudding cloth was that puddings of all kinds could be simmered and cooked along with the meat in one pot. Heavier puddings calling for suet could be formed into small cakes and fried in butter as an alternative to boiling.

Batter puddings, such as Yorkshire pudding, only became widely known in the eighteenth century and were either baked in an oven or cooked under the spit in the drippings that fell from the joint of meat as it cooked. Another eighteenth-century innovation was rice pudding, made by tying up rice and raisins or currants in a pudding cloth and boiling this in water until the rice had swelled, whereafter it was served with melted butter and sugar.

By the nineteenth century, the term "pudding" was being increasingly applied to those dishes that served as dessert. A "sweet" was any cold dessert; a pudding one that was served warm In addition, the pudding cloth was replaced, in some cases, with the new, mass-produced baking dishes.

Pudding Receipts

Boiled Rice Pudding: Gently stew ¼ lb. rice in 1½ pint new milk until tender. Pour into a bowl and add 2 ounces of butter then allow the mix to cool. Add 4 beaten eggs to rice mix, along with 4 large tablespoons of moist sugar and ½ teaspoon of salt. If desired, flavor with nutmeg, cinnamon or vanilla. Place the pudding in a greased dish, tie it up in your cloth and place in rapidly boiling water, cooking for 1¼ hours.

Oat Pudding (to be served with boiled beef): Grease a pudding cloth. Take enough beef broth to moisten 2 cups of coarse ground oatmeal, add seasonings and stir well. Pack this loosely into the pudding bag and hang it in the pan beside the beef. The oatmeal will swell until it fills the cloth and should be served with the meat once a little broth has been spooned on top.

Boiled Pork and Pease Pudding: Take the joint and put it into a thick pan with ample water. Bring to a slow boil, add carrots, swedes, onions, cabbage, celery and any other vegetable you choose. Take 2 handfuls of old peas and tie them in a muslin bag, which you will hang in the pan beside the joint. To the water you will add a large spoonful of sugar, peppercorns and 1 cup of cider. Cover and simmer for a few hours. When done, drain the meat, take out the bag of pease pudding, which will resemble a large ball, and unroll it onto a hot dish. Separate the ball into 2 halves and put a large pat of bacon fat on top of each.

Baked Bread Pudding: Into a saucepan put 1 pint of milk and 6 bitter almonds, letting them soak for 15 minutes. Bring milk and almonds to a near boil, strain liquid over ½ lb. breadcrumbs and allow the mix to cool. Then add 4 well beaten eggs, 4 ounces of butter, 4 ounces of moist sugar and 1 tablespoon of brandy. Beat well and mix thoroughly. Line the bottom of your dish with 2 ounces candied peel sliced thin, cover with pudding mix and bake for 45 minutes.

Yorkshire Pudding (serves 6): Put 6 large tablespoons of flour into a bowl, add 1 teaspoon of salt and add 1 pint milk to form a stiff batter. Remove all lumps, then add ½ pint milk more and 3 well beaten eggs. Beat together and transfer mix to a shallow baking tin, well greased with beef drippings. Bake in the oven for 1 hour, then place the tin under your roasting meat to catch the drippings. To serve, cut pudding into small squares.

Manchester Pudding: Boil 3 tablespoons of fine, white breadcrumbs in 1 pint of milk along with the rind of a lemon and sweeten with sugar or honey to taste. Remove from heat and beat into the mixture a good sized lump of butter and 2 beaten egg yolks. On the bottom of your dish, lay some apricot jam and cover with above mixture. Over this, spread another layer of jam. Take 3 egg whites and beat them, add a tablespoon of sugar and some vanilla and spread this mixture on the top layer of jam. Bake in a warm oven until the top layer is browned and forms a crust.

Baked Plum Pudding (serves 10): Finely chop 1 lb. suet and mix with 2 lbs. of flour, 1 lb. of currants, 1 lb. stoned raisins and a few slices of candied peel. To this add 2 well beaten eggs and enough milk to make a thick batter. Put the mix in a buttered dish and bake for 2½ hours. When cool, turn the pudding out onto a plate and cover with sifted sugar.

Christmas Pudding for the English Royal Family (serves 20–30): Mix together dry ingredients: 1¼ lb. suet, 1 lb. demerara sugar, 1 lb. each raisins and sultanas, 4 oz. citron peel and the same of candied peel, 1 teaspoon all spice, 1¼ teaspoon nutmeg, 1 lb. breadcrumbs, ½ lb. sifted flour. In a separate bowl, mix ½ pint milk and 1 lb. (before cracking) of eggs, whipped. Add this liquid to dry ingredients, plus 1 glass of brandy and put mix into well greased basins or fancy moulds. Boil at least 8 hours. Turn the pudding out of its mould and pour a glass of brandy over the pudding. Light the brandy and deliver to table whilst flaming.

BEVERAGES

Libations

Beer Casks, tilting: Casks should be set at least a week before use, longer in warm weather. You should use two barrel stands for each barrel. As soon as the barrel is delivered, set it on one pair of stands, and as the beer level lowers, get the next barrel and set it on the second stand. By the time one cask is finished, the next will be ready for use. It is customary for the brewer's man to collect one empty cask as he leaves a full one. Keep your pewter tankard in the cellar with the beer casks to keep it cool.

Beer Flip: Take 8 yolks of eggs, mix with sugar and orange juice and spices. Beat the whites separately until stiff. Make hot 1 quart of strong beer and pour over the yolks, then pour the mix back again from a height, so it will froth well. Add the white of the eggs to the froth and serve whilst still hot.

Blackberry Cordial: Take new cider from the press and equal parts of blackberry juice. Strain both together and mix with as much honey as will float an egg. Boil gently for 15 minutes in an earthenware pot. When it has cooled, barrel it and wait 6 weeks before drinking.

Hawthorn Flower Liqueur: Pick the blossoms that have the strongest almond scent, as they make the best liqueur. Gather the blossoms when they are in full flower and take the flowers only, not the small stems. Pack the flowers into a wide mouth bottle, shaking them to the bottom, but take care not to bruise them. Shake a very little crushed sugar candy over the flowers and fill the bottle with brandy before corking tightly. Stand the bottle in the full sun until it is warm and then store it in a dark, warm cupboard. Shake gently several times during the first few weeks. Then let it stand untouched for at least three months, when it can be gently decanted into a small flask.

AVERAGE WINE PRICES 1804
per dozen bottles (in shillings)

Superior Old Port	38
Prime Old Sherry	42
Prime Madeira	63
Superior Claret	70
Old Jamaica Rum	15
Holland's Geneva	10
Cognac Brandy	20 per gallon

Syllabub: Take 1 quart of sweet cream, ½ pint of white wine and ¾ of a pound pounded loaf sugar. Whisk the mix and take off the cream as it rises. Lay the cream atop thin muslin stretched over a sieve. Continue to whisk the mix, removing the cream as you go. When the mix will no longer froth, add the cream back to the mix, along with grated nutmeg, and half fill your glasses, laying the froth on the top.

English ozyat was made from ground almonds and sugar, orange flower water or citrus juice boiled together with spring water. It was a cold drink, similar to lemonade. Milk ozyat was made with boiled, spiced milk, which was cooled and mixed with ground almonds and then served in handled ozyat glasses.

In *Social England Under the Regency*, John Ashton says of a sale of fine wine, chronicled May 13, 1817: Friday, the cellars of Alexander Davidson, Esq., were emptied to the best bidders. The prices, at which the several lots were knocked down, were unusually high. Three dozen of red Madeira, bottled in 1801, were knocked down at eighteen guineas per dozen, it was supposed, for a distinguished member of the Royal Family. One lot of Hock, a hundred and seventeen years old, sold at ten guineas per dozen, and very little of Sherry went at less than five and six guineas per dozen."

The middle classes could not, of course, afford these wines, but they drank sound port, sherry and Madeira, brown brandy and gin. Whiskey was almost unknown.

Tea

Until the reign of Queen Victoria, customers blended their own teas at home, this task often being assigned to housekeepers. When blending tea at home, China teas were mixed with the less expensive Common Bohea or Common Green leaves, the more expensive leaves being Hyson, Congo and Gunpowder. Each tea was stored away in a tea chest, which had many drawers in which to keep the leaves separated. These chests were fitted with porcelain bowls, in which the tea was mixed, and a heavy lock, as the cost of tea was so dear.

Afternoon tea was served anywhere between three and six o'clock. Typically, the earlier a tea is served, the lighter the foods that accompany it. A tea served nearer to six o'clock would be a high tea, with the heavier dishes served making this more of a meal than a light, reviving snack. High tea is commonly mistaken for being somehow grander than afternoon tea service, but its origins are humble and it was never, in England, considered a fashionable meal. When laborers and factory workers arrived home from work at five or six o'clock, it was still too early for dinner, which during the nineteenth century was usually served at seven or eight o'clock. The men, however, were hungry for a meal, and so high tea evolved, being a cross between a snack and a hot meal.

Tea Adulteration

Tea was a product that consumers had to examine carefully before buying. Both servants and the poor sold used tea leaves to the tea vendor, who made these into "new tea." It was estimated that over fifteen hundred pounds of this new tea were processed in London each week. The old leaves were placed on heated plates and then both redried and redyed. To give the leaves a green hue, a dye containing copper was used. For the imitation of black teas, logwood was added.

Known as "smouch," this recycled black tea was mainly sold to "slop" shopkeepers, who in turn sold it to the lower classes.

THE DAIRY

Ideally, the dairy should face north, as should the larder, and have tiled floors and walls for both coolness and hygiene. Very strict rules for cleaning, maintaining and working in the dairy were always observed. For instance, only old linen was used to clean all wooden tools. The floors were scoured with white sand and lime; the walls were whitewashed with a mix of lime and skim milk. Using any type of soap in the dairy was to be avoided when possible, but if need be, the dairy maid reduced the soap to a fine jelly and used it with only cold water to prevent its sticking to any wood surfaces or tools. Wooden utensils were scalded with boiling saltwater and rinsed clean. Any wooden tubs and jars were set in the sun to dry.

Milk Collection

While both ewes and cows were used for milk during medieval times, the milking of ewes was abandoned altogether by the sixteenth century. The cows were milked until they were dry, and it was generally believed that the cows should be fed during the milking process to ensure the best milk. It was the housewife's or dairy maid's task to keep exact records as to how much milk each cow produced. Fresh milk was brought into the kitchen twice each day, in either a can or a wooden pail. It was strained and then poured into shallow milk pans, called creamers, and covered with cheesecloth.

After the cream had been allowed to rise, the morning's milk was skimmed in the afternoon; the afternoon's milk was skimmed the next morning. During the summer, milk was allowed to stand for butter production for twenty-four hours without skimming. In the winter, it was left to stand for forty-eight hours, the milk being skimmed very early in the day. The cream was used at table or for cooking and butter production. When cream was made into butter, the skim milk that was left was turned into cheese; the by-product of butter making was buttermilk. In lowland Scotland, milk was classified as being either sour, sweet or scum (buttermilk, ordinary milk or skimmed milk).

Butter Production

Cream, rather than milk, that was to be made into butter was first left to sour, which it did on its own if allowed to stand. However, if one could not wait until the cream soured naturally, a little soured cream could be added to hasten the process. This soured cream was then churned until it became butter. If the cream had been made sour enough and was at a temperature of about 65°F, the butter would appear within a few minutes. Then the excess water was squeezed out.

The Butter Churn

The butter churn was not in widespread use until the eighteenth century. To make butter, scalded, renneted cream was placed in large open bowls or tubs and churned by the dairy maid, who used only her hand as a tool. Later, a dog churn was sometimes used. This consisted of a large wooden wheel or round platform on which the dog ran, its weight serving to turn the wheel. The wheel was geared to a dasher, which in turn worked the churn. When butter was made in the churn, the milk was first left to stand for some time in wide shallow bowls so that the cream might rise. Three gallons of good milk yields one pound of butter.

The finest butter was produced using the first skimming of the cream. The second skimming of the cream, which took place hours later, produced a thinner cream. The worst butter of all was that made from the curds, which rose on the whey after full-cream milk had been renneted and drained for cheese. In any case, the cream collected by skimming was strained through clean cloths directly into the churn. It was agitated with quick strokes until the sound made by churning began to change as the butter began to form. The buttermilk was then poured off, and the butter left in the churn was rinsed with fresh, cold water.

Large wooden scoops were used to remove the butter from the churn and place it into a butter worker. This was a shallow, wooden trough that had a fluted wooden roller attached to it. The roller made its way down the length of the trough by means of a handle, thus squeezing more water from the butter. Clean water was again poured over the butter, and it was rolled some more. If the butter was not cleaned, and the water was not squeezed out of it, it would not keep. The butter was then salted and worked before being placed in earthenware pots. Before closing the pots, the air was removed by means of a wooden tool.

Butter Preservation

Because butter was liable to become rancid, especially if any buttermilk had been left in it, butter was always heavily salted. It was customary to wash out most of the salt in fresh water before using the butter. When used for cooking, the butter was clarified, melted and then strained before being stored in pots. Sweet butter intended for immediate use was beaten in fresh water until it was free of buttermilk and then salted; salted butter intended to be kept a long time was made by working out the buttermilk by hand and then beating strong brine or salt into it. The salted butter was packed into well-glazed earthenware pots or wooden casks, with a final layer of salt added before the pots were sealed. Contemporary instructions for another way of preserving butter read, "Make a good brine by boiling two pounds of salt, six lumps of sugar and as much saltpeter as will lie on a shilling in one gallon of water for ten minutes. When cool, wrap each pat of butter in wet muslin or cloth and put these into the brine. The butter must be kept beneath the surface of the brine and will keep good for months. Remove butter pats as needed; rinse before use."

Alternately, the dairy maid might have made the butter into blocks using butter hands or butter pats. These were wooden blocks that had grooved blades fitted into them. Holding one in each hand, the diary maid shaped and divided the butter into rectangular or square blocks. Then, with either a ribbed roller or a butter stamp made by a local tradesman, she set her stamp into each block of butter. Dairy maids also entered competitions during country fairs in which each maid created fanciful shapes, such as baskets, castle towers, flowers and animals, the only medium being butter.

Butter that was offered for sale was more often made into round pats, formed in wooden molds. Each portion of butter was stamped with a pattern, which indicated which farm had produced it. Some stamps were finely carved and were meant to be informative. When a swan was incorporated into the stamp, it meant that the producing farm had water meadows; corn sheaves indicated a farm also grew corn.

Clotted Cream

Clotted cream was produced by leaving new milk in shallow bowls over a low fire for several hours, taking care that it did not boil. The cream could be thickened further by adding more fresh cream. By 1650, clotted cream had become a popular dish, eaten on its own or flavored with sugar or honey.

A recipe of the day advised making clotted cream in the following manner: "Take the night's milk and put into a broad earthenware pan. In the morning, set over a slow fire and allow it to stand there from morn to night, making certain not to boil the liquid, only heat it. Take off the fire and set overnight in a cool place. Next morning, dish off your cream and it will be quite thick." Before serving, the cream could be made to resemble a cabbage if the skimmings of the cream were lifted carefully from the bowls. These skins were then built up in a dish, round and high like a cabbage, with sugar and rosewater sprinkled between the layers.

According to a recipe dated 1700, an alternative cream dish, orange flower cream, was made thusly: "Boil three quarts of sweetened water with the zest of two lemons and the juice. Beat eight eggs into one quart of cream and add to the water. Stir very slowly, only in one direction, and then let the mix stand. Skim off the curd into a pierced dish and drain. When cream has set, turn it out and pour around it whipped cream flavoured with orange flower water." Yorkshire cream cheese was made by placing a quantity of cream in a wet cloth that was tied up and hung in a cool spot for seven or eight days.

Cheese

The principal use of rennet was to curd new milk for cheese. To make rennet (or "curds and whey"), the calf's vell, or inner stomach, was removed, and the curd within was removed and cleaned, either by a butcher or dairy maid, and then hung in the chimney corners where it kept for a long while. The vell was washed, salted and stretched out to dry on planks of wood or on strong wooden skewers. It was then put into a pot that already contained a bit of curd, the thought being that it would "feed" the vell, thus increasing the flow of rennet.

Alternately, a small bit of rennet could be soaked first in half a teacupful of warm water for an hour or two. A spoonful of the resulting liquid was then added to a quart of new milk and kept in a warm place until the whey separated from the curd. The smaller the portion of rennet used, the softer and more delicate the resulting curd. When rennet-whey was required for the sick room, as it was considered to be easily digestible, a bit of rennet, rinsed first, was stirred into warm milk, which was strained of the curd and served to the invalid.

Dairy Receipts

Beistyn: This dish, thick and golden yellow, was produced using the first milk taken from a cow after calving. It is also called Beastlyns, Bestys and Firstings. As thick as double cream, it had to be thinned using four times its quantity of plain milk, sweetened. The mix was then placed in a cool oven and flavoured with a cinnamon stick or vanilla. Afterwards, the beistyn, which resembled egg custard, was topped with damp sugar and set under a grill until it formed a caramel crust.

Flavoured Rennet: Allow the calf to suck as much as it will before it is killed. Remove the milk bag from the calf and let it sit, covered in stinging nettles, for twelve hours or until it is red. Take out the curd and wash the bag clean. Salt it inside and out and lay in salt for twenty-four hours. Wash the curd in fresh milk and replace it in the bag with four streakings, the last milk from the cow, a beaten egg, twelve cloves and a blade of mace, and skewer the bag closed and hang it in a pot. In another pot, put half a pint of salted water, six tops of blackthorn, the same amount of burnt and two of sweet marjoram. Boil all together, cool, and put some of this water into the bag with the egg and thick milk and let the bag soak in the rest of the liquid. The water in which the bag rests is the rennet. The bag can be filled and left to exude another six or seven times before the action of the stomach juice lessens.

To Preserve Milk: *The Complete Servant* instructs that "Bottles must be perfectly clean, sweet and dry; draw milk from the cow into bottles and as they are fulled immediately cork them well up and fasten the corks with pack thread or wire. Then spread a little straw on the bottom of a boiler, on which place bottles with straw between them, until the boiler contains a sufficient quantity. Fill it up with cold water, heat the water and as soon as it boils draw the fire and let the whole gradually cool. When quite cold, take out the bottles and pack them with straw or sawdust in hampers and stow them in the coolest part of the house. Milk preserved in this manner, although 18 months in the bottle, will be as sweet as when first milked from the cow."

Ice Cream

Ice cream began to be produced in the eighteenth century, due to the development of proper icehouses on the grounds of country estates. At first, ice cream was made in tin icing pots with close-fitting lids, which were buried in pails of ice. Recipes for ice creams varied and included the addition of fruits that were worked together with sugar and scalded cream. Other flavorings included jams, such as raspberry, peach or strawberry.

To Make Ice Cream: Boil two quarts of milk, thicken with three tablespoons arrowroot and after it has cooled, add one pound of powdered sugar and the well-beaten whites of eight eggs. Flavor with lemon or vanilla.

To Freeze Ice Cream: You must use a peck of coarse salt to freeze two gallons. Pound ice very fine, mix with salt and pack around the ice cream freezer, which you must stand in a tub. By increments, the freezer should be turned half round and back until the whole is frozen. Cut the cream from the sides of the freezer every ten minutes. If any acid fruit is added, it should be at the last cutting to prevent souring. If the ice cream is to be moulded, fill the moulds just before the mix becomes solid and pack tightly, covering the moulds with ice and salt. When the ice cream is solid, cover the freezer with ice and salt until you want it, or store it in the ice house.

Icehouses

Icehouses had been built on vast estates since the Tudor period and survived until well into the twentieth century. They were stocked each winter with the ice blocks cut from nearby ponds, rivers or canals. The greater part of the structure was built underground, and for insulation purposes there were two doors through which one had to pass in order to reach the interior of the building. Once the building had been entered, one had to climb down a ladder to the level at which the ice was stored, this being on average twenty-five feet deep and fifteen feet in circumference. A drain was set into the floor, from which the runoff of melted ice could escape. Outside the structure, trees and shrubs were planted to supply shade.

By the nineteenth century, English winters were milder, and there

Icebox for use in home

was no longer a sufficient amount of ice formed to supply the increasing population and their demands for ice. Soon, ships that sailed to the Baltic carrying cargoes of coal began loading their empty holds with ice for the return trip home. By 1830, Britain's largest ports were home to massive insulated ice warehouses where the ice was kept until distribution. Iceboxes used in the home were made of wood and lined with either zinc or slate. An insulating layer of either felt, ash or charcoal was placed between the lining and the wood.

BIBLIOGRAPHY

Berriedale-Johnson, Michelle. *The Victorian Cookbook.* Northampton, England: Interlink Publishing Group, Inc., 1989.

Burgess, Anthony, ed. *The Book of Tea.* Paris: Flammarion, 1992.

Davies, Jennifer. *The Victorian Kitchen.* London: BBC Books, 1991.

Dickens, Cedrick. *Dining With Dickens.* Goring-on-Thames: Elvendon Press, 1984.

Hartley, Dorothy. *Food in England.* London: Futura Publications, 1985.

Chapter Three

Domestic Servants

By the nineteenth century, the middle class had grown wealthy enough to hire staff. To keep up appearances, they found it necessary to hire at least one servant, even if this was an untrained servant girl who worked for her keep and the smallest of wages. At the end of the nineteenth century, even those families at the bottom of the middle class had pride enough to engage a "step girl," who on Saturday mornings scrubbed the front steps and pavement, her presence intended to be noted by neighbors and passersby. The number of servants kept on staff, and their conduct and appearance, quickly became a mark of status, especially among those near the top of the class ladder. Doctors, lawyers, engineers and other professionals were quick to build a staff, believing it essential to employ at least three servants.

HIRING

In 1777, a heavy tax of one guinea per male servant was levied against employers. This was done to raise monies necessary to fight the American War of Independence. Though the tax was not lifted until 1937, it did little to discourage the hiring of male servants. Both male and female servants could be hired in various ways. A centuries-old institution was the mop fair, also called a statute or hiring fair. This was generally held in September and May, when new positions were entered into for a twelve-month probationary period. Typically, workers wore a distinctive article of clothing or carried a symbol that identified the position he or she was seeking to fill: Carters and wagoners twisted a piece of whipcord around their hats, while thatchers displayed a fragment of woven straw. Positions were entered into with the exchange of a handshake and the payment of earnest money, sometimes known as a fastening penny.

In addition, servants could be hired through statute halls or servant registries, the employment agencies of the day. A number of these early agencies printed advertisements that listed available servants, though this practice died out as newspaper distribution increased. Not all of these agencies were honestly run, and they soon gained a reputation for taking advantage of servants by charging them fees up front and later failing to find them positions or arrange for a single interview.

Word of mouth was another effective way in which a position might be applied for: Indeed, it might have been the most commonly used. From *Rose: My Life in Service*, by Rosina Harrison, lady's maid to Lady Astor, comes the following passage in her own voice: "By now I was well enough known to the staffs of the big houses to be able to put the word round that I was thinking of making a change, and something would be suggested to me through the grapevine. And one had the added advantage of learning in that way everything about the job and the person I'd be working for."

References

On the importance of a good reference, Harrison had the following to say: "Employers used to set great store by references. They had to be immaculate, otherwise you stood no chance of the job. [Likewise] we had a Who's Who and a What's What below stairs which contained more personal and colourful information about the gentry than ever the written version did. There was also a blacklist [against employers], and woe betide anyone who got on it. It could spell ruination for any hostess."

Servants could be dismissed with either a month's notice or a month's wages. Alternately, servants could not legally leave their positions until they had served out their notices, the advantage going to the employer. In some cases, an employer might get around the month's notice in the event of serious offenses on the servant's part. As might be expected, this clause was sometimes abused by employers, as they were the very persons who determined the seriousness of an offense.

No restraint of diet required during their use, and are certain to prevent the disease attacking any vital part. Sold by all chemists at 1s. 1½d. and 2s. 9d. per box.

TAMAR INDIEN, for Constipation, Headache, Bile, Indigestion, &c.—Special Caution.—The public are recommended to see that they get the real lozenge prescribed by the Faculty, as cheap and spurious imitations are now being extensively advertised. The genuine boxes bear the registered title, "Tamar Indien." Price 2s. 6d. per box, by post 2d. extra.—E. GRILLON, Wool Exchange, London, and of all Chymists.

A CERTAIN CURE for INDIGESTION.—CHARCOAL and PEPSINE LOZENGES. Prepared only by GODFREY and COOKE, Chymists, at 30, Conduit-street, W., and at 26, St. George's-place, S.W.; sole Manufacturers of the celebrated Godfrey's Smelling Salt and Spirit Sal Volatile. Specialities are protected by their trade mark. The oldest established firm in London; date 1680.

POWELL'S BALSAM of ANISEED, for coughs, bronchitis, influenza, colds, &c. The effect of one teaspoonful taken in a little water on going to bed is extraordinary. No family should be without it in the winter. Sold by chemists and medicine vendors throughout the world, at 1s. 1½d. and 2s. 3d. per bottle; a great saving in taking family bottles, 11s. each. Paris, Beral, Roberts, Hogg; Brussels, Pharmacie Delacre; Geneva, Baker; Rotterdam, Santen Koiff. Established over 50 years. Prepared only by Thos. Powell, Blackfriars-road London.

GOUT, Rheumatism, Spasms, Indigestion, Cramps, Nervous Complaints, &c., are greatly relieved by the use of OXLEY'S CONCENTRATED ESSENCE of JAMAICA GINGER, which has during 75 years been highly recommended by the Faculty. It shortens the duration of fits of gout, confining them to the extremities and mitigating the paroxysms; it warms and invigorates the stomach, removes flatulency, assists digestion, and strengthens the whole system. Sold by most chemists and medicine vendors throughout the world, in bottles, 2s. 9d., 4s. 6d., and 10s. 6d.

COCKLE'S COMPOUND ANTIBILIOUS PILLS. These pills consist of a careful and peculiar admixture of the best and mildest vegetable aperients with the pure extract of the flowers of the camomile. They will be found a most efficacious remedy for derangement of the digestive organs and for torpid action of the liver and bowels, which produce indigestion and the several varieties of bilious and liver complaints. They speedily remove the irritation and feverish state of the stomach, allay spasms, correct the morbid condition of the liver and organs subservient to digestion, promote a due and healthy secretion of bile, and relieve the constitution of all gouty matter and other impurities, which, by circulating in the blood, must injuriously affect the action of the kidneys; thus, by removing the causes productive of so much discomfort, they restore the energies both of body and mind. To those who indulge in the luxuries of the table, these pills will prove highly useful, occasioning no pain in their action, unless they meet with an unusual quantity of acrid bile and acid matter in the stomach and bowels. To Europeans on their arrival in India or China, they are recommended as a preservative against the fatal disorders peculiar to tropical climates. Their occasional use, if combined with the strictest attention to diet, will be frequently found to remove at once, by their influence over the secretions, that congestive and unhealthy condition of the liver which is so often the earliest antecedent of severe febrile and constitutional disturbance.

COCKLE'S COMPOUND ANTIBILIOUS PILLS.—This celebrated family aperient, long highly esteemed by all classes of society, being free from mercury, combines safety with efficacy. In boxes at 1s. 1½d., 2s. 9d., 4s. 6d., and 11s.—18, New Ormond-street, London.

COCKLE'S COMPOUND ANTIBILIOUS PILLS.—A good family medicine chest, with a prudent use, has saved many a life; and yet we think the idea might be improved upon, and reduced to a more simple form. Take some good compound, such as COCKLE'S ANTIBILIOUS PILLS, and we find that the desired end may be obtained without scales and weights, or little mysterious compartments and enchanted bottles with crystal stoppers. Others might be used, but Cockle's pills, as tested by many thousands of persons, and found to answer their purpose so well, may be set down as the best.—Observer.

COCKLE'S COMPOUND ANTIBILIOUS PILLS, in use by all classes 78 years, for indigestion, bilious and liver complaints, may be had throughout the United Kingdom in boxes at 1s 1½d., 2s. 9d., 4s. 6d., and 11s., as well as in India, China, New Zealand, and Australia.—18, New Ormond-street, London, W.C.

CHILBLAINS.—A Warranted Cure.—MARRIS'S ICELAND LINIMENT is a certain cure for all chilblains, broken or unbroken. Invaluable in all cases of rheumatism, lumbago, or neuralgia. 1s. 1½d., 2s. 3d., and 4s. 6d.; by post 18 or 33 stamps.—Marris, No. 37, Berners-street, London; Staircase, Soho Bazaar; and all Chemists.

MR. ADOLPHUS, Surgeon-Chiropodist to the Royal Family, may be consulted daily, for the removal of corns, bunions, defective toenails, &c. Terms moderate. Established. Address 43, Sackville-street, Piccadilly, W.

WANT PLACES.—All letters to be post-paid.

WET NURSE. Respectable, single, age 23. Very good reference. Baby 3½ months old.—M., 71, Cornwall-terrace, Regent's-park.

NURSE (LADY'S CERTIFICATED). Highly recommended by ladies she has nursed. Terms moderate.—Mrs. Stores, No. 24, Delancy-street, Camden-town, N.W.

NURSE to a lady's first baby. Respectable, age 23. Good character.—L. S., Leighton-lodge, Carshalton, Surrey.

NURSE to one or two children in a gentleman's family. 6 years' good character. Age 25. State wages.—L. H., 2, Harber-terrace, Stoke Newington-green.

NURSE in a gentleman's family. Age 31. Can take a baby from the month. Experienced. 4 years' personal character. Please state wages.—A. M., Wade's, 98, Kensington High-street.

LADY'S-MAID. Age 21. Good dressmaker, milliner, and hairdresser. Good references.—E. Gidley, 7, Fulbrook-road, Junction-road, N.

LADY'S-MAID. French Protestant, age 29. Dressmaker and needlewoman. Good character. London preferred.—M. S. D., Knoll Baildon, Shipley, York.

FEMME de CHAMBRE dans une bonne famille. Suisse Protestante. Parlant trois langues. Bonne couturière et coiffeuse. Pas d'objection à voyager.—M. B., 6, Park-row, Knightsbridge, S.W.

YOUNG LADIES'-MAID. Age 22. Protestant. Good hairdresser and dressmaker. Good references.—M., 186, Buckingham Palace-road, S.W.

MAID to one lady. No objection to travel. Good character. Town or country.—A. B., Woodcote-lodge, Epsom.

MAID (USEFUL) to one lady, or Housekeeper. Three years' personal character; 7 years' previous.—A. B., Johnson's Library, 106, Crawford-street, W.

MAID (USEFUL) to young ladies or children, or any

family where two or three are kept. Good character.—E. D., No. 8, Burford-road, Stratford, E., Essex.

KITCHENMAID. Age 20. Not been out before.—A. Cox, Owlswick Princes, Risborough, Bucks.

KITCHENMAID in a gentleman's family where a scullerymaid is kept. Wages £18 to £20, all found. Age 22. Good character.—M. B., Pellet's, Silver-street, Edmonton.

KITCHENMAID in a gentleman's family. Town preferred. Good references.—A. B., 63, Calverley-road, Tunbridge-wells.

KITCHENMAID in a gentleman's family. Age 22. Good character. Please state wages.—G. L., 12, Little Brook-street, Regent's-park, London, N.W.

KITCHENMAID (UNDER) in a gentleman's family. Age 16. Not been out before.—M. Thorne, 5, George-place, Queen's-road, Chelsea.

BUTLER where a footman or boy is kept. Good character. Age 40, height 5feet 9, single. Town or country.—H. H., Shaw's News Rooms, 256, Oxford-street, W.

BUTLER, or Butler and Valet where a footman or page is kept. Single, age 30. 2½ years' good character. Town or country.—J. P., Rampton Manor, Lincoln.

BUTLER. Age 43. Good character. Total abstainer. Town or country.—S. S., Broadbent's Stationer, High-street, Marylebone.

MAN-COOK (FRENCH), to do jobs or dinners in family, for a week or two, in London or the neighbourhood.—M. T. S., No. 75, Finchley-road, St. John's-wood, London, N.W.

TRAVELLING SERVANT, or Valet. Age 27. 4 years' good references.—F. K., Fredk. L. May and Co.'s, Advertising Agents, 159, Piccadilly.

TRAVELLING SERVANT and VALET, for Italy and the East. Experienced. Young. 12 months' reference to last employer.—A. Z., 24, Gilbert-street, Grosvenor-square.

VALET de CHAMBRE avec un gentleman seul. Un jeune homme Français. Arrivant de Paris. Connait un peu la cuisine. Hautes références.—O. T., Cholet and Benoist's, 67, Wigmore-st., W.

IN-DOOR SERVANT (thorough) where a footman or page is kept, or Single-handed in a small family. Age 32. 12 months' personal character. Now leaving.—F. B. W., 5, Victoria-grove, Kensington.

IN-DOOR SERVANT (thorough), Single-handed or otherwise. Age 26. Good character.—J. P., 15, William-street, Swanmore, Ryde.

IN-DOOR SERVANT, Single-handed or otherwise. Age 24. Good character.—G. B., 5, New Quebec-street, Portman-square.

IN-DOOR SERVANT, out of livery, where assistance is given. Single, age 27. 1 year and 10 months in last situation.—J. R., 20, Coleherne-mews, West Brompton, S.W.

IN-DOOR SERVANT. Age 28, married. 3 years and 10 months' character. Willing to make himself useful. Town or country.—S. H., 441, Liverpool-road, Islington, London, N.

IN-DOOR SERVANT in a family. German. Speaks French and a little English. Age 24, height 6ft. Good references. A. K., 2, Castle-street, Leicester-square.

IN-DOOR SERVANT, Single-handed in a gentleman's family. German. Just arrived. Age 23. Speaks English. High references.—O. D., 39, Brewer-street, Regent-street, W.

IN-DOOR MAN-SERVANT, Single-handed, out of livery. 3 years' good character. State wages. Country.—W. T., 47, Stamford-street, Blackfriars, London.

IN-DOOR SERVANT. Thoroughly understands his duties. Single-handed or otherwise. Good personal character. Age 40.—G. L., 39, Edward-street, Dorset-square, N.W.

IN-DOOR SERVANT, out of livery, Single-handed, or with a page. Height 5ft. 8. Good character.—G. L., 2, Campden-hill west, Kensington, W.

PAGE under a butler. Active. Age 16. Personal character.—O. M., 21, Warren-street, Fitzroy-square, W.

FOOTMAN (FIRST), or Single. Age 27, height 5ft. 8. 2½ years' character. Town or country. No objection to a job.—H. A., 9, Westmoreland-street, Pimlico, S.W.

FOOTMAN under a butler or otherwise. Age 20, height 5ft. 8. Town or country. Good personal character. Knows town well.—J. C. M., 8, Francis-street, Chelsea, S.W.

A Respectable MAN, age 22, height 5ft. 6, under a butler. Willing to make himself generally useful.—H. W. B., No. 61, Frith-street, Soho.

COACHMAN (HEAD). Age 40, married, no encumbrance. 2 years' good character from last situation.—G. H., 14, Livingstone-terrace, Oak-hill, Beckenham, Kent.

COACHMAN. Middle age. Long character. Good testimonials.—J. G., Ryan's, Saddler, Spring-street, Paddington.

COACHMAN. Married, light weight. 3 years and 7 months' good character, 8 years and 6 months' previous.—A. B., Hearn's Library, 125, Seymour-place, Bryanston-square

COACHMAN. Experienced, married, age 38. Knows town well. 2 years' good personal character.—H. P., Ivall and Large's, Coachmakers, Victoria-street, S.W.

COACHMAN where one or more grooms are kept. Married six years, no family. Excellent character from last and previous masters. Country preferred.—A. W., 20, Tachbrook-st., Pimlico.

COACHMAN. One or a pair. Knows town. Country preferred. Good character. Age 33, married.—W. N., 2, Prospect-cottages, Woodford, Essex.

GROOM. Can ride or drive well. Town or country. Can wait at table. Excellent character.—M., 29, Queen's-road, Bayswater.

GROOM under a coachman, or Single-handed. Age 21. Good character from last and previous situation.—F. A., Froyle, Alton, Hants.

GROOM, Single-handed or under a coachman. Age 26, single. Country preferred. 3 years' character from last situation.—A. K., Vine-cottage, Peckham-rye, London.

GARDENER (WORKING) where two or more are kept. Thoroughly practical man. Over 35 years' experience. Married, no encumbrance. Good character.—A. B., 1, Edinburgh-ter., Herne-hill.

GARDENER (UNDER), or to look after a horse and trap and small garden. Age 21. Good character.—B., Leacroft, Staines, Middlesex.

PORTER, or Waiter in an hotel, restaurant, or tavern. Age 23, single. Tall, steady. In or out of house. Good character from hotel.—J. D., 72, Grange-street, St. John's-road, Hoxton.

WAITER. Sitting or coffee room. Town or country. In large or small hotel. 3 years' good character from last situation. Age 25, single.—M. D., 92, Drummond-street, Euston-sq., N.W.

WAITER. French. Speaks English

Advertisements in newspapers listed available servants

WAGES

During the mid-nineteenth century, a maid-of-all-work in London was receiving six to eight pounds per year and an allowance for tea, sugar and beer. Or, according to the terms of employment, she might have received from nine to fourteen pounds per year if she herself purchased the tea, sugar and beer. A typical lady's maid was earning twelve to fifteen pounds and an allowance, a valet from twenty-five to fifty pounds, and a liveried footman fifteen to twenty-five pounds per year.

Board wages and tea money were also decided upon at the time of employment. Board wages were the sums allowed the servants whenever the employer's family spent time away from the household, as when taking up residence at a country home, taking the cook along with them. Board wages were then used by the servants to buy meals at a pub or cookhouse. In 1825, board wages amounted to about ten shillings per week for females, twelve shillings a week for males. Also, a man was allowed a pot of ale per day and a woman a pint per day, in addition to the table beer served during meals. Tea money was paid to a servant in lieu of an employer providing daily tea and sugar.

PERQUISITES

Traditionally, presents of money were made by employers to their servants either at Christmas or the new year. Additionally, an upper servant might realize additional income from the perks that went along with certain positions. It was understood that a lady's maid expected to receive her mistress's cast-off clothing, and this would have been defined in the terms of employment. The valet often enjoyed the same perk. These clothes could be worn by the servants on their days off or sold for cash to secondhand clothes dealers. Upon the death of her mistress, it was usual for the lady's maid to receive her lady's entire wardrobe, with the exception of any personal articles specifically bequeathed elsewhere.

Another form of extra income available to certain servants was vails, or tips. Upon joining the staff, an upper servant was informed of the approximate amount of vails and tips he could expect to realize each year. The master also provided details regarding the scale of entertaining that typically went on in the house, which helped the servant estimate just how much he might hope to realize in vails.

The distribution of vails took place upon a guest's departure, with the house servants lining up in two files by the front door. As the guest walked to the door, he was expected to tip the various servants according to the amount of personal service he'd received from each, as well as to the social standing of the master. In some homes, only the male servants were entitled to vails, but as a rule these vails were shared among all upper staff, with a small portion distributed to the lower servants as well. Potential visitors who did not themselves possess a small fortune were often forced to turn down invitations, as the payment of vails was not within their means. Another disadvantage to paying vails was that a guest might pay a servant less than the servant felt he deserved. Upon the guest's return to the house, he would find his orders ignored or continually "misunderstood."

Before the nineteenth century, annual holidays and days off during the week or month were usually not allowed. It was generally accepted that from the time servants entered into service, their every moment belonged to the master or mistress, and they were expected to abandon thoughts of conducting any sort of private lives outside the house. It was frowned upon for servants to have friends or relatives call at the back door, and any female servants who had "followers" were dismissed. Later, the masters of many large houses allowed the servants to receive friends or family at the house upon certain occasions. In some houses, especially those in town, the servants were required to attend church on Sunday evenings. A cold dinner would have been served to the family in order that the servants might get away in time for the service, which lasted an hour or so.

During their time off, servants most often visited the homes of nearby friends and relatives or some public house that catered to the servant classes. Often, grand events were held for servants at the larger houses during the Christmas holidays, including themed dances and masquerades. On March 13, 1819, the Prince of Wales personally hosted a supper in the kitchen of the Brighton Pavilion for his servants, and each year Queen Victoria hosted a Ghillie's Ball for her servants at Balmoral Castle.

Many members of the aristocracy included their servants in family celebrations as well. John Ashton relates the story of such a celebration, which took place on January 4, 1814: "The day of the Christening of the little Marquis of Granby was also the birthday of his father, the Duke of Rutland, so that the two events [were], combined with the

Royal visit [of the Regent]. Mr. Douglas, the Duke's butler, entertained the tenantry with an oval Cistern of strong punch, containing 50 gallons. . . . [This hospitality went on for days.] The house contains more than two hundred individuals, who partake daily of the festivities. The Cistern of punch, under the management of Mr. Douglas, administered in the Servants' Hall on Tuesday to the household and tenantry, laid many a brave fellow prostrate. The passages of the house reminded one of a Castle taken by storm. . . . Many were found the next day in subterraneous passages of the Castle, with symptoms of recovering animation. The punch was not out at 10 o'clock on Wednesday morning."

Prince Puckler-Muskau, visiting England in 1827, wrote a similar account: "I rode to Cobham Hall, to spend a few days there on occasion of Lord Darnley's birthday, which was celebrated today in a rural and unpretending manner. Excepting myself, there was no one but the family. . . . We dined early, in order that we might be present at a supper in the open air, which Lord Darnley gave to all his labourers, about a hundred in number. It was managed with the greatest decorum. We sat next to the iron fence in the pleasure-ground, and the tables for the people were placed on the new-mown grass. First, about fifty young girls, from the Lancasterian school which Lady Darnley has established in the Park, were regaled with tea and cakes. They were all dressed alike, and very prettily too: they were children of from six to fourteen. After them came the labourers, and seated themselves at a long table plentifully furnished with enormous dishes of roast beef, vegetables and pudding. Each brought his own knife and fork and earthen pot. The servants of the house set out the dinner, did the honours and poured out the beer from great watering-pots. The village musicians played all the while."

RETIREMENT

By saving their money, servants could retire in comfort, especially if they had been remembered in deceased employers wills or with annuities or pensions. Along with these monies, upper servants familiar with the ways of the gentry could easily enter a community and live in comfort. Retired male servants might set themselves up in some respectable trade, with many keeping public houses.

In 1837, the Department of Treasury proposed the following pensions for retiring royal servants: Samuel Jemmet—Senior page of backstairs in constant attendance upon the late king upward of thirty-five years, is sixty-seven years of age and much entitled to favorable consideration. Income 440 pounds per annum with apartments. Margaret Yeackle—personal housemaid to George IV and William IV, twenty-five years in service, very infirm. Proposed allowance 50 pounds per annum.

Upper female servants were often kept in places within the family, rather than send them into a lonely retirement. Lady Sarah Spencer wrote from Wimbledon on June 12, 1808: "I must tell you that two days ago Papa made Nurse Strode a present of twenty guineas, I believe, and announced to her that she was to establish herself here for her future life as a sort of housekeeper, or rather, what Mary Carter called, 'house-creeper.' She was so delighted, and so overcome, that the conference ended in their both crying together."

In 1851, the census found that 40 percent of female servants in England and Wales were under the age of nineteen, with 66 percent being under twenty-four years in age. A bit later, *The Times* of January 10, 1870, listed the following servants who were seeking positions:

2 Housekeepers
5 Cook/Housekeepers
29 Cooks
13 Lady's Maids
2 Under Housemaids
2 Maids
4 Chambermaids
7 Parlormaids
4 Kitchen Maids
2 Laundry Maids
1 Scullery Maid
5 Upper Nurses
1 Nursemaid
10 Butlers
3 Valets
3 Footmen
2 Pages
22 Coachmen
1 Second Coachman
5 Grooms
1 Head Gardener
1 Gardener
1 Stillroom Maid
2 Head Nurses
8 Nurses
2 Needlewomen

SERVANTS IN MOURNING

Mourning garments, usually completely black in color, were provided to the staff when a death occurred in the family. If the deceased was a child, an unmarried woman or a lady who had died in childbirth, the color of mourning was white, and black armbands were worn. Sometimes the band was placed on the coachman's right arm and on the footman's left so that they looked symmetrical when seated upon the box. Livery crest buttons were changed to black, as were the horses' harnesses.

Should the master of the house have died while at his country estate, the body would have lain in state before burial. Along with friends and neighbors, the servants, tenants and local tradesmen filed past the coffin to pay their respects. At the funeral, after the coffin had been lowered into the grave, the family's upper servants symbolically broke their staffs of office and threw these down upon the coffin lid.

By the late nineteenth century, simple black dresses and bonnets, collars and cuffs of crepe were worn by female servants. After a prescribed period of time, half-mourning attire would be worn, when the severity of unrelieved black was broken. A servant might then don white trimmings. Male servants wore black suits, sans shiny buttons, appropriate ties and armbands. All servants were given two sets of mourning clothes, one to work in, the other to be worn on Sundays and reception days, with this second set of clothing being made from a better-quality cloth. For at least eight years after the death of Prince Albert, royal servants continued to wear armbands of black crepe upon the direction of Queen Victoria.

SERVANTS' LIVERY

Distribution of livery varied from house to house, but the following extract from *The Household Regulations for Hatfield House* (1896) is typical of the period: "Liveries are given 1st April and 1st October of each year. Evening liveries every twelve months. Tweed Jackets every Twelve Months (except the Hall Porter and Steward's Room Boy, they have a tweed suit). Hats, Gloves and Stockings for them will be issued from time to time as required. Mackintoshes are given according to wear. When Evening Liveries have been worn Six Months from date of entry into service, the wearer is entitled to a New Suit on the 1st of April approximately. . . . When Morning Liveries have been worn Three Months from the date of entry (into service), the wearer is entitled to a New Suit either in April or October, according to date of entry, but if not worn Three Months the wearer is not entitled to a Suit until the next term, or issue of Liveries."

BIBLIOGRAPHY

Dawes, Frank Victor. *Not in Front of the Servants.* London: Random Century, 1989.

Hartcup, Adeline. *Below Stairs in the Great Country Houses.* London: Sidgwick & Jackson, 1980.

Roberts, Robert. *Roberts' Guide for Butlers and Household Staff.* Bedford: Applewood Books, 1988.

Stanley, Liz, ed. *The Diaries of Hannah Cullwick: Victorian Maidservant.* New Brunswick, N.J.: Rutgers University Press, 1984.

Vince, John. *The Country House: How It Worked.* London: John Murray, Ltd., 1991.

Chapter Four

Home Furnishings

Perhaps the most important nineteenth-century interior design innovation was the coordination of elements in a single room to achieve a specific look. The originator of this concept was Robert Adam, who brought neoclassical design to England, and who went so far as to plan room design down to the doorknobs, accent medallions and carpets. In addition, rather than limiting himself to design concept alone, Adam worked with such craftsmen as Thomas Chippendale and Josiah Wedgwood to conceive original designs to match his clients' tastes and preferences. Carpets became fitted to the floor and furniture lines cleaner, with French windows now letting more light into rooms. In addition to Adam's neoclassical trends, other popular Regency styles included the Empire, based upon Napoleon's Egyptian campaigns, which was in vogue 1804–1815, and the Chinese design inspired by Chippendale and taken to the extreme by the Prince Regent.

WILLIAM MORRIS

While the middle class put their rooms together impulsively, the wealthy began to use classical themes in their decorating plans, modeling these upon Greek, Renaissance and rococo influences. A major decorating innovation was the rise of that most intimidating of species, the interior decorator, the most well known of these being William Morris, who greatly influenced the second half of the nineteenth century. In the beginning, the interior decorator did not merely make decisions as to fabric and paint, or advise on the merits of one dining table over another. Instead, decorators were schooled in various principles of design and influenced everything from preliminary building plans to garden design. In 1861, Morris's firm was either personally producing or supervising the production of wall murals, architectural carving, stained glass, metalwork, furniture, fabrics, paper hangings and more.

CHARLES EASTLAKE AND CHRISTOPHER DRESSER

Never before had there been such a mass shaping of national tastes nor so concerted an effort to educate the public in the domestic arts. Even those Victorian consumers unable to afford the services of an interior decorator benefited from the knowledge of period designers and arbiters of good taste, such as Charles Eastlake and Christopher Dresser. Each gentleman wrote books that have become classics in their fields, with Eastlake having published his *Hints on Household Taste in Furniture, Upholstery, and Other Details* in 1868 and Dresser producing his *Principles of Victorian Decorative Design* in 1873. As a member of the Royal Institute of British Architects, Eastlake's credentials were impressive, but his true passion lay in the design of furniture and interior fittings. His book was so popular that it underwent five reprintings, and there is no doubt that, along with its sound decorating advice, its success was due to the ease with which readers could employ Eastlake's suggestions in their own homes.

So concise was the presentation of Eastlake's book that it was broken down into such chapters as "The Entrance Hall," "The Floors and Walls" and "Table Glass," among others. Dresser, on the other hand, structured his book and teachings around the basics, such as curtain material, paint colors, carpets, hardware and the like. The result of these and other books of their kind was that the public was provided with a measure of knowledge and confidence that allowed for sound decorating decisions.

COMMERCIALIZATION

During the first half of the nineteenth century, a unique marketing advancement was born—the pattern book. These were sold to the public, who could then pore over designs when considering purchases, and they were also used in the shops themselves. Customers could see many more designs in both furniture and ornamentation than a tradesmen could possibly stock, and the coordination of interiors could be achieved more easily than ever before. Instead of the resulting haphazard interior design previously achieved by the less wealthy, consumers in all income brackets could now depend upon a "finished" look within their homes. In addition, it was about this time that industrialization allowed for ready-made furniture. By midcentury, aniline dyes had been developed and were producing a broader spectrum of color options, and carpets, fabrics and wallpaper were all being mass manufactured in factories.

HIGH VICTORIAN STYLE

In addition to the factors above, an increase in jobs due to the industrial revolution and wage stabilization made for a middle class who not only aspired to ape their betters, but who could, for the first time, afford to do so. During the third quarter of the century, William Morris initiated a trend away from mass-produced designs by introducing the Arts and Crafts movement, which featured handmade patterns. While these were beyond the finances of most of the population, the machine age allowed Morris's designs to be cheaply reproduced, so that the masses could surround themselves with a semblance of Morris's ideas for "good taste."

"THE ICING ON THE CAKE"

London's Great Exhibition of 1851, for which Prince Albert was chiefly responsible, introduced the public to the myriad possibilities for interior design. It also served as a showcase for the various tradesmen who produced ornamental objects, such as pottery, porcelain, silver and glass. The Victorians embraced these and took to covering every available flat surface within their homes with such objects as liquor sets, urns, picture frames, china sculptures, vases and lamps. Advances in the mass manufacture of various types of ornamental glass allowed for their purchase by all levels of society. Silver, whether used in pieces that were ornamental or functional, such as vases or eating utensils, also underwent a change in production. The process of electroplating had been developed and meant production at lower costs, the savings being passed on to the eager consumer. Gilt, japanning and decoupage all became popular methods of decoration for items in most rooms in the house, being used upon decorative boxes, fire screens and tea trays.

As surprising as it may seem to the modern-day decorator, the entrance hall received perhaps the most thought and planning when being decorated. Anyone who has ever visited a Victorian house will recall a large hall stand or mirrored coat/umbrella/hat stand taking the place of pride just within the entrance door. Though serving a function, these stands were status symbols as well. Should the hall be large enough, a center table might also have been added, as well as oil paintings, geometric floor tiles and elaborate lighting fixtures, either suspended from the ceiling or hung in pairs on the walls. Should any empty space be left, the Victorian housewife might have added a piece of sculpture or large vase to complete the decor.

THE PARLOR

The largest public room within a house was the drawing room or parlor. This was where visitors would be entertained and where family celebrations took place. Newly constructed houses were built to designs that made the most of available space. As most rooms in middle-class homes had a specific purpose, parlors became an increasingly important status symbol, as they were strictly nonfunctional and seen as a luxury. Parlors were reserved for entertaining guests and displaying heirlooms, a nod to aristocratic drawing rooms. From the 1850s on, everyone aspired to have a parlor, as it served to elevate a residence above the strictly functional cottage homes of the lower classes.

The main difference between Regency and Victorian parlors is that the molded and gilded decoration that had been lavishly added to ceiling and wall moldings during the Regency fell out of use. Thereafter, the bulk of ornamental interest was transferred to the furnishings and decorative pieces themselves. High ceilings and wallpapered walls were the norm, with a floral pattern being the most popular. A machine-woven, wall-to-wall carpet would have covered the floor, while large pieces of wall furniture, such as massive fireplaces with overmantels, bookcases, writing desks and display cabinets, were placed throughout the room. Paintings, photographs and homemade samplers were hung upon any remaining wall space. The tall windows

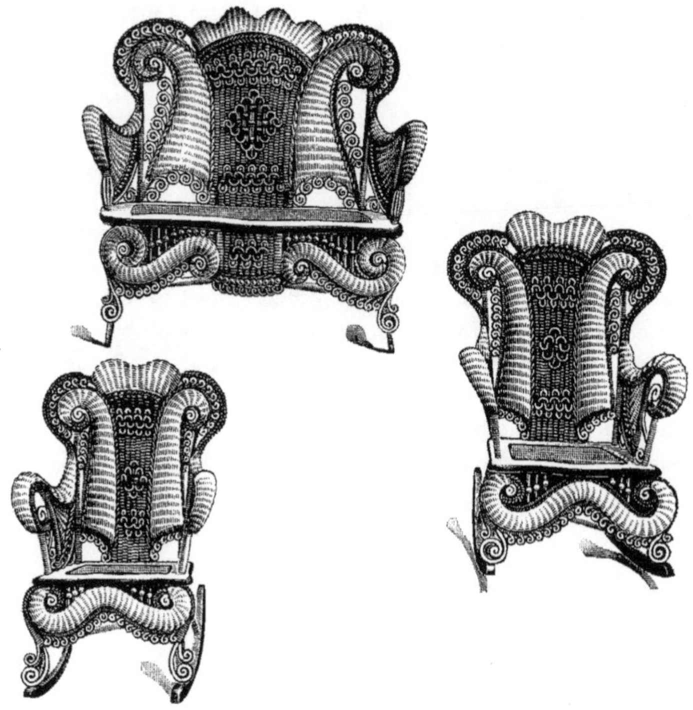

Parlor suit

would have been decorated with elaborate curtains in a heavy fabric and a valance. In order to achieve the "cluttered" look most associated with Victorian design, cording, tassels, pillows, skirting and other fabric details were used.

THE DINING ROOM

The Victorian dining room most often seems to present-day minds to have been as crowded, or more so, than the parlor. This results from the fact that the room was most often somewhat smaller in size, heavily paneled, either in wainscoting or full wall panels. Dark paint and heavy drapes served to further the illusion of closeness. In addition, the dining room table and chairs were heavy pieces of furniture, often elaborately carved and of dark wood such as walnut or mahogany. Paintings upon the walls, sideboards, china cabinets and the manner in which the Victorian table was laid for service all played their parts in reducing the size of the room. Each place would have been set with a dinner and side plate, heavy silverware and two or three glasses, as well as the table being decorated with an epergne, candelabra, decanters and serving dishes.

THE BEDROOM

Regency bedrooms tended to be eclectic in arrangement, as it was not until circa 1840 that matching bedroom suites were introduced to consumers. The furniture most often found in Regency bedrooms included a bed, wardrobe, washstand, chair and perhaps writing desk or vanity and a standing, full-length mirror. By the early Victorian period, half tester or canopied beds had returned to vogue. Bedrooms were heated by fireplaces and, with the heavy draperies, bed hangings and other decorative upholstery, many advocates for hygiene and health felt that the rooms should be less cluttered in order to prevent vermin and the breeding of germs.

As the Victorian bed became larger, so did the other furnishings. And as ladies' garments became wider in design, with more underclothing being worn with them, wardrobes and armoires necessarily became larger as well. Even after bathrooms began to be fitted into homes, a washstand would still have been used in the bedroom, with a vanity or dressing table being sold along with the washstand as a set. A major factor in the transition of the bedroom from Regency function to Victorian sanctuary can be found in population growth. Families became larger, the middle classes adopted servants and the house became necessarily some degrees more crowded. The bedroom became a place into which one could escape in order to enjoy a bit of privacy, and so they were fitted out and contained everything one might need for comfort.

BIBLIOGRAPHY

Blackie and Son Staff. *The Victorian Cabinet-Maker's Assistant.* New York: Dover Publications, 1970.

Chippendale, Thomas. *The Gentleman and Cabinet-Maker's Director.* New York: Dover, 1966.

Cunningham, Colin. *Building for the Victorians.* Cambridge: Cambridge University Press, 1985.

Eastlake, Charles L. *Hints on Household Taste: The Classic Handbook of Victorian Interior Decoration.* New York: Dover Publications, 1969.

Girouard, Mark. *The Victorian Country House.* New Haven: Yale University Press, 1985.

Guild, Robin. *The Victorian House Book.* New York: Rizzoli, 1989.

Hoskins, Lesley, ed. *The Papered Wall: History, Pattern, Technique.* New York: Abrams, 1994.

Joy, Edward, ed. *Pictorial Dictionary of British Nineteenth-Century Furniture Design.* Wappingers Falls, N.Y.: Antique Collectors' Club, 1977.

McClelland, Nancy. *Duncan Phyfe and the English Regency 1795–1830.* New York: Dover Publications, 1980.

Miller, Judith, and Martin Miller. *Victorian Style.* London: Mitchell Beazley, 1993.

Watkins, Susan. *Jane Austen's Town and Country Style.* New York: Rizzoli, 1990.

CHAPTER FIVE

Fashion

There has been much written about nineteenth-century fashions, and there are innumerable books devoted to the description and illustration of dress. It would be redundant to recount the same details here. The laborer, industrial worker and those living and working in the countryside would typically have worn more serviceable, rather than fashionable, clothing. The majority of the population sought to keep up with the fashionable minority, copying their clothing in less expensive materials, the results often being that their everyday wear would have been at least a season or two out of date. What has previously been neglected, and what is perhaps more valuable to the researcher, are firsthand accounts of the fashions and rules regarding the wearing of various costumes. The following are accounts from *The Habits of Good Society*, in which the anonymous author offers insight into both male and female dress.

MALE ATTIRE

"A well dressed man does not require so much an extensive as a varied wardrobe. He wants a different costume for every season and occasion; but if what he selects is simple rather than striking, he may appear in the same clothes as often as he likes, as long as they are fresh and appropriate to the season and the object. There are four kinds of coats which he must have: a morning coat, a frock coat, a dress coat and an over coat. An economical man may do well with four of the first and one of each of the others per annum. George the Fourth's wardrobe sold for fifteen thousand pounds, and a single cloak brought no less than eight hundred pounds. But George was a king and a beau, and in debt to his tailor. The dress of an English gentleman in the present day should not cost him more than the tenth part of his income on an average. But as fortunes vary more than position, if his income is large it will take a much smaller proportion, if small a larger one. But generally speaking, a man with three hundred pounds per year should not devote more than thirty pounds to his outward man. The seven coats in question will cost about eighteen pounds. Six pairs of morning, and one of evening, trousers will cost nine pounds. Four morning waistcoats and one for evening make another four pounds. Gloves, linens, hats, scarves and neck ties about ten pounds, and the important item of boots, at least five pounds more. . . . The frock coat of very dark blue or black, or a black cloth cut away, with white waistcoat, and lavender gloves, are almost indispensable.

"For all evening wear—black cloth trousers. The only evening waistcoat for all purposes for a man of taste is one of simple black cloth, with the simplest buttons possible. The only distinction allowed is in the neck tie. For dinner, the opera, and balls, this must be white, and the smaller the better. The black tie is only admitted for evening parties, and should be equally simple. The gloves must be white, not yellow. Gloves should always be worn on entering the room, and drawn off for dinner. There are shades of being 'dressed'; and a man is called 'little dressed,' 'well dressed,' and 'much dressed,' not according to the quantity but the quality of his coverings. To be 'little dressed' is to wear old things, of a make that is no longer the fashion, having no pretension to elegance, artistic beauty, or ornament. To be 'much dressed' is to be extreme in fashion, with brand new clothes. To be 'well dressed' is the happy medium between these two.

"For hunting . . . cord-breeches and some kind of boots are indispensable. So are spurs [and] a hunting whip or crop. The red coat is only worn by regular members of a hunt. . . . In any case you are better with an ordinary riding-coat of dark colour, though undoubtedly red is prettier in the field. If you will wear the latter, see that it is cut square, for the swallow tail is obsolete. Again, your cords should be light in colour and fine in quality; your waistcoat, if with a red coat, quite light too; your scarf of cashmere, of a buff colour, and fastened with a simple gold pin; your hat should be old, and your cap of dark green or black velvet, plated inside. Lastly, for a choice of boots, the Hessians are more easily cleaned, and therefore less expensive to keep.''

FEMALE COSTUME

''For married women of rank, five hundred [pounds] a year ought to be the maximum; a hundred a year the minimum. The wives of ministers, and more especially of diplomatists, who require to appear frequently either in foreign courts, or in our own, may require five hundred, or even more. . . .'' Speaking of the current fashion for crinolines, the anonymous author attributes its popularity to the Empress Eugenie: ''The infatuation has spread from the palace to the private house; thence even to the cottage. Your lady's maid must now need to have her crinoline, and it has even become an essential to factory girls. . . . That there are some advantages in this modern fashion, cannot be denied. . . . The peeress, or the baronet's lady, or the wife of a minister, or of an opulent M.P., or of a very wealthy commoner, should, when she appears dressed for the morning, be richly dressed. Silk, or if in winter, some material trimmed with silk or velvet, should compose her dress. The morning dress of the present day is worn close up to the throat, and the sleeves are loose and large; so that underneath them, sleeves, richly worked, or trimmed with lace, may be seen hanging down, or fastened round the wrist with a bracelet. If stockings are visible, they should be of the finest silk or thread; the shoe well made, slight, and somewhat trimmed; the fashion of wearing gloves indoors, or even mittens, has much died away lately.

''There is another style of morning dress is elegant, that of the 'peignoir,' a loose robe, which admits of great richness of texture; it may be of Cashmere or of fine Merino; of anything but silk, which is more appropriate to gowns; but this dress is scarcely suitable to any but the early morning hours, and ceases to be consistent in the gay afternoons. . . . The morning coiffure, be it a cap, or be it the dressing of the hair, should be simple, compact and neat.

''One point of dress has been much amended lately, owing to the good sense of our Queen. It was formerly thought ungenteel to wear anything but thin Morocco shoes, or very slight boots in walking. Clogs and galoshes were necessarily resorted to. Victoria has assumed the Balmoral petticoat, than which, for health, comfort, warmth, and effect, no invention was ever better. She has courageously accompanied

Street and house dresses showing English sleeve and new method of decoration (from Petit Courrier des Dames*)*

it with the Balmoral boot, and even with the mohair and coloured stocking.

"The carriage or visiting dress should be exceedingly handsome; gayer in colour, richer in texture than the morning dress at home. . . . A really good shawl, or mantle trimmed with lace, are the concomitants of the carriage, or a visiting dress in winter. . . . In ordinary evening costume at home the hair should now be fully dressed, and with care; flowers may be worn by the young; caps with flowers by the elder. The full dinner dress, in England, admits, and indeed, in the present days of luxury, demands great splendour. The dress may be blue, silver grey, maize, lavender, or very pale green; pink is suitable alone to balls; it may be of any thick texture of silk in vogue; but in the fashion it must be. Trimmings of Brussels lace, or of Mechlin, or of Maltese, are preferable to blonde or tulle, which are for balls or soirees. At large dinners, diamonds may be worn, but only in a brooch, or a pendant from the throat; a full suite of diamonds is suitable for very full dress alone. The same rule applies to emeralds, but not to pearls. Rows of pearls, confined by a diamond snap, are beautiful in every dress.

"Ball dressing requires less art than the nice gradations of costume in the dinner costume, and small evening party dress. For a ball, everything in married women may be light, somewhat fanciful and airy. . . . The heavy, richly trimmed silk, is only appropriate to those who do not dance. . . . For the married lady 'moire' dresses, either trimmed in lace, or tulle and flowers, or white silk or thin dresses over white satin are most suitable. Small feathers are even worn at balls; and, for the married, produce perhaps more effect than any other 'coiffure'; but they are wholly out of fashion on a young lady's head.

"Under the head of festive occasions, the court dress must not be admitted. This costume consists, first, of an entire dress, generally made of some plain but costly silk. The dress, therefore, forms one component part; next comes the petticoat, usually of some lighter material; and lastly, the train. The dress is made, even for elderly ladies, low; and the bodice is trimmed in accordance with the petticoat and the train. The petticoat is now usually formed of rich Brussels lace, or of Honiton lace, or tulle; and often looped up with flowers. The train is of the richest material of the whole dress. Formerly it was often of satin; now it is of moire or glacé silk, though satin is again beginning to be worn. It fastens half round the waist, and is about seven yards in length, and wide in proportion. It is trimmed all round with lace, in festoons, or on the edge, with bunches of flowers at intervals, and is lined usually with white silk. The petticoat is ornamented with the same lace as the train, sometimes in flounces, sometimes in puffings or bouffons of tulle, sometimes 'en tablier,' that is down either side. The bodice and sleeves are all made in strict uniformity with the train and petticoat.

"The head-dress consists of feathers, and comprises a lappet of lace, hanging from either side of the head down nearly to the tip of the bodice. Diamonds or pearls, or any other jewellery sufficiently handsome, may be worn in the hair, but the two former are most frequently adopted. The same ornaments should be worn on the bodice around the neck and arms. The shoes should be of white satin, and trimmed

Evening dress of the 1830s (from Le Follet Courrier des Salons*)*

accordingly to fashion. The fan should be strictly a dress fan; those [that are]spangled are the most suitable for a costume which requires everything to be as consistent as possible with the occasion."

RIDING DRESS

"In this particular several changes have been made during the last two or three years. The round hat, of masculine appearance, is almost always exchanged for a slouched hat, sometimes of a round form, and turned up round the brim—sometimes turned up on either side, and coming with a point low down upon the forehead—and sometimes three-cornered: all these different forms have their votaries; but it must be acknowledged that the more simple and modest the shape, the more becoming. . . . The habit has sustained some changes, and, as far as appearance is concerned, not for the better. It used to be invariably tight, well shaped, with close sleeves. It is now often made loose, with deep cuffs, or, if worn tight, a loose jacket, or 'casaque,' can be put over it. . . . A plain white collar of fine lawn should be worn with the habit, deep lawn cuffs underneath the sleeves, while gauntlet gloves of thick leather, and no ornaments, save perhaps a delicately twined whip, need be displayed. Compactness and utility are the requisites for the riding-dress."

BIBLIOGRAPHY

Ackermann, Rudolph. *Ackermann's Costume Plates: Women's Fashions in England 1818–1828.* New York: Dover Publications, 1978.

Alexander, Helene. *Fans.* Aylesbury, England: Shire Publications, 1989.

Bailey, Adrian. *The Passion for Fashion: Three Centuries of Changing Styles.* Limpsfield: Dragons World Ltd., 1988.

Blum, Stella, comp. *Victorian Fashions and Costumes From Harper's Bazaar 1867–1898.* New York: Dover Publications, 1974.

————. *Fashions and Costumes From Godey's Lady's Book.* New York: Dover Publications, 1985.

Boehn, Max von. *Ornaments: Lace, Fans, Gloves, Walking-Sticks, Parasols, Jewelry, and Trinkets.* North Stratford: Ayer Company Publishers, Inc., 1989.

Bradfield, Nancy. *Costume in Detail: Women's Dress 1730–1930.* Boston: Plays, Inc., 1983.

Buck, Anne. *Victorian Costume and Costume Accessories.* Bedford: R. Bean, 1984.

Buxton, Alexandra. *Discovering Nineteenth-Century Fashion.* Cambridge: Hobsons, 1989.

Byrde, Penelope. *A Frivolous Distinction.* Bath: Bath City Council, 1980.

Calder-Marshall, Arthur. *The Grand Century of the Lady.* London: Gordon Cremonesi Ltd., 1976.

Cunnington, C. Willet. *A Dictionary of English Costume 900–1900.* London: A. & C. Black, 1960.

Cunnington, Phyllis. *Charity Costumes of Children, Scholars, Almsfolk and Pensioners.* London: A. & C. Black, 1978.

————. *Children's Costume in England From the Fourteenth to the End of the Nineteenth Century.* London: A. & C. Black, 1972.

————. *Costume for Births, Marriages and Deaths.* London: A. & C. Black, 1972

————. *English Costume for Sports and Outdoor Recreation From the Sixteenth to the Nineteenth Centuries.* London: A. & C. Black, 1969.

————. *Occupational Costume in England From the Eleventh Century to 1914.* London: A. & C. Black, 1968.

————. *Your Book of Nineteenth-Century Costume.* London: Faber & Faber, 1970.

Davidson, D.C. *Spectacles, Lorgnettes and Monocles.* Aylesbury, England: Shire Publications, 1989.

Davis, R.I. *Men's Garments 1830–1900: A Guide to Pattern Cutting and Tailoring.* Studio City, Calif.: Players Press, 1994.

Dawes, G.R. *Victorian Jewelry: Unexplored Treasures.* New York: Abbeville Press Publishers, 1991.

Earnshaw, Pat. *Lace in Fashion: From the Sixteenth to the Twentieth Centuries.* London: B.T. Batsford, 1985.

Eckstein, E. *Gentlemen's Dress Accessories.* Aylesbury, England: Shire Publications, 1987.

Ewing, Elizabeth. *Everyday Dress 1650–1900.* New York: Chelsea House Publishers, 1989.

————. *History of Children's Costume.* London: B.T. Batsford, 1977.

Foster, Vanda. *A Visual History of Costume: The Nineteenth Century.* London: B.T. Batsford, 1984.

Gernsheim, Alison. *Victorian and Edwardian Fashion: A Photographic Survey.* New York: Dover Publications, 1981.

Gibbs-Smith, C.H. *The Fashionable Lady in the Nineteenth Century.* London: H.M. Stationery Off., 1960.

Giles, Edward B. *The Art of Cutting and History of English Costume.* Lopez Island, Wash.: R.L. Shep, 1987.

Harris, Kristina. *Victorian and Edwardian Fashions for Women, 1840–1919.* Atglen, Penn.: Schiffer Publishing Co., 1995.

Hawthorne, Rosemary. *Bras: A Private View.* London: Souvenir Press, 1992.

————. *Knickers: An Intimate Appraisal.* London: Souvenir Press, 1991.

————. *Stockings and Suspenders: A Quick Flash.* London: Souvenir Press, 1993.

Jarvis, Anthea. *Liverpool Fashion: Its Makers and Wearers.* Liverpool: Merseyside County Museums, 1981.

Johnson, Barbara. *A Lady of Fashion: Barbara Johnson's Album of Styles and Fabrics.* New York: Thames & Hudson, 1987.

Johnson, Judy M. *French Fashion Plates of the Romantic Era in Full Color: 120 Plates From the "Petit Courrier des Dame" 1830–34.* New York: Dover Publications, 1991.

Lansdell, Avril, *Fashion a la Carte, 1860–1900: A Study of Fashion Through Cartes-de-Visite.* Aylesbury, England: Shire Publications, 1985.

————. *Occupational Costume and Women's Clothes.* Princes Risborough: Shire Publications, 1990.

————. *Seaside Fashions 1860–1939.* Princes Risborough: Shire Publications, 1990.

————. *Wedding Fashions 1860–1980.* Aylesbury, England: Shire Publications, 1983.

Le Bourhis, Katell, ed. *The Age of Napoleon: Costume From Revolution to Empire, 1789–1815.* New York: Metropolitan Museum of Art, 1989.

Leisch, Juanita. *Who Wore What?: Women's Wear 1861–1865.* Gettysburg: Thomas Publications, 1995.

Leneman, Leah. *Into the Foreground: A Century of Scottish Women in Photographs.* Edinburgh: National Museum of Scotland, 1993.

Levitt, Sarah. *Victorians Unbuttoned: Registered Designs for Clothing, Their Makers and Wearers 1839–1900.* London: Allen & Unwin, 1986.

Manchester Museum, The Gallery of English Costume. *Women's Costume: The Eighteenth Century.* 1952.

————. *Women's Costume: 1800–1835.* 1952.

————. *Women's Costume: 1835–1870.* 1951.

————. *Women's Costume: 1870–1900.* 1953.

Oakes, Alma. *Rural Costume: Its Origin and Development in Western Europe and British Isles.* London: B.T Batsford, 1970.

O'Day, Deirdre. *Victorian Jewellery.* London: Letts Collectors Guides, 1974.

O'Hara, Georgina. *The Encyclopedia of Fashion: From 1840 to the 1980s.* London: Thames & Hudson, 1986.

Peacock, John. *Men's Fashion: The Complete Sourcebook.* London: Thames & Hudson, 1996.

Rothstein, Natalie. *The Victoria and Albert Museum's Textile Collection: Woven Textile Design in Britain From 1750–1850.* New York: Canopy, 1994.

Saint-Laurent, Cecil. *A History of Ladies' Underwear.* London: Michael Joseph, 1968.

Schoeser, M. *English and American Textiles From 1790 to the Present.* London: Thames & Hudson, 1989.

Schroeder, Joseph, comp. *The Wonderful World of Ladies' Fashion 1850–1920.* Northfield, Ill.: Digest Books, 1971.

Ulseth, Hazel. *Victorian Fashions: 1880–1890. Vol. 1.* Grantsville: Hobby House, 1988.

Walker, Richard. *Savile Row.* New York: Rizzoli, 1989.

Walkley, Christine. *Crinolines and Crimping Irons: Victorian Clothes: How They Were Cleaned and Cared For.* Chester Springs, Penn.: Dufour, 1985.

————. *Dressed to Impress, 1840–1914.* London: B.T. Batsford, 1989.

Waugh, Norah. *Corsets and Crinolines.* London: B.T. Batsford, 1954.

————. *The Cut of Men's Clothes 1600–1900.* London: Faber, 1964.

————. *The Cut of Women's Clothes 1600–1930.* London: Faber, 1968.

Wilson, Eunice. *A History of Shoe Fashion.* New York: Theatre Arts Books, 1974.

Chapter Six

Medicine

By the nineteenth century, great strides had been made by surgeon John Hunter in understanding the role the body's organs played in illness, while physician Edward Jenner's work enabled medical practitioners to attribute various sicknesses to their true causes, rather than to such things as "bad humours" or astrology. A vaccine against smallpox had been discovered, and at the dawn of the century, medicine was on the verge of discovering two of its greatest advances: antiseptics and the use of anesthetics during surgery.

In 1800, English chemist Sir Humphrey Davy discovered that patients inhaling nitrous oxide gas were rendered unconscious, and that this could "probably be used with advantage in surgical operations." However, although laughing gas was used at parties by socialites in the United Kingdom and United States, it would be another fifty years before it was used in surgery. Another anesthetic, chloroform, was adopted for surgical use in 1847, but the public remained leery of accepting it until Queen Victoria was given it during childbirth in 1853.

ANTISEPTICS

Building upon Louis Pasteur's discoveries about the prevention of bacteria, Yorkshire surgeon Joseph Lister began experimenting midcentury with carbolic acid in the treatment of infected wounds. He concluded that when the acid was applied directly to a wound it had no effect, but when it was sprayed about a room and used to clean instruments and the hands of caregivers, carbolic acid was a powerful deterrent to infections common to injuries, childbirth (puerperal fever) and surgical recovery. Not only did more patients recover from their illnesses and more mothers and infants survive labor, but without the great threat of infection, surgeons could now attempt to operate on parts of the body they dared not treat with surgery before.

HOSPITALS

During the Georgian era, hospitals still retained their medieval description. They were not intended as places where one went to be treated for illness or injury and then released. Rather, hospitals were where those who had no place else to turn—the poor, the insane, the drunk and the contagious—were deposited. Patients were not nursed, but rather minded, in unsanitary and overcrowded conditions by too little staff.

Between 1700 and 1825, 154 new hospitals were opened throughout Great Britain due to increased public awareness and aristocratic funding, as the government allocated no monies toward public health. In addition to the larger hospitals found in major cities, cottage hospitals were erected in rural areas, the first of which opened in Surrey in 1859, and by 1880, every county had at least one such hospital. These were staffed by local doctors, who used the facilities to perform operations that would have been impossible in a home setting. As they were purpose built, they were all modern in design and as sanitary as the period allowed.

These new hospitals increased the need for doctors. While medical universities in London and Edinburgh had no shortage of students, they did have a shortage of subjects for anatomical dissection—cadavers—and even the most reputable surgeons and teachers were made to resort to body snatchers for specimens. Since the time of Henry VIII, the bodies of criminals hanged in Great Britain were to be turned over by the hangman to surgeons, for which the hangman received a fee. This gave rise to the public belief that to be dissected was an end reserved for the worst sort of humanity, and people were loathe to bequeath their own or their loved ones' remains to the medical schools.

BODY SNATCHERS

The body snatchers, or "resurrection men," sought to meet the demand for cadavers by robbing fresh graves or by claiming the bodies of persons without family who had died in a hospital or a parish workhouse. They charged exorbitant fees, sometimes up to fifteen guineas per cadaver, as well as a fee at the start of every new anatomy course meant to ensure that they would supply enough specimens to meet the demand. Soon, grave robbers were turning to other outlets in which to find corpses, namely, murder. William Burke and William Hare became notorious for these crimes, wherein they murdered elderly and incompetent lodgers in rooming houses in Edinburgh in the early nineteenth century; John Bishop and James May operated in London's East End in 1831.

A sharp-eyed surgeon at King's College, London, upon being delivered a specimen by Bishop and May, noted that the body of a fourteen-year-old lad appeared quite fresh, that it displayed no signs of recent burial and, further, had a bloody cut upon its forehead. The police were called, and the pair were arrested, tried and executed. Some months after this, in 1832, the Anatomy Act was passed by the Houses of Parliament, doing away with the giving over of criminals' bodies to the hangmen, and therefore removing some of the stigma from anatomical dissection. The act also made death certificates mandatory and allowed for relatives or friends of a deceased person to direct the corpse into the hands of a surgeon, anatomist or medical school. A final note: The bodies of both Burke and Bishop were delivered to the anatomists after their executions.

NURSING

Florence Nightingale studied nursing in 1851 at Kaiserwerth, near Dusseldorf. Upon returning to England, Nightingale endeavored to interest women in the nursing profession. Typically, nurses in England worked daily shifts, with patients being left in the care of watchwomen, who had no formal training in the evenings. In 1854, she was prompted by the appalling state of war hospitals near Constantinople to take thirty-eight women to the war zone to treat English soldiers. After reorganizing the field hospitals and improving conditions, she returned to England an exhausted heroine. Her efforts brought fruits, as she was given forty-four thousand pounds with which to found the Nightingale School of Nursing at St. Thomas's Hospital, London, the first students being admitted in 1860. In 1907, she became the first woman to receive the Order of Merit.

CHILDBIRTH

Childbirth in the nineteenth century was accomplished, as it had been for centuries, at home, with the help of a midwife. Midwives, and "men midwives," had no formal training in delivery, usually learning their skill from family members. Though there were many who knew their craft well and carried it out with compassion, there had always been a high mortality rate due to ineptitude, unsanitary conditions and overdosing with both laudanum and opium, which were used to lessen the mother's pain and to quiet the cries of the child. In 1864, a Ladies' Obstetrical College was founded in London, which sought to train women in the art of midwifery, the theories behind procedures and the follow-up care of both mothers and newborns.

PATENT MEDICINES

The nineteenth century gave rise to the popularity of patent medicines, those with names protected by trademarks and used to treat a variety of the public's ills. At the age of thirteen, Jesse Boots went to work in his mother's herbal shop in Nottingham. He took over the business in 1877, and within six years had opened ten branches in surrounding towns. In 1892, Boots began to manufacture drugs on a wider scale, and when Jesse died in 1931, having been made first Baron Trent, his company, known then and now as Boots the Chemist, had over one thousand outlets in Great Britain.

Another well-known purveyor of British patent medicines was the Beecham family. In 1847, Thomas Beecham began selling Beecham's Pills, containing laxative properties. He was one of the first British entrepreneurs to appreciate the value of advertising and did so on a large scale. In 1891, his son Joseph was spending 120,000 pounds per annum on ads, with the family business by then being worth several million pounds.

HOME REMEDIES

Though patent medicines were widely available, many nineteenth-century housewives continued to prepare their own remedies at home. The following are just a few of the popular medicinal receipts available during the era.

To apply leeches: The leeches [must] be kept out of water for half an hour before applying, and the skin they are to be applied to [must] be well washed and rubbed dry. A little sweetened milk placed on the part will make them bite, and in placing them on the patient put the mouth, which is in the tapering end of the body, against the patient. Place the leeches in a glass and turn it over upon the spot to be bitten. They must not be pulled off; when they have done their work they will fall off naturally, and can be put into a plate of salt to vomit the blood. The leech bites should be bathed in cold water until the bleeding stops and then covered with linen. *Never* put leeches directly over a vein.

For asthma or shortness of breath: Take one quart aqua vitae, one ounce aniseed, bruised, one ounce licorice sliced and a half pound of stoned raisins. Mix together and steep for ten days, then pour off the liquid into a container, add two spoonfuls of fine sugar and stop close.

For the bite of a mad dog: Take a spoonful of common salt, add as much water as will make it damp and apply like a poultice every six hours, and it will be sure to stop the hydrophobia.

Or: Beat a new laid egg and put in pan with oil of olives. Into this put powdered oyster shells, enough to absorb the liquid. Give doses to patient, whilst making him to fast, for nine days. At the same time, wash the wound regularly with salt water. This cure is for both man and beast.

For a bruised eye: Take conserve of red roses and rotten apple in equal parts, wrap them in a fold of thin cambric or old linen and apply to the eye. This will remove the blackness.

Chamomile tea: Take two dozen flowers and infuse them in a pint of boiling water for half an hour; decant, sweeten with honey, and drink a half gill. When taken in not too strong a dose, from its tonic and antispasmodic qualities, strengthens the digestive organs and tends to dispel dyspepsia.

To cast a broken bone: Pick comfrey roots in March, when they are full of clear juice which has a slimy texture. Grate up the roots, set the broken limb and use the mash to cover the limb well. Make a joint in the cast to use when sawing off the cast later. The mash will be slow to set and will also promote healing.

For chapped hands: Mutton fat taken from around the sheep's udders is best. It is very hard when clarified and must be warmed before use. Dip the whole hand into the warm fat and work in thoroughly. Hold the hands under cold water and wipe gently.

A lotion for the chilblains: Take one drachm of sugar of lead, two drachms white vitriol and reduce these to a fine powder; add four ounces water. Shake the mix well before using, and then rub on affected parts, in front of a good fire in the evenings. Do not use on broken chilblains.

For a consumptive cough: To make spirit of saffron, take four drachms of the best saffron, open and pull apart. Put in a quart bottle and pour in one pint of ordinary spirit of wine, and half a pound of white sugar candy beaten small, and stop up the bottle with a cork. Set in the sun and shake twice a day until the candy is dissolved and the liquid is of a deep orange colour. Let the bottle stand and settle then clear it off into a fresh bottle and keep for use. Give a spoonful of the mix for a child, or a large spoon for an adult.

A certain cure for corns: Take two ivy leaves and put them into vinegar for twenty-four hours; apply one to the corn and, when you find its virtue extracted, apply the other, and it will effectually and speedily remove the corn without the least pain.

Cordial water for gripe in babies: Take one ounce of aniseed, one pint pure water, two tablespoons treacle and three drachms tincture of opium and mix well. A teaspoon or two may be given occasionally.

To cure a dog of mange: Take four ounces of Tar, mix with some fresh Grease, so as it may run, then put to it some Brimstone powdered, half a spoon of Gunpowder powdered, and two spoons honey, mix well, and anoint the Dog. In summer tie him in hot Sun, that the ointment may soak into him; in winter lay him on thick fresh hay, and there keep him that the heat of his body may heat and melt it. Thrice dressing it will cure him.

For the hiccough: Put a drop of cinnamon on a sugar cube and dissolve in the mouth.

For the itch: Heat lard and melt into it some brimstone. Apply to the body three times at night, before a warm fire, and rub in well.

For piles: Roast quick snails in their shells, pick out their meat with a pin and beat them in a mortar with some Powder of Pepper to a Salve, then take the dried roots of Pilewort in powder, and strew it thin on the plaster and apply it as hot as you can suffer it.

For the poison of the adder: Olive oil is an absolute specific for the bite of the adder, the oil should be well rubbed upon the bitten part; in case of violent symptoms a glass or two should be taken inwardly. Common sweet oil will also answer the purpose.

To prevent hysterics: Mix finely pounded caraway seeds with a small measure of ginger and salt, spread upon bread and butter. Eaten each day, especially early in the day and at night before retiring, this is a good remedy against hysterics.

For the rheumatism: Take goose grease, melted with horse radish juice, mustard and turpentine. Shake till white and creamy and spread on affected areas.

To procure sleep: Chop chamomile and crumbs of brown bread and boyl them with white wine vinegar. Stir it well and spread it on a cloth, and bind it to the soles of the feet as hot as you can suffer it. You may add to it dried red rose leaves or red rose cakes with some red rose water and let it heat till it be thick and bind some of it to the temples and some to the soles of the feet.

Saline wash for headache: Take of fine salt a half ounce, four ounces each of vinegar and soft water, two ounces whiskey or brandy and mix together until the salt is dissolved. This is a good cooling wash for headache and inflammation of the brain.

To stop a nosebleed: Put a nettle leaf upon the tongue and then press this against the roof of the mouth, or place a large key flat against the naked back.

To destroy vermin in the hair: Take one ounce vinegar, one ounce stavesacre well powdered, half ounce of honey, the same of sulphur and two ounces sweet oil; mix the whole together into a liniment, rub the head repeatedly with this mix until the vermin is gone.

For warts: Cut an apple and rub it for a few minutes over the wart, the juice will loosen the wart and in a few days it will drop off.

For a wasp's sting: Over the spot where the sting has entered, apply the pipe of a key, press it for a minute or two, and the pain and swelling will disappear.

TIME LINE

1800 Humphrey Davy publishes *Researches, Chemical and Philosophical, Concerning Nitrous Oxide.*
The Royal College of Surgeons is founded in London by Henry Cline, John Abernethy and Sir Everard Home.

1805 F.W.A. Sartuner isolates morphine.

1812 While in South America, Englishman Charles Waterton discovers curare, a poison that acts on nervous system, and later uses it as an anesthetic during surgery.

1816 R.T. Laennec invents the stethoscope.

1823 The British medical journal *The Lancet* is first published.

1832 The Anatomy Act is passed.

1834 German chemist F.F. Runge discovers carbolic acid.

1841 Scottish surgeon James Braid discovers hypnosis.

1847 The use of chloroform during surgery is tested and adopted by the medical community.

1852 Plaster bandages (casts for broken bones) are introduced.

1853 Dr. John Snow administers chloroform to Queen Victoria during the birth of Prince Leopold.

1858 Joseph Lister studies coagulation of blood.

1859 England's first cottage hospital opens in Surrey.

1860 The Nightingale School of Nursing opens in London.

1864 The Ladies' Obstetrical College opens in London.

1865 Lister begins carbolic acid experiments.

1872 The first attempts at blood transfusions are made.

1877 Robert Koch develops technique of staining and identifying bacteria.

1878 Thomas Forster receives British patent for improved rubber gloves to be used in surgery.

1885 Pasteur develops rabies vaccine.

BIBLIOGRAPHY

Aveling, James H. *English Midwives: Their History and Prospects.* London: Elliott, 1967.

Ayers, Gwendoline M. *England's First State Hospitals and the Metropolitan Asylums Board 1867–1930.* London: Wellcome Institute of the History of Medicine, 1971.

Ball, James Moores. *The Body Snatchers.* New York: Dorset Press, 1989.

Godlee, R.J. *Lord Lister.* Oxford: Clarendon Press, 1924.

Loudon, Irvine. *Medical Care and the General Practitioner 1750–1850.* Oxford: Clarendon Press, 1986.

Porter, Roy, and Dorothy Porter. *In Sickness and In Health: The British Experience, 1650–1850.* London: Fourth Estate, 1988.

Williams, Guy. *The Age of Miracles: Medicine and Surgery in the Nineteenth Century.* Chicago: Academy Chicago Publishers, 1987.

Woodham-Smith, Cecil. *Florence Nightingale 1820–1910.* London: Constable, 1950.

Part Two

Government, War and the Economy

CHAPTER SEVEN

The Courts

In London's great Scotland Yard there stood the Palace Court, over which the knight marshal presided. This court was formerly concerned with matters connected to the royal household, but by the dawn of the nineteenth century, it had become a minor court of record for actions of debt within Westminster and an area comprising twelve miles around the city. The court had its own prison, the Marshalsea, which stood at No. 119 High Street, before moving southward to new quarters in 1811. The last cases were heard in this court in 1849. As to the Central Criminal Court, founded in 1834, proceedings were held in the Sessions House in Old Bailey. This was rebuilt in 1809 on the site of the old Sessions House and intended as the center of the criminal jurisdiction of the kingdom.

DOCTOR'S COMMONS

Doctor's Commons was the name given to the College of Advocates and Doctors of Law, which stood near St. Paul's Cathedral, London. It consisted of five courts, one pertaining to the see of Canterbury, one to the see of London, one to the Lords Commissioners of the Admiralties, one to the office of registrary of the archbishop of Canterbury and another to the office of the bishop of London. Between them, these courts heard such causes as matrimony, divorce, bastardy, tithes, reparation of churches, probate of wills, administrations, incest, adultery and commutation of penance. The five courts that comprised Doctor's Commons were as follows.

The Court of Arches: This court belonged to the archbishop of Canterbury. At one time it was located in Bow Church, Cheapside, whose tower was arched and from which the court was given its name. All appeals directed in ecclesiastical matters, including testamentary and matrimonial causes, within the province of Canterbury were heard here.

The Court of Audience: Also belonging to the archbishop of Canterbury, this court heard both causes and complaints.

The Prerogative Court: Wills and testaments were proved here, and all administrations, or final decisions, were the prerogative of the archbishop, as he had special preeminence over ordinary bishops in his province.

The Court of Faculties and Dispensations: The court had the power to grant privilege or special power to a person to which by law he was otherwise not entitled, such as the right to marry without first posting banns or the right of a son to succeed his father in his benefice.

The Court of Admiralty: This court belonged to the high admiral of England and heard all causes relating to merchants and mariners. It also ruled on any death or mayhem committed in rivers and could take ships for the king's use during war.

There also existed a Court of Delegates, which served as the high court of appeals for any of the above courts and was also the highest court of appeal for civil cases.

The Court Probate Act

The Court Probate Act of 1857 established a Court of Probate and abolished the jurisdiction of the ecclesiastical courts. The reforms of this act made it possible for the public to prove wills or obtain letters of administration without professional assistance; admitted jurors to try the validity of wills and questions of divorce; allowed those persons seeking to establish legitimacy, the validity of marriages and the right to be deemed natural born subjects the means of doing so; enabled persons needing copies of wills that had been proven since January

1858, in any part of the country, to obtain them from the principal registry of the Court of Probate in Doctor's Commons.

Wills

If a person died owning property situated entirely within the diocese where he died, then a probate or proof of the will was made, or an administration taken out, before the bishop or ordinary of that diocese, and the matter could be closed. However, if the deceased had owned goods and chattel amounting to as little as five pounds (ten in London) within any other diocese from that in which he had died, then the jurisdiction in proving his will lay in the Prerogative Court of the archbishop of the province; that is, either at York or at Doctor's Commons.

Legal Matters

As can be expected, since the London courts also served as the main courts of the land, they were horribly backlogged. At Queen Victoria's accession in 1837, there were nearly a thousand causes waiting to be heard by the lord chancellor, the master of the rolls and the vice-chancellor of England, who presided over the Court of Chancery. Many of the cases had been pending for a quarter of a century. Besides the judges having their regular political functions, they had to preside in the House of Lords when their own appeals were heard, and had an additional caseload of matters regarding bankruptcy and the insane.

The courts were also bogged down by the antiquated ways in which cases had to be drawn up. For instance, in order to bring an action in the King's Bench, it was necessary for the writ to describe the course of action as "trespass," and then to put the true charge in an *ac etiam* clause. The reason behind this was that trespass was still a criminal offense, and the defendant would, technically, be considered to be under the custody of the marshal of the Marshalsea once such a charge was filed—and therefore the case might be heard within the jurisdiction of the King's Bench. While this tangle of red tape seems baffling to the present-day reader, it was just as confusing to the majority of the public in the nineteenth century. Add to this the fact that it was not until 1851 that the plaintiff and defendant in a case could enter the witness box on their own behalfs, and one can see the reasons for justice having moved slowly.

Again, it should be remembered that the state of London courts affected the states of courts throughout Great Britain, since in those days all matters intended to be heard at the assizes were in form prepared for trial at Westminster. The record was delivered to the officers of the King's Bench, Common Pleas or Exchequer, and the cause was set down for trial at Westminster. In the meantime, the judges went on circuit into the county in which the cause of action had originated. While there, the assize judges took down evidence, tried the action with a jury comprised of residents from the county and pronounced judgment according to the jury's verdict. The judges then brought back the verdict and judgment, which were entered into record at Westminster.

Matters of probate, and all suits relating to testacy and intestacy, were disposed of in the ecclesiastical courts, which were tribunals attached to the archbishops, bishops and archdeacons. The Court of Arches, the Ecclesiastical Court for the Province of Canterbury, the Prerogative Court and the Admiralty Courts were held at Doctor's Commons. Evidently, the Courts had long ago gained a reputation for exacting heavy fees. In his *Journey Through England* Daniel DeFoe wrote "England was a fine country, but a man called Doctor's Commons was the devil, for there was no getting out of his clutches, let one's cause be never so good, without paying a great deal of money."

CRIMINAL LAW

Criminal law was at least as convoluted as civil law. Justice dealt harshly with the accused via procedures and penalties. In a case of felony, for instance, until 1836, a prisoner could not be defended by council and had to represent himself in court. The prisoner, often poor and uneducated, was often ignorant of the technical points of law. The indictment, often lengthy and legally worded, was read to him in court, with separate counts for each offense. Defense depended as much upon the prisoner uncovering some legal flaw as in proving his innocence. But what chance did an illiterate prisoner have of fighting the law, especially when he wasn't to be given a copy of the indictment to study prior to trial?

If a person were fortunate, or educated, enough to be aware of the finer legal points, he did have one option open for freedom. If a difficult legal point arose in any criminal case heard at the assizes or elsewhere, the judge reserved the point and brought it before his peers.

The point could then be argued by counsel for the defendant, not in a court but at Serjeants Inn, of which all judges were members. If it was decided that the prisoner had been improperly convicted, he received a free pardon. In 1848, this tribunal became known as the Court for Crown Cases Reserved.

The Bankruptcy Courts

The bankruptcy courts were perhaps the most daunting of all. In 1839, nearly four thousand people were arrested for debt in London alone, with nearly four hundred of these remaining permanently in prison. Traders owing more than three hundred pounds could obtain a discharge upon full disclosure and surrender of all their property, but even then the proceedings were protracted to an almost interminable length. The legal machinery was both tedious and costly. Until 1831, the bankruptcy law in London was administered by commissioners appointed separately for each case by the lord chancellor. In 1831, a Court of Review was established, consisting of a chief judge and two minor judges, and this served to control and supervise the proceedings. In the country, however, the old procedure prevailed.

If a bankrupt did not surrender to his commission within forty-two days of notice, nor make discovery of his estate and effects, nor deliver up his papers and books, he was considered a felon and liable to be transported for life. An adjudication, the first stage in bankruptcy proceedings, was granted upon the mere affidavit of a creditor; a fiat was issued, the commissioners held a meeting and, without hearing any testimony from the debtor himself, he was then declared a bankrupt. Thus, it was quite possible for a trader to find himself in prison while still being solvent. He did have recourse, via actions for trespass or false imprisonment against the commissioners, but this was a long and costly process.

Insolvent debtors, those not in trade, were yet worse off. Imprisonment on "mesne process," or on affidavit of a creditor, was the leading principle behind this branch of the bankruptcy law, with the debtor languishing in prison until he either found security or paid off the debt. The anomaly that exempted real estate from the payment of debts had been removed in 1825. After that, a debtor who was in prison could obtain a release by surrendering all his real and personal property, while remaining liable for all the unpaid portion of his debt, to be satisfied whenever the court deemed him able to pay.

DIVORCE LAWS

Divorce was only available to the wealthy, as it was a costly process. The motion for divorce began with an action for recovery of damages against the corespondent and a suit in the ecclesiastical courts for a separation "from bed and board," both of which were tedious and expensive. Once these charges had been successfully prosecuted, they were followed by a divorce bill, which had to pass through all its stages in both the Lords and Commons before a divorce or "a vinculo matrimonii" could be obtained. It was not until 1857 that a separate Court for Divorce and Matrimonial Causes was created.

Pleas for judicial separation were heard in the King's Bench court by a jury or in the guildhall in the evenings, and were termed "actions for criminal conversation," which amounted to charges of adultery. Louis Simond, a visitor to England in 1810–1811, left a vivid picture of the proceedings: "This criminal conversation is not prosecuted criminally, but produces only a civil suit for the recovery of damages, estimated in money. The jury determines the amount of these damages, by the degree of union and conjugal happiness existing before the criminal conversation which destroyed it, and by the rank and fortune of the parties. The smallest appearance of negligence or connivance on the part of the husband deprives him of all remedy against the seducer, who owes him nothing, if he only took what was not of value to him, and which he guarded so ill. I have heard of ten thousand pounds Sterling awarded in some cases, which is certainly rather dear for a conversation! The husband pockets this money without shame, because he has the law on his side, and in the world ridicule alone produces shame. A divorce is generally granted by act of Parliament in these cases; and marriage as generally takes place between the lovers. The publicity which such prosecutions necessarily occasion, and all the details and proofs of the intrigue, are highly indelicate and scandalous. The testimony, for instance, of servants, of young chambermaids, who are brought into open court to tell, in the face of the public, all they have seen, heard or guessed at, is another sort of prostitution more indecent than the first. Morals are far from being purified by this process; but the substantial infringement is prevented."

Neither the defendant nor the plaintiff was allowed to give testimony in person in court. A guilty verdict against a corespondent could destroy a man both financially and socially. If he could not pay damages immediately, a warrant was issued, and he was sentenced to prison until such time that he was able to pay.

Parliamentary divorce was created about 1690 by a private act of Parliament, in a society in which divorce was legally prohibited. As the process could cost several hundred pounds, it was reserved for the aristocracy. These divorces could be obtained between 1690 and 1857, but only by those men who could afford it and whose wives had committed adultery. What made parliamentary divorces so desirable was that, once granted, both parties were allowed to remarry. By 1810, the requirements for allowing a bill of divorce were that a wife's adultery had to be proven and testified to by two witnesses; that the marriage had been sound before the adultery was committed; and that there was no evidence that the husband had neglected, abandoned or otherwise given his wife cause to commit adultery. The House of Lords also required proof that a successful action of criminal conversation tried in common-law courts had been decided in the husband's favor, and that deed for separation had been granted him in the ecclesiastical courts. After 1700, a husband was allowed to keep his wife's marriage portion, but in return he was made to provide an annuity for her maintenance. After 1811, this amount was to be decided by both parties and entered into a deed of settlement, which was to be drawn up prior to presenting a bill for parliamentary divorce. However, in order to receive this, the divorced woman had to promise to remain unmarried and to conduct herself in a manner above reproach.

Creevey, May 12, 1823: "A piece of news in the fashionable world which has been referred to in the papers is the separation of Henry B—from his wife. She has long been known to be a 'neat un,' but her vagaries at Paris were so undisguised that some friend wrote and advertised her husband of it here, and he, to justify himself before proceeding to extremities, took to breaking open her boxes in pursuit of evidence against her. In one of these he is said to have found 20 locks of hair, with a label on each containing the name of the love to whom it belonged, such as 'dear John Warrender's.' So having collected his trophies of this kind, with letters equally instructive, he sallied forth to meet her return, and Rochester was the place they came together. Here, upon giving her solemn word of honor that all the children 'but one' were his, he banished her and 'the one' from his sight for ever, and has taken all the other children from her."

In 1870, Sir Charles Mordaunt, of the Prince of Wales's Marlborough House set, brought a suit for divorce against his twenty-one-year-old wife after she attributed the blindness of their newborn child to her having committed adultery with a number of partners, including the Prince of Wales. In an unprecedented step, the Prince of Wales took the witness box, denying adultery but admitting to having written her a handful of letters. The prince was not cross-examined, and the petition for divorce was dismissed. A second petition, making no mention of the Prince of Wales, later succeeded. And when Lady Charlotte Wellesley had an affair with Lord Paget, Henry Wellesly, brother of the duke of Wellington, was awarded thirty-four thousand pounds in damages against Paget for criminal conversation. Paget and Lady Charlotte later married.

Farington, June 7, 1804: "Lord Ferrers has an estate which may be ten thousand pounds a year, and He has saved much money. He is very little visited or respected. He married when young a lady in Kent privately & by her had one Son. The marriage became known, & He used means to sully the character of His Wife, but in vain. She sued Him for a maintenance and He was obliged to pay Her eight hundred pounds a year."

Wife Selling

An alternative to divorce was wife selling, a practice mentioned in Thomas Hardy's novel *Mayor of Casterbridge*. Little is known about how or why these sales took place, and many modern-day skeptics doubt that they took place at all. However, records indicate that such sales were in fact conducted, though they were prohibited by law and were never considered a substitute for legal separation. In many of the cases, the sales appear to have been both a form of public entertainment and a way for an unhappy couple to move on with their lives, with both parties having agreed to the proceedings. In some instances, the "highest bidder" was known to all beforehand and was, in fact, usually the wife's lover. The following are contemporary accounts of wife selling.

Ashton, January 1815: "MATRIMONIAL SALE—Tuesday s'en night, a man named John Osborne, who lived at Gondhurst, came to Maidstone, for the purpose of disposing of his wife by sale; but, it not being market day, the auction was removed to the sign of 'The Coal-barge,' in Earl Street, where she was actually sold to a man named William Serjeant, with her child, for the sum of one pound. The business was conducted in a very regular manner, a deed and covenant being given by the seller, of which the following is a literal copy:

> I, John Osborne, doth agree to part with my wife, Mary Osborne, and child, to William Serjeant, for the sum of one pound, in consideration of giving up all claim whatever, whereunto I have made my mark as an acknowledgement. dated 3 January.

Ashton, July 1815: "Smithfield Bargain—One of those scenes, which occasionally disgrace even Smithfield, took place there about five o'clock on Friday evening (14 July), namely—a man exposing his wife for sale. Hitherto, we have only seen those moving in the lowest classes of society thus degrading themselves, but the present exhibition was attended with some novel circumstances. The parties, buyer and seller, were persons of property; the lady (the object of sale), young, beautiful, and elegantly dressed, was brought to the market in a coach, and exposed to the view of her purchaser with a silk halter round her shoulders, which were covered with a rich white lace veil. The price demanded for her, in the first instance, was eighty guineas, but that finally agreed on, was fifty guineas, and a valuable horse upon which the purchaser was mounted. The sale and delivery being complete, the lady, with her new lord and master, mounted a handsome curricle which was in waiting for them, and drove off, seemingly nothing loath to go. The purchaser, in the present case is a celebrated horsedealer in town, and the seller, a grazier of cattle, residing about six miles from London. The intention of these disgusting bargains is, to deprive the husband of any right of prosecution for damages. . . .

Ashton, September 1815: "On Friday last, the common bell-man gave notice in Staines Market, that the wife of Issey was then at the King's Head Inn, to be sold, with the consent of her husband, to any person inclined to buy her. There was a very numerous attendance to witness this singular sale, notwithstanding which only three shillings and four pence were offered for the lot, no one choosing to contend with the bidder, for the fair object whose merits could only be appreciated by those who knew them. This, the purchaser could boast, from a long, and intimate, acquaintance."

Deeds of Private Separation

Deeds of Private Separation were contracts drawn up between husband's and wife's trustees stating that they had agreed to separate.

Most provided that the husband agreed to allow his wife an annual allowance for her maintenance, and that the wife ceased to hold her husband responsible for any future debts. Additional clauses might involve custody of children and promise of the husband not to molest or make his wife return to him by force. As these agreements meant that both parties would achieve their ends (that is, to be rid of the other), most went along this course and thus avoided the almost impossible alternative of going through church or courts, neither of which officially recognized the validity of these deeds. In every way, these deeds arranged for a separation of the parties only, and no one deceived themselves into believing that they equaled a divorce.

THE HOUSES OF PARLIAMENT

Catholic Emancipation

William Pitt the younger and some of his cabinet had supported full Catholic emancipation, which would have allowed Catholics to sit in the House of Commons, early in the nineteenth century, but faced opposition from George III and Tory politicians. In response to this, the Irish founded a league and elected Daniel O'Connell as their representative to the House for County Clare. The majority of the members of Parliament in England favored emancipation, but Sir Robert Peel opposed them from the Cabinet. In the wake of this opposition, national unrest simmered until Wellington stepped in. While in theory the duke favored maintaining the status quo in most things, he wisely advised the king to give way in the matter of Catholic emancipation, and the act was passed in 1829.

The first bill laid before Parliament, seeking that Jews be allowed to sit in the House of Commons, was presented in 1830, but was defeated. Jews were first admitted to the House of Commons in 1858, and to the House of Lords in 1885. Banker Lionel Nathan de Rothschild was the first Jew to be elected as a member of Parliament. First elected in 1847, he would be reelected five times. However, due to the wording of the parliamentary oath, which read in part, "taken on the true faith of a Christian," Rothschild did not take his seat until 1858, when the oath was rewritten.

The Reform Acts

The reform acts consisted of three separate acts. The act of 1832, originated by the Whig government under Lord Grey, disenfranchised most rotten boroughs, which were boroughs that were entitled to votes that were no longer viable to the outcome of an election. For instance, it might consist of an area composed mainly of parkland, which had few residents; another ancient borough, Dunwhich, had for centuries been buried under the North Sea. In effect, a rotten borough was once whose parliamentary vote was decided by a single power or landowner, rather than by a majority of borough residents. Disenfranchisement brought about the release of seats in rotten boroughs and redistributed them among counties and previously unrepresented boroughs. Franchise, or the right to vote, was extended in the counties from the freeholders of property worth forty shillings per annum to fifty-pound short-leaseholders and tenants; in the boroughs, ten-pound householders were granted the vote. The electorate in England and Wales was increased by 50 percent, but these sums extended the electorate only to the prosperous middle class, while agricultural and factory workers were still unrepresented.

A second reform act in 1867, instrumented by Disraeli and supported by Lord Derby's conservative government, extended the franchise to another 938,000 voters, and extended the vote to five-pound leaseholders and twelve-pound occupiers in the counties and to all householders and renters paying ten pounds per annum in the boroughs. Forty-five parliamentary seats were thus redistributed. The third act, introduced by Gladstone's government in 1884, extended household franchise to the counties, increasing the total electorate from three to five million.

PRISONS

Conditions and Reforms

Throughout England, prisons before the nineteenth century consisted of either local gaols or, fewer still, houses of correction capable of housing a larger prison population. An idea of the treatment received by prisoners in these local jails can be gotten by looking at London's notorious prisons, including the Fleet, a debtor's prison, and Newgate Gaol, the main criminal prison in the city.

Typically, prisoners were made to pay garnish, or fees, to the prison keeper for everything necessary to survival, including clean water, food, clothing, bedding and better accommodations. This last was necessary because prisoners were housed in dank, dark cells with upward of ten prisoners in each. Much more often, cells were so tightly packed by prisoners that there was no space for beds of any sort, and they slept instead on a layer of straw laid over the stone floor. This straw was rarely changed. These fees were paid from any money a prisoner might have had upon him when coming to the prison, or by friends and relatives.

Prisons were not only places in which to hold criminals, but a lockup for the insane as well. There was no move to separate these two classes of prisoners, and there was no attempt at reforming or rehabilitating the criminal until a report by the Holford Committee, formed to examine prison conditions in 1811, called for prison reforms. These included the establishment of penitentiaries, with Millbank Prison in London being the first model completed, in 1816.

For the first time, prisoners were kept in separate cells; there was a large staff, which included reformers, clergy, health officials and others; and prisoners were put to labor during the day. More such prisons were built throughout Great Britain, and perhaps the most important change was that these fell under the control of the central government, which oversaw conditions in each by committee. In 1850, the Board of Directors of Convict Prisons was set up and headed by Chairman Sir Joshua Jebb.

The Hulks and Transportation

The transportation of criminals was legalized in 1719, and it became common practice to send criminals who had escaped the gallows into servitude overseas. The sale of convicts to both American and West Indian plantations had been going on for decades prior to this, but was never before sanctioned by law. Prisoners were sold for ten pounds per head, though agents charged forty pounds to the government to meet their expenses in transporting them.

In 1776, the Revolutionary War interfered with the transport of prisoners, and the English government was forced to look elsewhere for a place to send its criminals, a search that lasted ten years. Finally, it was decided to house convicts in the hulks of old ships moored on the Thames at Portsmouth, Woolwich and Plymouth. However, these quickly became overcrowded, and in 1786, it was decided to once again transport prisoners, this time to the Australian colonies.

Problems arose from a shortage of transport ships, and as the number of convicts awaiting sail rose, antiquated prisons became still more crowded, necessitating the use of still more hulks.

In 1816, there was a population of twenty-five hundred housed aboard five hulks. It is not surprising that the hulks became a school of vice for younger prisoners, and discipline a problem. By 1841, the governments in Australia and New South Wales refused to take any more English convicts. With transportation no longer a viable housing option for prisoners, the English government was forced to take control of the newer penitentiaries of Millbank, Dartmoor, Portland, Parkhurst and Pentonville and place them under national administration.

Country Prisons

Before prison reforms by the government, rural or country prisons were most often under the control of local noblemen or owners of a lot of land, with the dukes of Leeds and Portland overseeing Halifax and Macclesfield prisons, respectively. On a daily basis, the prisons were under the control of the local justice of the peace, who had been empowered since 1720 to commit vagrants and idlers as well as criminals, to these places.

In most cases, it wasn't thought necessary to raise funds to build a separate jail, and so existing buildings, such as gatehouses, barns, cellars, storerooms, etc., were used instead. Some of the buildings chosen to serve as gaols had long since fallen into disrepair, necessitating the prisoners being chained to walls to prevent easy escape. The gaoler on duty was not an elected official, but would have bid to win the position, knowing full well that he could recoup these monies through the sums he would raise through garnish. In addition, upon his release, each prisoner was charged a separate fee for the jailer's "turning the key."

TIME LINE

1829 Catholic Emancipation Act is passed.
1831 Court of Review is established.
1832 The first reform act is passed.
1834 Central Criminal Court is founded in London.
1836 Defendants in felony cases are permitted council.
1848 Court for Crown Cases Reserved is established.

1850 Board of Directors of Convict Prisons is established.
1857 Court Probate Act is passed.
A separate Court for Divorce and Matrimonial causes is created.
1858 Jews are admitted to the House of Commons.
1867 The Courts of Admiralty and Probate are removed to Somerset House.
The second reform bill is passed.
1884 The third reform bill is passed.
1885 Jews are admitted to the House of Lords.

BIBLIOGRAPHY

Byrne, Richard. *Prisons and Punishments of London.* London: Grafton, 1992.

Gordon, Charles. *The Old Bailey and Newgate.* London: T. Fisher Unwin, 1902.

Howard, D.L. *The English Prisons.* London: Methuen, 1960.

Mayhew, Henry. *The Criminal Prisons of London and Scenes of Prison Life.* London: F. Cass Publications, 1968.

Pearce, Robert R. *A History of the Inns of Court and Chancery.* Littleton, Colo.: Rothman, 1987.

Radzinowicz, Leon. *A History of English Criminal Law and Its Administration From 1750.* New York: Macmillan, 1948.

Salbstein, M.C.N. *The Emancipation of the Jews in Britain: The Question of the Admission of the Jews to Parliament, 1828–1860.* Rutherford, N.J.: Farleigh Dickinson University Press, 1982.

Tobias, J.J. *Nineteenth-Century Crime in England: Prevention and Punishment.* Newton Abbot: David & Charles, 1972.

Walkowitz, Judith R. *City of Dreadful Delight: Narratives of Sexual Danger in Late-Victorian London.* London: Virago, 1992.

Webb, Sidney, and Beatrice Webb. *English Prisons Under Local Government.* London: Longmans, 1922.

Chapter Eight

Military

The nineteenth century proved to be a time of much activity and growth for the British army and navy. England's role as a world power was strengthened, and at the same time, new ideas concerning the organization and operations of its armed forces were put into place. Many of these changes affected the daily lives of the soldiers and sailors, while others ensured that, for most of the century, Britain remained unmatched in her fighting strength.

COMMISSIONED ARMY OFFICERS

Commissioned officers had always been culled from the upper classes, many being the younger sons of the aristocracy and gentry. Until 1871, commissions and promotions were purchased in the infantry, cavalry and guards regiments to the rank of lieutenant colonel. An officer candidate, having reached the age of sixteen, had to be nominated or approved by either the commander in chief of the Horse Guards or the colonel of his chosen regiment. Once approved, the candidate's name was placed on a waiting list.

Payment for an army commission was not made to the government, but rather to the officer who was retiring from the position being sold. A wealthy officer could advance quickly through the ranks, buying vacancies in either his own or another regiment, as long as he was willing to pay top dollar. While the prices of commissions were regulated, many times an additional premium was added to the sum, and a sort of private commission auction ensued among the officers. In the event an officer died while in service, his commission reverted to the Crown, and so could not be sold by his family.

REGULATION PRICES SET BY ROYAL WARRANT OF 1821 ON COMMISSIONS (IN POUNDS)

	Cornet	*Lieutenant*	*Captain*	*Major*	*Lieutenant Colonel*
REGIMENT					
Foot	450	700	1,800	3,200	4,500
Cavalry	840	1,190	3,225	4,575	6,175
Life Guards	1,260	1,785	3,500	5,350	7,250
Royal Horse Guards	1,200	1,600	3,500	5,350	7,250
Foot Guards	1,200	2,050	4,800	8,300	9,000

Half Pay

To facilitate promotions within the ranks, the War Office allowed half-pay line officers to retire by selling their commissions to lower ranking full-pay officers. Officers would typically have been placed on half pay when they were between postings or tours of action. However, even if a junior officer possessed the means with which to buy a higher rank, it was not possible to do so without seniority. Army ranks above that of lieutenant colonel were not open for purchase and had to be earned through promotion. Therefore, once an officer had been promoted above the rank of lieutenant colonel, he could no longer sell his commission, and so lost his initial investment.

An officer could leave the army before realizing a senior rank, but officers were not entitled to pensions unless they had been wounded in action. An officer could opt to take half pay instead of selling his commission, and this was usually done when he was waiting to return to active service, usually at a higher rank. In 1822, there were 8,676 officers on half pay, representing more men than were on active duty either at home or abroad. In light of this, the government attempted to shorten the half-pay list by returning officers to service and full pay, whereupon these officers would not be entitled to go on half pay again during their careers, and could only retire by selling their commissions.

Expenses

Officers were paid according to rank, but unless an officer had a private source of income, he could not support himself on half pay alone. Upon joining his regiment, each officer had to buy his own uniform, barracks furniture, horses and weapons, and to pay the salaries of his groom and manservant. These costs could total anywhere from two hundred pounds for an infantry officer to one thousand pounds for a cavalry officer. Therefore, in order to meet expenses, an infantry officer would have needed a private income of at least one hundred pounds, a cavalry officer six hundred pounds.

Though troops were housed in purpose-built barracks or at inns that had been requisitioned by the army, officers might have taken rooms in a nearby hotel or had private residences. In addition, they were expected to lead the life of an aristocratic gentleman about town. Cavalry officers were obliged to hunt, and to pay for their own horses, hounds and equipment. In return, the officer received minimum pay, certainly not enough to compensate for these expenses, although he could realize a gain on his initial investment when he sold his commission.

Prince Puckler-Muskau recorded his impressions of a typical officers' mess in 1827: "I was invited to dine in barracks by a Major of the Horse Guards. There is a most advantageous custom prevalent throughout the English army, I mean the so-called 'Mess.' Each regiment has its common table, to which every officer is bound to contribute a certain sum, whether he choose to avail himself of it or not. By this he is entitled to the privilege of dining at it daily, and of bringing an occasional guest according to some established regulations. A committee superintends the economical part. Each officer presides at the table in turn, from the colonel down to the youngest lieutenant, and is invested, so long as he is 'en functions,' with the requisite authority. The tone of the officers is excellent; far more 'gentlemanlike' than that commonly to be found on the Continent; at least so I am bound to conclude from this sample. Although the strictest subordination prevails in service, yet when that is over, they meet as gentlemen, so entirely on an equality, that it were impossible for a stranger to discover from their deportment the superior from the subordinate officers. The table was admirably served. There was not wanting either the elegant service of plate, or champagne, claret, or any of the requisites of luxury."

Joseph Farington adds the following on officers' expenses, written November 1, 1803: "In the evening, Philip Hamand [Farington's nephew] came from Canterbury where his regiment, the Blues, is quartered. . . . A Cornetcy in the Blues costs 2,000 guineas & the income is about two hundred pounds a year. The recruiting parties do not offer bounties to those who enlist, nothing more than a Sixpence or Shilling, a retaining fee. The pay of the privates is 2s. 6d. a day; but their subsistence only one shilling, which with the advantages they have is quite sufficient. A Captain is allowed the keep of 3 Horses, a Cornet of two, at the daily expense of 8d. for each Horse; the remainder is paid by the Government. A Cornet may live with the Regiment if He has one hundred fifty pounds a year besides His pay. . . . Officers at their Regimental Mess pay 4s. 6d. each for their dinners, besides wine. If an officer who belongs to the Mess dines one day in the week there He is charged for the whole week, but not other ways. They also pay 2s. 6d. for breakfast and 2s. 3d. for supper; at the former they have grills, &c. Those officers who are married and live separate from the Mess are equally respected, and it does not appear that an officer suffers anything in the opinion of his comrades if He adopts a frugal plan."

Officer Training

At the beginning of the nineteenth century, officers were not given compulsory military training, such as that later instituted at the Royal Military College at Sandhurst and the Royal Military Academy at Woolwich. It was not until 1849 that all applicants for commissions were made to pass an exam before receiving an appointment in the Horse Guards. In 1850, exams became mandatory before promotion from the rank of ensign to lieutenant, and from lieutenant to captain. The duke of York, as commander in chief of the army, ruled that no officer could be promoted to field rank without at least six years of service, nor to captain without at least two years of service. In 1871, the purchase system was finally done away with due to the efforts of war secretary Edward Cardwell, and officers were required to have formal military education at either Sandhurst or Woolwich.

As to the officers' dress, Captain Gronow states, "Nobody in the present day can conceive the inconvenience of our military costume when I first entered the guards in 1813, or the annoyance to which we were subjected at being constantly obliged to seek the assistance of a coiffeur to powder our hair. Our commanding officers were very severe with respect to our dress and powdering; and I remember, when on guard, incurring the heavy displeasure of the late Duke of Cambridge for not having a sufficient quantity of powder on my head, and therefore presenting a somewhat piebald appearance. I received a strong reprimand from HRH, and he threatened even to place me under arrest should I ever appear again on guard in what he was pleased to call so slovenly and disgraceful a condition. The hairdresser was not only required at early dawn, before our field days or parades, but again in the evening if we dined out, or went to parties or balls.

"The most fashionable coiffeur was Rowland, or Rouland, a French émigré. His charge for cutting hair was five shillings, and his shop was next door to the Thatched House Tavern in St. James's Street. He was the inventor of the famous Macassar oil, and made a large fortune."

ENLISTED MEN

Of course, the army did not operate entirely upon the purchase system. The artillery, foot soldiers, engineers and lesser ranking officers came from all classes of society. Rank-and-file troops were recruited in large towns. Sergeants and their recruiting staff received a fee of fifteen shillings per every man they signed up in the 1830s. Recruiters were notorious for plying prospective recruits with drink before offering them what was known as the sovereign's shilling. By accepting a shilling, the recruit indicated his willingness to join the army.

Once enlisted, the man was brought before a local magistrate or justice of the peace within ninety-six hours so that details regarding his background could be taken down. Poverty was the greatest incentive for enlistment as, once enlisted, a man could not be arrested for abandoning his wife and children as wards of the parish. Along with the sons of soldiers, the enlisted ranks were swelled by orphans and children from the workhouses.

Meager pay, harsh discipline and a rigorously structured daily routine did nothing to tempt men who had any other recourse available to them. In addition, recruiters often went round to local courts during quarter sessions and culled new soldiers from the ranks of those criminals who would otherwise have been sentenced to transportation. Once in the army, many continued their illegal activities. The Duke of Wellington called his men at Waterloo the "scum of the earth" and stated that, "In ninety-nine instances out of one hundred, soldiers enlisted on account of some idle or irregular, or even vicious, motive."

In 1847, Lord Grey introduced a short-term enlistment plan in the hope of making military service more desirable. Soldiers were to serve ten years and could then join a reserve company and be paid an annual portion, later receiving pensions at age fifty-five or sixty. Due to the intervention of the duke of Wellington, commander in chief of the army, the revised terms of service at first applied only to new recruits, as he feared that the new plan would disrupt the existing organization of the army.

Army Pay

During the first half of the nineteenth century, army pay remained the same, one shilling per day in the infantry to one shilling, three pence per day in the cavalry, with an allowance of one pence per day for beer. After 1866, these wages were nearly doubled. Those soldiers who were skilled in some trade—tailors, carpenters and the like—could supplement their wages by providing the army with their services, and army wives could do regimental washing for five shillings per week. Extra wages were paid to men who served in the officers' mess or performed extra labor such as road work or bridge building. Cavalrymen earned extra as grooms and farriers. Paydays were the first, eighth, fifteenth and twenty-second of each month.

Living Conditions

Army barracks were overcrowded, with the men often sleeping four to a wooden crib as late as 1816. Added to the populations were the wives and children of those men who were allowed to marry. As the army frowned upon the men marrying, no man could marry without receiving the permission of his regimental colonel, and only six men out of every one hundred who applied were allowed to wed. During the Peninsular War, barracks were built for the troops who were no longer housed in public houses or the older barracks, which had unsanitary drainage and poor ventilation.

The daily army diet, which had been set in 1813, consisted of one pound of bread and three-quarters of a pound of meat per man. After 1833, another half pound of bread was allowed. However, the only cooking facilities typically available within the barracks were two copper boilers, one used for cooking meat and the other for potatoes, so that the menus were confined to beef broth and boiled beef with potatoes. Breakfast was eaten at 7:30 A.M., dinner at 1:30 P.M.; an evening meal was not regulation until the 1840s. Proper kitchens were installed in most barracks after 1858, as the findings of the Sanitary Commission deemed them necessary to the health of the men. In 1870, a cooking school was founded at Aldershot, where soldiers were trained in culinary routine.

Battlefield Conditions

While living conditions during battle are necessarily inconvenient, the nineteenth-century British soldier faced additional hardships. By 1811, each troop had been assigned its own farrier, who held the rank of corporal, and there was a farrier attached to each squadron. The farrier branded horses, docked tails and shod the horses, though each man was supplied with enough iron to make a spare set of horseshoes if the need arose. The farriers had with them two mules, one carrying a small anvil and bellows, the other charcoal and iron. Farriers were necessary, as the army would be unable to advance without their services, but this level of attention given to equine needs was not extended to the daily lives of the servicemen themselves. Meager rations and contaminated water supplies led to an alarming number of illnesses.

In the late 1830s, Lord Howick, secretary of war, investigated the high rate of mortality in the army and found a direct correlation between poor rations and illness, prompting a reduction in the army's purchase of salted meat, and bulls were marched along with the troops in order to supply fresh meat. In an effort to lessen the consumption of liquor by troops overseas, the rations of free spirits routinely issued to soldiers was checked.

During the battles of the Crimean War in 1854, the horrid living conditions of British troops could no longer be ignored. Supply shipments were backlogged, and food supplies were low. The temporary shelters were unsanitary, with many troops living in wet trenches and suffering from exhaustion. For those who had been wounded in action, conditions grew dire, as doctors were scarce and the injured were left to lie in the mud with no medicine or medical care available. Field hospitals, where they existed at all, were poorly outfitted, and medicine and equipment were virtually nonexistent.

Due to the efforts of Florence Nightingale, a Commission of Inquiry began investigations into the sanitary conditions within the army in May 1857. Nightingale then worked to make these findings public and had them brought before the House of Commons by Lord Ebringon. These efforts resulted in an Army Medical School being founded at Chatham in 1860, and the organization of the Barrack and Hospital Commission, which visited every barrack and hospital in Britain between 1857 and 1861 to assess the conditions.

Punishment

Before 1829, there existed three types of court martial within the British army: general, garrison and regimental. The power of these courts had been unchecked before 1829, when the general and garrison courts were restricted to imposing five hundred lashes upon a man as punishment, and the regimental courts to three hundred lashes. In 1833, officers in the Horse Guards maintained that corporal punishment should be used for certain offenses, including violence toward superior officers, insubordination, mutiny, theft and drinking on duty. By 1836, flogging was being used as punishment in cases of mutiny, insubordination, desertion and theft of army property. By the mid-1840s, army prisons were being built both at home and abroad, but flogging remained the usual form of punishment, with twenty-five lashes being the maximum allowed in 1879.

THE ARMY IN INDIA

By the beginning of the eighteenth century, the British East India Company had established a series of posts in India, and the British Army had settlements there as well. By the nineteenth century, there came to be a certain prestige attached to Indian service, as well as the opportunity for private dealings, which could result in monetary profits.

The voyage to India lasted anywhere from two to six months, with both water and food being in short supply by the end of the trip. Most of the English gathered in Cairo until there were a number of people traveling on, and then proceeded as a group, in order to defend against bandits. In 1830, the first steamer service was begun between

Suez and Bombay. Experienced travelers booked cabins on the north side of these ships to avoid the constant heat of the sun. These cabins, booked "port out, starboard home," were the most desirable, and the initials of the phrase resulted in the coining of the word *posh.*

Living Conditions

India was the place where middle-class men could go to find opportunities unavailable to them in England. The pay for Indian service was good and, due to the currency exchange rate, allowed for more luxuries than a man was used to at home. On the other hand, living conditions included intense heat, monsoons and hordes of insects. The Indian women went about in veils and heavy robes, while English ladies strove to maintain their status by dressing in the latest fashions. Europeans, who existed outside of the Indian caste system, were considered untouchable, and the Indians would not shake their hands or eat at the same table with them.

British Wives

British bachelors stationed in India took Indian mistresses, but it was understood that these women would be pensioned off should a more suitable English bride be found. Very few British soldiers were allowed to marry, so the majority instead entered into liaisons with local women, with many deserting these women once their tours of duty were up. Some men found wives while they were home on leave; others chose from among the daughters or other female relations of the European community, whom they met at social functions. Still other men became engaged before beginning their service in India, with their fiancées then left behind to wait, sometimes for years at a time, while the men went on to India to make their fortunes.

If an English couple did marry in India, every effort was made to hold the ceremony in a church and to adhere to English traditions. The women banded together to make wedding favors, and food and champagne were often ordered from France. Brides wore white tulle, with the dresses either being brought from one of the larger stores in India or sent from England by a relative. No doubt many a bridal gown was handed from bride to bride, as they were hard to come by. Many brides who had married in England considered the long voyage to India with their husbands to be their honeymoons. Those who married after arriving in India had short honeymoons at hill stations, which were military camps or settlements.

Loneliness was a great drawback for English wives, as there were few other females and opportunities to enjoy the niceties of life, such as paying calls, attending tea parties, etc. They could not volunteer in local charities or hospitals due to the restrictions on mingling with the natives. Most European women had nannies, or ayahs, to watch their children, as the fees charged by ayahs were relatively low. However, most European children were sent home to be educated as soon as they were old enough, causing still more loneliness for most women.

Pastimes

The lack of a ready social life made what little intercourse that did exist that much more important. New brides arriving in India waited to be called upon by ladies already in residence, but otherwise new arrivals took it upon themselves to make the initial calls, thus setting the social machinery in motion. At hill stations, where houses were set back from the road, making for a difficult climb, a box would be erected at the beginning of the paths leading to the houses, into which calling cards could be placed when the lady of the house was "not at home," this fact being indicated by a sign near the box to save the caller from having to make the long trek uphill.

The cooler hours of the morning were reserved for housekeeping, so visits were made in the heat of the afternoon sun. In India, horses were inexpensive both to buy and to keep, and many ladies rode during the mornings, sometimes before dawn, in order to avoid the heat. Garden parties were rather formal affairs in India, and usually included bands or entertainment of some sort. Dinner parties were formal, as well, complete with menu cards written in French and evening dress required. Drinks were first served in the drawing room or on the verandah, and then the party moved into the dining room, where the revolving overhead fans would be set into motion by servant boys.

While senior officers at the military bases held balls on special occasions, such as the monarch's birthday, other entertainments were routinely organized as well, including regimental balls, military club dances, fancy dress balls, concerts, amateur theatricals and tableaux vivants.

Vacations home to England were rare, but the ladies could travel throughout India in order to sightsee. Alternately, those women who lived in small settlements or who were isolated by geography chose to vacation at hotels and boarding houses that sprang up near hill stations. Here, they could spend time in the company of a larger European community and take advantage of libraries, churches and company stores.

As for shopping trips, in the 1820s, Calcutta's Taylor's Emporium sold elegant china and furnishings, and by the end of the nineteenth century, Calcutta boasted several department stores, including a branch of the Army and Navy Stores and a Whiteaway and Laidlaw, which was much like a miniature Harrod's and was run by Europeans. For the most part, however, shopping was accomplished at local street markets and bazaars. Box wallahs, or traveling salesmen, visited far-flung outposts and sold everything from perfumes and fabric to household goods and sardines, and there were also mail-order catalogs to shop from.

Servants

The problems that arose from differences between the Indians and the Europeans extended to servants as well. Some Indians refused to perform certain household tasks due to their castes; Muslim cooks would not touch pork and Hindu cooks would not handle beef, so that chicken and goat were most often served. The English ladies encountered problems in teaching their servants to do things in the British manner, and attempting to get them to adhere to these new rules and requirements was a constant struggle. Laundering European garments presented a problem for Indian servants, and many clothes were ruined during the learning process. Most hill stations kept registries of dependable servants, but servants who were knowledgeable in the English ways were hard to find. The problem was compounded by the fact that ten servants was considered the absolute minimum to be kept. The middle class employed nearly sixty servants, while the wives of officials employed hundreds.

Mutiny

The Indians had been given little say in matters concerning their country since the beginning of British rule. Increasingly, the dictates of the British government led to disquiet among the Indian people. The matter came to a head when Governor General Marquess of Dalhousie (1848–56) ruled that those Indian states without ruling princes who were legal heirs would revert to the British crown. Additionally, Dalhousie placed the few existing regions of fertile Indian land, including Oudh, under British rule. Together, these dictates led to the Indian Mutiny of May 1857. English citizens were slaughtered, their houses robbed, and those who survived were taken prisoner by the Indians.

Englishwomen who escaped these consequences were left with no news of their husbands' fates. Many found that they had no servants left and were forced to live a hand-to-mouth existence. The local rajah of Cawnpore further organized the wholesale massacre of British troops in that city, and there ensued a wholesale slaughter of English women and children. Their bodies were afterward thrown down a well into a mass grave, which was then sealed. In mid-November, English troops captured Delhi and ended the Mutiny. From that date forward, British troops carried live ammunition for their weapons at all times and were ever on the lookout for signs of mutiny among the Indians.

THE ROYAL NAVY

As in the army, naval officers were recruited from the upper classes and were usually the younger sons of aristocrats. In the navy, these men could look forward to making their fortunes via the prize money they were awarded for capturing enemy ships, not to mention the extra money they could realize from their shares of booty. Through influential patronage, a young officer would have no trouble achieving the rank of captain, but to further his career beyond this point was often difficult. The Admiralty had a policy of not retiring naval officers, and so the lines of promotion often ground to a halt. During peacetime, senior officers were placed on half pay when they had no ships to command nor any postings on land, and promotions were stalled until an elder officer died.

During the Napoleonic Wars, fleets of British ships were launched, and all officers were returned to active duty. Calls for officer recruits went out, and junior officers easily advanced through the ranks. However, once the war had ended, ships were taken out of active duty and so the need for active officers was diminished. In order to stop the bottleneck of advancing officers that ensued, the Admiralty began to regulate the number of cadets entering naval service in 1815.

Seamen

During times of war, when the need for sailors was great, the navy recruited sailors by apprehending all vagrants and men who could not give satisfactory accounts of themselves and giving them the option of serving in His Majesty's navy or being sent to prison. *The Times* of July 7, 1803, recorded "Public Office, Bow Street—Yesterday upwards of forty persons were taken into custody, under authority of privy search warrants, at two houses of ill fame; the one in Tottenham Court Road, and the other near Leicester Square. They were brought before N. Bond. Esq., and Sir W. Parsons, for examination; several of them, not being able to give a satisfactory account of themselves, and being able-bodied men, were sent on board a tender lying off the Tower."

Men who had been recruited in such a fashion could hardly be expected to have been content with their situations, and therefore it is not surprising that mutinies occurred. From Ashton (1890): "The Navy was a rough school then, and the officers mainly came from a very different class to that from which they are now recruited." What a midshipman's berth was like then, we can learn from the following extract from a letter, also from Ashton: "The Midshipman is easily distinguished amongst his more fortunate companions in arms; you generally see him attired like the prodigal son returning from his occupation of a swineherd, [rather] than a British officer. His perforated worsted hose, shoes which have a very great resemblance to sandals, threadbare pantaloons which were once blue, a tattered 'uniform' coat and a slouched hat show that poverty, and not his will, consents."

Treatment of Sailors

The daily life of a nineteenth-century sailor was difficult. At sea, rum was the only beverage fit to drink once the supply of fresh water had been exhausted. Food rations were predictable and often stale, leading to cases of scurvy and tuberculosis, and many men were maimed by service or the cat-o'-nine-tails. Trusses were issued by the government to sailors, who routinely ruptured themselves while lifting heavy cargo and canvas sails. During times of war, wealthy individuals and business firms came forward as volunteers, offering their money and ships for government use. However, little was done to alleviate the daily lot of the sailors.

Ashton (1818): "This year did not open as one of national prosperity.

There was one subject that especially appealed to the country's benevolence. Of course, when the long, long war was over, the Navy was reduced to a peace footing, and thousands of men-of-war's men were paid off; and those who were obtained with such difficulty, who, in spite of being pressed, and forcibly taken from all that was dear to them, bullied by their officers, flogged nearly to death for comparative trifles, yet fought like lions, and laid the foundation of England's present prosperity, were cast adrift to shift for themselves as best they might. They were no longer wanted. Had trade been good, nothing more would have been heard of it, they would have been absorbed into the merchant navy, and the Government would have had all the credit of retrenchment and dutifully administering the funds of the Nation.

"As it was, people could see for themselves the streets teeming with old sailors, unable to obtain employment, and walking about almost in a state of nudity, and with empty stomachs. I am not exaggerating. In a Newspaper of January 10th, we find the following: 'We can confidently inform our readers that the Society for the Aid of Destitute Seamen are proceeding with much energy: Officers in the Royal Navy are, with much patience, and unwearied assiduity, examining the various objects as they present themselves. The greater number are men-of-war's men. Near two hundred and fifty seamen have been housed in a temporary lodging. Yesterday morning they breakfasted on wholesome porridge. . . . The applications were so numerous, yesterday, that the Committee, with much regret, have been obliged to suspend granting temporary relief for a day or two, to give time for investigation of the cases already before them.' Thanks to private Charity, this scandal was ended, and we hear no more of distressed seamen."

Naval Uniforms

Officers wore blue coats with blue (admiral, warrant officer) or white (captain) lapels and cuffs and white breeches. In 1797, epaulettes were introduced to officers' uniforms, with the following distinctions being laid down:

Admiral:	Two gold epaulettes, three silver stars on each.
Vice Admiral:	Two gold epaulettes, two silver stars on each.

Rear Admiral:	Two gold epaulettes, one silver star on each.
Captain (after 3 years service):	Two plain gold epaulettes.
Captain (under 3 years service):	One plain epaulette on right shoulder.
Commander:	One plain epaulette on left shoulder.

In 1812, two epaulettes were allowed all captains and commanders. Senior captains wore two anchors on their decoration; junior captains wore one. Commanders and lieutenants began to wear a single epaulette on the right shoulder. In 1825, officers were given new dress uniforms, with the following specifications: a blue coat with lapels turned back and sewn down with nine plain buttons on each side. Three buttons were to be placed on the cuffs and hip pockets, and two buttons on each side of the vent at the back of the coat.

Meanwhile, the sailors themselves had no regulation dress code, though officers were by this time attempting to inject some uniformity to their appearance. Some captains spent their own monies to purchase clothing for the crew. Though there may have been many ships at sea that were built along the same lines, each could be identified by the clothes worn by its crew. In 1840, the captain of the *HMS Blazer* ordered a blue-and-white striped coat for his men, with the name of this garment, the blazer, later passing into civilian usage.

Beginning in 1827, officers began wearing blue or white trousers, and knee breeches were reserved for royal drawing rooms only. The double-breasted coat was cut more to the lines of the civilian tailcoat, rather than having a distinctive, flaring skirt. Finally, in 1857, a uniform dress code was laid down for seamen, consisting of a blue cloth jacket and trousers, white duck trousers, a white frock coat, a pea jacket, a black silk scarf and a black canvas hat with the ship's name embroidered on it in gold letters.

NAVAL REFORMS

By 1852, the navy had recognized the problems inherent to enforced service. In that year, the Admiralty instituted a new system of recruiting, whereby young men were asked to volunteer and to serve a ten-year term, after which they could leave the navy. The idea was successful and allowed for seamen to be properly trained in a variety of shipboard occupations. Despite these great strides, at the end of the Crimean War, there was once again a vast number of officers who were put on half pay and who had not been assigned positions, making the advancement of officers difficult.

While Queen Victoria's Order in Council of 1840 made it mandatory for a certain number of naval captains to be retired from service each year, additional headway was made in thinning the ranks in 1869. Before this, flag officers were able to nominate as many recruits as midshipmen as they saw fit. After 1869, these nominations were limited to three names. By 1870, elderly officers were being officially retired, clearing the way for promotion from within the ranks.

The navy's objective changed also. Free trade and the Congress of Vienna served to reformat the duties of active ships. The congress served to officially outlaw the slave trade, and the British navy was given the task of stopping and inspecting all ships suspected of carrying slaves, regardless of their nationalities. While this meant that naval frigates were sent to the West African coast, the larger warships were dispatched to Gibraltar, where they fought organized piracy.

THE AGE OF STEAM

More changes were in store for the navy, in the form of new technology in shipbuilding. The Admiralty first adopted steam in 1816, when it ordered dredgers for use around its ports. The first naval steamship was the *Dee*. Weighing seven hundred tons, she carried six guns and was driven by paddle wheels. In time, four more steam vessels closely resembling the *Dee* would be ordered, but steamships were not officially recognized until 1827, when they were accorded the prefix *HMS*. In 1837, new steamships, with an underwater screw propeller replacing the bulky and inhibiting paddle wheels, were commissioned by the navy. The first of these was the *Francis B. Ogden*. Soon after, ironclad ships and those boasting armored decks would be commissioned, and in 1876, the Royal Navy's first torpedo boat, the *Lightning*, was launched. In 1897, the year of Queen Victoria's Diamond Jubilee, the Royal Navy presented a most impressive representation of its fleet to mark the event. On hand at Spithead were 165 ships, including 40 cruisers, 22 battleships and 20 torpedo boats.

IRREGULAR RECRUITS

While naval duty was notoriously difficult, it appears that some nineteenth-century patriots took extreme measures in order to enlist. Ashton: "In September [1813] the master of a Collier, belonging to Ipswich, had reason to believe that one of his apprentices who had made two voyages was a girl, and so it proved, and the girl appeared to be a respectable, steady, young man; whilst she was on board she conducted herself with great propriety, and was considered a very active, clever lad. In September 1815, when the Crew of the Queen Charlotte, 110 guns, was paid off, one of the Crew, an African, was discovered to be a woman. She had served as a seaman in the Royal Navy for upwards of eleven years, during several of which she had been rated able on the books of the above ship, by the name of William Brown, and had served for some time as Captain of the foretop, highly to the satisfaction of the officers.

"But ladies did not confine themselves to 'ploughing the main.' We know what an attraction a red coat has for them, and therefore no surprise need be manifested if some of them tried the Army. In January, 1813, was a rather romantic case: a girl, in man's clothes, was enlisted in the 53rd Regiment. Her sex was afterwards discovered when she said her lover was in the 43rd Regiment on foreign service, and she wanted to be near him.

"In 1814, Old Phoebe Hassel was alive, and at Brighton, aged 99. She had served in the army for seven years. The Regent, after seeing her in 1814, allowed her half a guinea a week, and at her death ordered a stone to be put up to her memory."

TIME LINE

1798 Napoleon occupies Egypt.
Russo-British Alliance is established.

1801 British liberate Egypt.
First Battle of Copenhagen occurs.

1802 Treaty of Amiens is established between Britain and France.

1803 Hostilities resume with France.

1804 Napoleon becomes emperor of France.

1805 British invade Hanover.
Battle of Trafalgar takes place.

1806 Prussians are defeated at Jena and Auerstadt.
1807 Russians are defeated at Friedland.
Second Battle of Copenhagen is fought.
France invades Portugal.
1808 France invades Spain.
1809 Battles of Corunna, Oporto and Talavera occur.
1810 Second French invasion of Portugal is conducted.
1811 Duke of York becomes commander in chief of the army (until 1827).
Battles of Fuentes d' Onoro and Albuera are fought.
1812 Wellington has victories at Ciudad Rodrigo, Badajoz and Salamanca.
War with America takes place.
1813 Battles of Vitoria and Pyrenees occur.
1814 Napoleon abdicates.
Gurkhas Wars begin (last until 1816).
1815 Napoleon abdicates for second time.
Battles of Ligny, Quatre Bras, Wavre and Waterloo are fought.
Second Peace of Paris ends Napoleonic Wars.
1824 First Burmese War begins (lasts until 1846).
1827 Duke of Wellington becomes interim commander in chief of the army.
1828 Lord Hill becomes commander in chief of the army.
1833 British Colonial slavery is abolished.
1842 Duke of Wellington becomes commander in chief of the army.
1846 Earl Grey becomes colonial secretary.
1847 Short Term Enlistment Act is introduced.
1852 Wellington dies.
Lord Hardinge is made commander in chief of the army.
Second Burmese War begins (lasts until 1853).
1854 Treaty of Paris (March) is established.
France and Great Britain declare war on Russia (May)—start of Crimean War.
1856 Duke of Cambridge becomes commander in chief of the army.
1857 Indian Mutiny takes place.
1858 East India Company's forces transferred to British Crown.
1859 Sidney Herbert becomes secretary of state for war.

1860 Indian Army is amalgamated.
1868 Edward Cardwell is secretary of state for war (until 1874).
1871 Purchase system is abolished.
1873 Ashanti War begins.
1879 Zulu Wars take place.
1880 First South African War starts.
1882 Egyptian War occurs.
1895 Duke of Cambridge resigns as commander in chief of the army.
1896 British take control of Sudan.
1899 Second South African War begins (lasts until 1902).

BIBLIOGRAPHY

Bromley, J.S. *The Manning of the Royal Navy: Selected Public Pamphlets 1693–1873.* London: State Mutual Books, 1987.

Bruce, Anthony. *The Purchase System in the British Army, 1660–1871.* London: Royal Historical Society, 1980.

Colledge, James J. *Ships of the Royal Navy: An Historical Index.* 2 vols. New York: Kelley, 1969.

Duncan, John. *Heroes for Victoria.* Speldhurst: Spellmount, 1993.

Hartfield, Alan. *British and Indian Armies in the East Indies, 1685–1935.* London: State Mutual Books, 1987.

Keay, John. *The Honourable Company: A History of the English East India Company.* New York: Macmillan, 1994.

Lavery, Brian. *Nelson's Navy: The Ships, Men and Organization.* Annapolis, Md.: Naval Institute Press, 1990.

Lees, James. *The Masting and Rigging of English Ships of War, 1625–1860.* Annapolis, Md.: Naval Institute Press, 1984.

Makepeace-Warne, Antony. *Brassey's Companion to the British Army.* London: Brassey's, 1996.

Rothenberg, Gunther. *The Art of Warfare in the Age of Napoleon.* Bloomington, Ind.: University Press, 1978.

Sherwig, John M. *Guineas and Gunpowder: British Foreign Aid in the Wars With France, 1793–1815.* Cambridge, Mass.: Harvard University Press, 1969.

Stanley, Jo, ed. *Bold in Her Breeches: Women Pirates Across the Ages.* London: Pandora, 1995.

Strachan, Hew. *From Waterloo to Balaclava: Tactics, Technology and the*

British Army, 1815–1854. Cambridge, Mass.: Cambridge University Press, 1985.

Sutton, John. *From Horse to Helicopter: Transporting the British Army in War and Peace, 1648–1988.* North Haven, Conn.: Shoe String Press, Inc., 1989.

Webber, William. *With the Guns in the Peninsula: The Peninsular War Journal of Second Captain William Webber, Royal Artillery.* London: Greenhill Books, 1991.

Chapter Nine

Economics and Banking

Specialist banking came to the English provinces in the second half of the eighteenth century. Before this, banking functions outside London had been handled by provincial attorneys. Provincial towns and villages acquired an extensive banking system in the 1780s, with individual banks issuing their own bank notes, which customers used to settle their debts locally.

THE ECONOMY

The British economy expanded during the period from 1822 to 1824, when employment was at an all-time high. When the boom ended in 1825, a liquidity crisis ensued in the banking sphere. A panic for cash depleted the banks' reserves, and the public lost confidence in the ability of country bankers to meet their obligations.

As panic over the state of the economy spread, bank notes were presented to country banks by customers who demanded either coin or Bank of England notes in return. Widespread hoarding of cash ensued. In 1826, Parliament grew concerned and sought to abolish the right of country banks to issue small notes, thus checking the possibility of their overextending themselves again in the future. In 1829, notes under five pounds were banned in England and Wales. Strong lobbying by the Scots prevented the ban from extending to Scotland and Ireland.

The Country Bankers Act

The ban on small notes hardly affected the Bank of England, as it had been taking its small notes out of circulation since 1821 and had only reissued them during the liquidity panic. In conjunction with the small note ban, the government also believed that the abolition of the Bank of England's joint stock monopoly would strengthen both the country and commercial banking systems. It would allow them to withstand any future runs, as larger partnerships would produce larger banks that had access to larger capital resources. In addition, creditors could take legal action against these larger partnerships in cases of failure, and this knowledge would instill renewed confidence among depositors.

The Country Bankers Act became law in May 1826, and permitted the formation of banks with an unrestricted number of partners outside a sixty-five mile radius of London. It also allowed new banks to sue and be sued in the name of public officers.

BANK NOTES

When cash payment for bank notes resumed in May 1821, many new styles of notes appeared in England. The Bank of England's notes, though, remained, for the most part, unchanged. Country banks incorporated detailed vignettes, double-sided printing techniques and colored ink. Engraver and printer W.H. Lizars, of Edinburgh, began incorporating hand-engraved vignettes on his note designs, and landscapes became another popular note theme. Most often, country bank notes depicted local landmarks. The Bank of England continued to use a single black-and-white note, its only decoration being the Britannia medallion. The directors believed that the public, familiar with this design, would be better able to spot forgeries. The Bank of England finally issued a newly designed note in 1855, which depicted a newly fashioned Britannia and used a shaded watermark. This same design would be used on all Bank of England notes until 1957.

Transfer of Funds

To conduct business efficiently, bankers needed a speedy and reliable means of remitting cash, securities and other documents. By the 1820s, banks were relying on the stagecoach system, and later on the railway network, which was established in the 1830s. Steam locomotives were dependable and fast, and by the 1880s, they could reach Edinburgh from London in eight and a half hours. Additionally, the extension of the electric telegraph in the late 1830s, as well as reforms to the postal system and the introduction in 1840 of a uniform rate of one pence per letter, speeded communication.

Still, provincial banks remained local in nature, and their isolation was a problem. They needed a means of remitting funds between different towns and of keeping abreast of investment opportunities. To deal with these factors, the banks developed a provincial agency network, which allowed them to arrange payments or collection of debts. The network also served as a clearinghouse for information regarding the state of annual harvests, frauds, bankruptcies, forgeries and the like.

Forgery

By 1797, bank note forgery was becoming so widespread that the public was asked to submit antiforgery suggestions. These were taken and debated until 1802. Some suggested that bank notes be wrought in silk, that colored paper be used and that parts of the paper be raised. None of these suggestions were adopted. In fact, no successful means of stemming forgery was introduced until the first quarter of the nineteenth century.

The dating and numbering of bank notes by hand was a tedious business, and early in the nineteenth century, Joseph Bramak devised a machine capable of dating and numbering two thousand bank notes per day. The type of print Bramak devised would continue to be used on notes until 1945. His printing technique proved effective against forgery, as it was actually a combination of two printing methods: intaglio and letterpress. However, by 1819, convictions for forgery of Bank of England notes rose again, and the public protested against the harsh punishment of hanging for the crime.

Artists and engravers spread propaganda and satirical broadsides against the bank and its directors. George Cruikshank's bank restriction note was one of the most famous examples. It was a caricature of a Bank of England note, the pound sign being a noose and signed by "Jack Ketch," the name applied to all London hangmen. Cruikshank was moved to draw the note, which took him all of ten minutes, after seeing a woman forger hung outside Newgate Prison.

Notes and Coins

The monetary system of the nineteenth century was used for three hundred years, until 1968, when it was decimalized. Before 1968, each pound had been divided into twenty shillings; each shilling was divided into twelve pence, or pennies, enabling the pound to be divided into 240 equal parts. This meant that a pound could be divided into halves, thirds, quarters, fifths and so on, down to one hundred and twentieths. A decimal system only allows halves, quarters, fifths, tenths, twentieths, twenty-fifths and fiftieths.

Many British coins were named for their Latin equivalents: In Latin, *libra* was the word for pound, *solidus* the word for shilling and *denarius* the word for penny. When writing monetary amounts, £ was used to indicate a pound, *s.* for the shilling and *d.* for pence. When writing amounts that included pounds, shillings and pence, these were abbreviated £ 9.6.2, or nine pounds, six shillings and two pence.

THE POST OFFICE

The Penny Post

Before 1801, the postal letter rate was one penny, but in that year it was raised to two pence, and in 1805 to three pence. During this time, it was the recipient who paid the cost of postage upon delivery of a letter, not the sender. Many recipients could not afford the high fees, and so letters went undelivered. In order to lower rates and improve service, Member of Parliament Robert Walles began a campaign for uniform penny postage in 1833. Rowland Hill joined the effort, and in January 1840, the Penny Post was established. Hill immediately began a campaign to bring about an adhesive stamp, which would allow postage to be prepaid by the sender. This first stamp, the Penny Black, was introduced on May 6, 1840.

The Penny Post routes operated six days a week, and letters were delivered to any house on the routes. For those who lived away from these routes, receiving houses, at which mail could be picked up, were set up in most villages. A late posting fee was sometimes charged if mail was received after normal reception hours. The fee was meant to save the postmaster's inconvenience, and usually amounted to a penny.

At the beginning of the nineteenth century, private postal boxes were available but not in widespread use. In 1837, the Bromley postmaster had six subscribers from whom he received an annual fee of a

BANK OF ENGLAND NOTES

(All notes were white and measured between 7 and 8 inches by 4 to 5 inches.)

Value	*First Issued*	*Last Issued*
One pound	March 2, 1797	1826
Two pounds	March 2, 1797	1821
Five pounds	1793	1957
Ten pounds	1759	1943
Fifteen pounds	1759	1822
Twenty pounds	1725	1943
Twenty-five pounds	1765	1822
Thirty pounds	1725	1852
Forty pounds	1725	1943
Fifty pounds	1725	1943
Sixty pounds	circa 1730	before 1803
Seventy pounds	circa 1730	before 1803
Eighty pounds	circa 1730	before 1803
Ninety pounds	circa 1730	before 1803
One hundred pounds	1725	1943
Two hundred pounds	circa 1730	1928
Three hundred pounds	circa 1730	1885
Four hundred pounds	circa 1730	before 1803
Five hundred pounds	circa 1730	1943
One thousand pounds	circa 1730	1943

guinea each. The use of these boxes was explained in the *Second Report on Postage* (1838): "Persons having private boxes enjoy generally the advantage of receiving their letters as soon as the window is open and the Letter-carriers dispatched, by which means, those Subscribers who reside at any distance from the post office obtain their letters so much earlier than they would do by the ordinary Delivery; they have also the opportunity of ascertaining at once whether there are any letters for them, and are usually allowed credit by the Postmaster."

COINS

Coin	*Denomination*	*Metal*	*First Minted*	*Last Minted*
Sovereign	£1 or 20s.	gold	1817	1968
Half sovereign	10s.	gold	1817	1926
*Guinea	£1. 1s. 21s. or 252d.	gold	1663	1813
Crown	5s.	silver	1662	1937
Half crown	2s. 6d.	silver	1663	1946
Florin	2s.	silver	1849	1946
Shilling	12d.	silver	1663	1946
Sixpence	6d.	silver	1674	1946
Two penny	2d.	silver	1797	1797
Penny (pence)	1d. or 4 farthings	copper	1797	1860
Half penny	2 farthings	copper	1672	1860
Farthing	¼ penny	copper	1672	1860
Half farthing	⅛ penny	copper	1842	1856

(While no longer minted after 1813, guineas remained in circulation. Guineas would be replaced in 1817 by the sovereign. The guinea was considered a gentleman's coin. Tradesmen were paid in pounds, but gentlemen, artists, barristers, etc., were paid in guineas.)

Postmistresses

In October 1792, the post office declared itself against the appointment of innkeepers as postmasters, as they rarely provided separate rooms for postal business, and so left the mails vulnerable to theft. By March 1836, only one post town in England still had an innkeeper as postmaster. More common were post offices combined with some other business, such as a drugstore, stationery shop, grocer, news agent or bookseller.

Women were allowed to serve as postmistresses, or allowed to take over existing post offices upon the deaths of husbands who had acted as postmasters. Of the twenty-nine Kentish post towns in March 1836, four had postmistresses. One of these was the bustling Ramsgate office, the salary attached to which was roughly 178 pounds per annum. When a postmistress married, it was the ruling of the post office that she give up her appointment, though it could be transferred to her husband. At Faversham, the widow of Mr. Plowman, the late postmaster, took over the post upon his death, but in 1800 she married Andrew Hill, who became postmaster in her place. After Hill died in July of the same year, Sara was reappointed as postmistress.

Commercially produced postcards became popular in the late 1880s, when the post office instituted a fee of half a penny for their delivery. Envelopes had been invented in the 1830s but were not widely used until the Great Exhibition of 1851, when Jeremiah Smith displayed his gummed envelopes. Still, the use of envelopes did not become popular until well into the 1860s. Most people preferred the old-fashioned method of folding a blank sheet of paper over a letter and then fastening it shut with a wafer, which was a small disk made of gum and flour. This disk was moistened with water and then pressed closed with a seal.

BIBLIOGRAPHY

Andreades, A. *History of the Bank of England.* New York: Gordon Press Publishers, 1973.

Austen, Brian. *British Mail-Coach Services, 1784–1850.* New York: Garland Publishing, 1987.

————. *English Provincial Posts, 1633–1840.* London: Phillmore, 1978.

Bagehot, Walter. *Lombard Street: A Description of the Money Market.* London: John Murray Ltd., 1915.

Butchart, M. *Money in the English Tradition 1640–1936.* New York: Gordon Press Publishers, 1936.

Challis, C.E., ed. *A New History of the Royal Mint.* Cambridge, Mass.: Cambridge University Press, 1992.

Clapham, Sir John. *The Bank of England: A History.* 2 vols. Cambridge, Mass.: Cambridge University Press, 1970.

Collins, M. *Money and Banking in the U.K.: A History.* London: Rutledge, Chapman and Hall, 1988.

Kay, F. George. *The Royal Mail.* London: Rockliff, 1951.

Robinson, Howard. *The British Post Office: A History.* Princeton, N.J.: Princeton University Press, 1948.

CHAPTER TEN

The Laboring Classes

Perhaps the darkest shadow to have fallen over the nineteenth century was the harsh and often inhumane treatment of Britain's laboring classes, and especially of the women and children who made up so many of its numbers. The poorest classes, despite the mitigating causes of their reduced circumstances, were looked upon as a drain to the public purse, and even the lot of the able country laborer and his family was a hard one.

CHILD LABOR

In the year 1801, the overcrowded conditions in most factories and mills, combined with long hours, poor food and ventilation and overwork, caused an outbreak of epidemic fever among workers in England. For the first time in history, not only was the public conscience roused, but the House of Commons was urged to intervene. An act of 1802 limited the daily work hours to twelve for children, with an hour and a half for meals and rest. This meant that child laborers still worked, on average, from 6 A.M. to 7 or 8 P.M. In 1833, another act limited children under thirteen to not more than forty-eight hours per week, and they could not work between the hours of 8:30 P.M. and 5:30 A.M. Lord Althorp's Factory Act of 1833 set legal limits on the working hours of children and young persons, enforced by factory inspectors. The Ten Hours Bill of 1833 limited daily work of women and children in textile factories to ten hours per day.

Climbing Boys

Youngsters continued to be used as climbing boys by chimney sweeps despite legislation, until 1875, when the continued deaths of children in flues aroused public outcry. Since 1817, efforts to secure the abolition of such labor had been made and constantly renewed. In 1834, a halfhearted act was passed ordering that before a boy was bound to a sweep as an apprentice, he should be examined by two magistrates and made to state that he was "willing and desirous to follow the business of a Chimney Sweep."

Climbing boys, or "chummies" as they were known, usually started at the age of five and were employed until they were killed or grew too large to climb up inside a chimney flue. In the poorer districts across England, where children were plentiful and wages low, children of any age from four upward were sold to master sweeps, who were under no obligation to look after them, physically or morally.

In 1848, a case came before the Hull magistrates in which it transpired that a boy of ten had been sold from sweep to sweep five separate times, and though the injuries he had sustained in chimney climbing had crippled him for life, he had been driven up no less than twelve flues in the space of the few days prior to the case being heard. Two years later, at Nottingham, a boy became jammed within a chimney above a smoldering fire. He was pulled out by force but died a few hours later, and no inquest into his death was ever held. Additional chimney sweeps acts, in 1840 and 1864, remained largely disregarded by householders, local authorities and magistrates. The Society for the Prevention of Cruelty to Children was founded in 1884, when further reforms were instituted.

Conditions were worse still in the coal pits. In every mining district throughout England, children were commonly employed at the age of seven; in many pits, they were sent underground at age five or six as "trappers" and taught to work the trapdoors upon which the ventilation system of the mines depended. Once below ground, the children often spent twelve or more hours in complete darkness and silence. Youngsters were also used for pushing trucks from the face of the mine to the bottom of the shaft. These carts were drawn by children who were harnessed to them like animals and forced to crawl through the shafts on all fours.

FEMALE LABOR

There were few ponies used in the coal pits, as it was found that female workers were less costly to keep. The women were employed by foremen and not by the mine owners. Lord Shaftesbury's Mines Act of 1842 forbade women and children under ten to work below ground in the mines. Yet even after these conditions had been brought to light, they were met with disbelief or, worse yet, complacency from an upper-class society who lived in an entirely different world. This separation of classes is best illustrated by the lot of London seamstresses.

The industrial revolution allowed for the production of large quantities of inexpensive fabric, allowing women from the middle class to follow new changes in fashion. Seamstresses became much in demand, and for girls from the lower classes, entering the dressmaking field was seen as a step toward bettering oneself. While it was deemed a ladylike occupation, the realities of the seamstress's daily life were harsh. A girl might serve as an apprentice for two or three years, beginning at around the age of fourteen. Her family paid twenty pounds or more to the dressmaker for this apprenticeship, for which she received room and board and was taught the trade, but the girl received no salary. After the girl's skills had been deemed competent, she might be moved up through the line of production, doing finer tasks, which brought with them more responsibility. However, some employers attempted to keep the girls from advancing in order to keep them at minimal pay.

In order to make the sumptuous dresses in which society women dressed themselves, sweated labor was needed. Seamstresses generally worked from 8 A.M. until 11 P.M. during the winter and from 6 A.M. until 12 A.M. in summer. During the fashionable season (April through July), when the number of balls, dances and other entertainments increased the demand for dresses, it frequently happened that these hours were extended in order to meet increased demand. For special orders, such as for court drawing rooms, general mournings and weddings, the women might work through the night for up to three months at a time. These conditions lasted well into the 1860s.

THE POOR LAWS

By 1818, the annual national poor rate, taxes collected in each town by parish officers, had reached nearly eight million pounds. Thousands of small farmers and laborers, unable to pay their shares of these increased taxes, lost their properties or had their incomes dangerously reduced. In order to curb expenditures to support the poor, reforms in the Poor Law were sought, and attempts were made to mark the distinction between the laboring poor, who were temporarily in need of support, and those persons who were paupers or vagrants. The commission for Poor Law Reform approved the continuance of outdoor relief to the aged and sick, who would continue to receive help in the form of clothing, food and housing, and who would not be impressed to enter a workhouse.

Almshouses were only for those who met the criteria of an individual charity or those who had a friend or patron among the trustees who could make application on their behalf. Still, almshouses could only serve a few of the needy in each town, and the remaining families were placed in workhouses, their upkeep paid for by poor rates.

One reason for such financial distress was that the casual laborer could not depend on a steady income, with most unskilled jobs being contingent on the need for temporary workers or on the seasons. In addition, landlords might lease a ten-room house for twenty to forty pounds per year, or convert a house into single rooms, which were rented for five to ten shillings per week. Even though these rooms offered only the barest amenities and were rarely kept in good repair, many people could not afford these rents, and so many families often lived together in the same single room in order to share the rent.

Such persons were rarely able to put any money by for the hard times, and often found themselves either in debt or buying on credit. Should a landlord unexpectedly decide to raise the rent or the breadwinner suffer an unforeseen illness, such families could very well find themselves in workhousees. In *Life and Labor of the People of London*, Charles Booth wrote the following graphic account of the plight of such a family: "This family live, to the greatest possible extent, from hand to mouth. Not only do they buy almost everything on credit from one shop, but if the weeks tested are a fair example of the year, they every week put in and take out of pawn the same set of garments, on which the broker every time advances 16s. charging them the no doubt reasonable sum of 4d. for the accommodation. 4d. a week or 17s. 4d. a year, for the comfort of having a week's income in advance. On the other hand, even on credit they buy nothing until actually needed. They go to their shop as an ordinary housewife to her canisters; twice a day they buy tea, or three times if they make it so often; in 35 days they made 72 purchases of tea, amounting in all to 5s. 2¾d. Of sugar there are 77 purchases in the same time."

The Workhouse

The 1834 Poor Law Amendment Act sought to separate those who would not support themselves, such as vagrants, from those who had fallen upon hard times by refusing them outdoor relief and instead placing them in workhouses. Living conditions within the workhouses were so harsh that most avoided them at any cost. Husbands and wives were placed in separate wards, and meals consisted of gruel, broth, dry bread or potatoes. Workhouse inmates could only see visitors by special permission and under supervision. Of course, the inmates were free to leave whenever they wished, and if they did but had no other means of support, they were also made to leave the area so they would not be a further burden upon the parish.

AGRICULTURAL LABORERS

Nearly two thousand land enclosure acts were passed between 1802 and 1844, encompassing over six million acres, which represented roughly one-quarter of the cultivated land in England. There were three reasons for enclosing land: Arable land was converted to pasture for livestock, individual parcels of arable strips were consolidated into a single holding, or common or uncultivated land was enclosed into arable holdings. Enclosure was deemed necessary, as there was often no cooperation between individual owners of small plots of land. The planting, sowing, fertilization and irrigation of these parcels were accomplished randomly. Enclosure sought to make local agriculture more efficient by the cooperation of neighboring farmers.

Enclosure commissioners, who divided the parcels of land after they had been enclosed, were respectful of the rights of those landowners who had legal title to the land. But those landowners who had based their claims upon custom or tenancy were often displaced.

Female Agricultural Laborers

Many agricultural workers were women. During the Napoleonic Wars, when the majority of men were fighting, women workers were a common sight in the fields. In 1851, 11 percent of the two million workers engaged in the trade were women; by 1901, women made up 6 percent of the workforce. While women were often hired temporarily at harvest times, they also worked full time at potato gathering, turnip pulling, weeding, hoeing, hop binding and all manner of vegetable and fruit picking. Often, their children worked alongside them, and it was not unusual for employers to advertise for entire families of farm workers.

While many farm families might be able to live off the land in terms of food and fuel, cash money was still necessary for the purchase of clothing, medicines and other essentials. The wives and children of farmers might earn extra money from the sale of butter or craft items, or by performing such tasks as sewing for the gentry or doing daily cleaning work. Women, children and the elderly could likewise make money at any of a number of localized cottage industries, which were types of labor that could be performed in the home. In the Midlands, pillow-lace making was common; in Buckinghamshire, Bedfordshire, Hertfordshire and Essex, there was straw plaiting for the hat trade; in Nottinghamshire and Leicestershire, there was hosiery work; in Oxfordshire, Worcestershire and the West Country, there was glove making; in east Dorset, there was button making; and on the coasts of East Anglia and Dorset, there was net making.

Cottagers

Many farmers rented small areas of land, usually measuring one hundred acres or less, from the gentry and aristocracy. In addition to what he earned from the land, a farmer might have been given the use of a cottage for a token rent or rent-free, and would usually have been given a share of food at harvest time. These rural farm cottages were never elaborate buildings, with most having but two rooms, resulting in crowded living quarters. The farmer's diet was also inadequate, consisting of whatever could be grown by the family, with such items as tea and bacon fat being considered luxuries. Beginning in the 1850s, the publication *Punch* and other venues began to advertise these scandalous living conditions. The Prince of Wales purchased and renovated Sandringham during the 1860s, and over the next twenty years erected over seventy new cottages for his laborers, each having three bedrooms and two common rooms, prompting other landowners to follow his example.

The small-farm worker, or cottager, was given little say in the running of country government, and his children did not regularly receive an education, even after the 1850s and 1860s, when country schools were set up. An act of 1870 made the provision of education for all English children a law, and local landowners and clergy sought to erect schools in their towns and villages. Still, the amount of money a child might contribute to a family's income took precedence over education. It was also feared that education would broaden the minds of country children and make them want for things above their station, or prompt them to leave home in order to seek out their own fortunes.

Many owners of large areas of land were accustomed to hosting annual feasts or other entertainment for their workers, tenants and the poor of the parish. From Charles Greville, May 12, 1834: "On Monday last I went to Petworth, and saw the finest fete that could be given. Lord Egremont has been accustomed some time in the winter to feast the poor of the adjoining parishes (woman and children, not men) in the riding-house and tennis-court, where they were admitted by relays. His illness prevented the dinner taking place; but when he recovered he was bent upon having it, and, as it was put off till the summer, he had it arranged in the open air, and a fine sight it was; fifty-four tables, each fifty feet long, were placed in a vast semicircle on the lawn before the house. Nothing could be more amusing than to look at the preparations. The tables were all spread with cloths, and plates and dishes; two great tents were erected in the middle to receive the provisions, which were conveyed in carts, like ammunition. Plum-puddings and loaves were piled like cannon-balls, and innumerable joints of boiled and roast beef were spread out, while hot joints were prepared in the kitchen, and sent forth as soon as the firing of guns announced the hour of the feast. Tickets were given to the inhabitants of a certain district, and the number was about 4,000; but, as many more came, the old Peer could not endure that there should be anybody hungering outside his gates, and he went out himself and ordered the barriers to be taken down and admittance given to all. . . . At night there was a great display of fireworks, and I should think, at the time they began, not less than 10,000 people were assembled."

FACTORY HOUSING

Factory owners realized early on that worker morale and productivity could be strengthened by providing their employees with low-cost, nearby housing that was let at reasonable rents. In 1842, William Cooke

Taylor wrote his *Notes of a Tour in the Manufacturing Districts of Lancashire,* which includes the following description of this type of housing (provided by Ashwoth's cotton mill in Turton, near Bolton, Lancashire): "The cottages are built of stone and contain from four

MAP OF ENGLISH SOCIETY IN 1814

(From Patrick Colquhoun's *A Treatise on the Wealth, Power, and Resources of the British Empire,* 1814)

Class	*Heads of Families*	*Total Family Members*
HIGHEST ORDERS: royal family, lords spiritual and temporal, great officers of state, peers above the degree of a baronet	576	2,880
SECOND CLASS: baronets, knights, country gentlemen, others with large incomes	46,861	234,305
THIRD CLASS: clergy, doctors, merchants and manufacturers on a large scale, bankers	61,000	112,200
FOURTH CLASS: lesser clergy, doctors, lawyers, teachers, ship owners, merchants and manufacturers of the second class, shopkeepers, artists, builders, mechanics, persons of moderate income	233,650	1,168,250
FIFTH CLASS: lesser freeholders, shopkeepers, innkeepers, publicans, persons in miscellaneous occupations	564,799	2,798,475
SIXTH CLASS: working mechanics, artists, craftsmen, agricultural laborers	2,126,095	8,792,800
SEVENTH CLASS: paupers, vagrants, gypsies, idle persons supported by criminal activity	3,371,281	16,165,803
ARMY AND NAVY: officers, including half	10,500	69,000
pay noncommissioned officers, soldiers, seamen, marines, pensioners	120,000	862,000

to six rooms each; back-premises with suitable conveniences are attached to them all. . . . Daughters from most of the houses, but wives, as far as I could learn, from not, worked in the factory. Many of the women were not a little proud of their housewifery, and exhibited the Sunday wardrobes of their husbands, the stock of neatly folded shirts, etc. . . . I was informed by the operatives that permission to rent one of the cottages was regarded as a privilege and favour; that it was in fact a reward reserved for honesty, industry and sobriety."

Another factory town was Bournville, begun in 1878 near Birmingham by Cadbury's, a Quaker cocoa processor, and completed in 1895. Only half of Bournville's residents worked in the nearby factory, so it could not be wholly termed a company town, such as the town of Port Sunlight, built by Lever Brothers in Merseyside.

BIBLIOGRAPHY

Alderman, Geoffrey. *Modern Britain 1700–1983: A Domestic History.* London: Routledge Chapman & Hall, 1986.

Bovill, E.W. *English Country Life, 1780–1830.* London: Oxford University Press, 1962.

Briggs, Asa, comp. *How They Lived: An Anthology of Original Documents Written Between 1700 and 1815*, Vol 3. Oxford: Blackwell, 1969.

Cadbury, Edward. *Women's Work and Wages.* London: T. Fisher Unwin, 1906.

Charles, Lindsey. *Women and Work in Pre-Industrial England.* London: Routledge Chapman & Hall, 1986.

Donajgrodzki, A.P., ed. *Social Control in Nineteenth-Century Britain.* Totowa, N.J.: Rowman & Littlefield, 1977.

Driver, Felix. *Power and Pauperism: The Workhouse System, 1834–1884.* Cambridge, Mass.: Cambridge University Press, 1993.

Falkus, M. *Britain Transformed: An Economic and Social History, 1700–1914.* Ormskirk: Causeway Books, 1987.

Hewitt, Margaret. *Wives and Mothers in Victorian Industry.* London: Rockliff, 1958.

Horn, Pamela. *A Georgian Parson and His Village: The Story of David Davies, 1742–1819.* Abingdon: Beacon Publications, 1981.

Kain, Roger. *An Atlas and Index of the Tithe Files of Mid-Nineteenth-Century England and Wales.* Cambridge, Mass.: Cambridge University Press, 1986.

Morsley, C., ed. *News From the English Countryside, 1750–1850.* London: Harrap, 1979.

Perkin, Harold. *Origins of Modern English Society 1780–1880.* London: Routledge Chapman & Hall, 1972.

Pyne, W.H. *Picturesque Views of Rural Occupations in Early Nineteenth-Century England.* New York: Dover Publications, 1977.

Robinson, Geoffrey. *Hedingham Harvest: Victorian Family Life in Rural England.* North Pomfret: Trafalgar Square, 1989

Schmiechen, James A. *Sweated Industries and Sweated Labor: The London Clothing Trades, 1860–1914.* Urbana, Ill.: University of Illinois Press, 1983.

Sinclair, John. *The History of the Public Revenue of the British Empire.* New York: Kelley, 1966.

Webb, Sidney, and Beatrice Webb. *English Poor Law History.* London: Longmans, Green & Co., 1927.

Part Three

Society

CHAPTER ELEVEN

Arts and Entertainment

READING

During the first half of the nineteenth century, reading was hardly a popular pursuit. Much of the population was unschooled, and, more importantly, printed matter was too expensive for the common man. The Stamp Act of 1797 placed a tax of sixpence on each copy of a newspaper. In 1815, this tax was raised to four pence, and a tax of three shillings was placed on pamphlets. Additionally, there was a tax of three shillings, sixpence placed upon newspaper advertisements. After 1836, the newspaper duty was reduced from four to one pence. These taxes, added to the already high cost of printing, made newspapers a luxury only the wealthy could afford. The price for a single issue of such papers as *The Times* and *Morning Chronicle* was seven pence, and the newspaper tax was not abolished until 1861.

The high cost of newspapers led to the formation of newspaper societies, which existed in every parish and totaled five thousand in number in the 1820s. In a society, a group of people each contributed sixpence a week to subscribe to a London paper and two or three provincial papers. Poorer districts had more subscribers who each paid less fees, say a penny a week, in order to subscribe to a provincial paper, which was published once or twice a week.

Libraries

Books were also expensive and were considered luxuries, which is why it was a sign of wealth and prestige for a private home to include a library, the shelves well stocked with leather-bound volumes. Thomas Creevey, a member of Parliament, found the purchase of books to be beyond his reach, illustrated in a letter he wrote from Brooks's Club, London, on October 4, 1835: "When I was at Stoke I fell in love with Wellington's Peninsular dispatches, published by Gurwood; but as my supply from that library is now cut off, and the book itself too dear to buy, I am living upon Napier's Peninsular War."

Many local printers and booksellers started their own libraries, such as the Book Society begun in 1808 by Messrs. Thomas and Wrightson, booksellers, at the Stamp Office. They opened a news room to be supplied with four London dailies, *Lloyd's List,* a Sunday paper, three provincial papers, three Birmingham papers, reviews and popular magazines. *The Monthly Magazine* for June 1821 estimated that there were 65,000 reading societies in Great Britain, providing families with reading material for an annual subscription that varied from half a guinea to two guineas per annum. In addition, most towns had subscription and circulating libraries, where books could be borrowed in exchange for an annual fee. And, from 1850 on, the larger employers, such as factories and mills, provided their workers with an on-site reading room or library.

Book Publishing

London was the capital of the book publishing world. Chapman and Hall, and Longmans were leading publishers, and John Murray, a Scot who settled in London, published such authors as Jane Austen, Leigh Hunt, Byron, Scott and Coleridge. Public taste in reading matter between 1816 and 1851 can be gauged by a contemporary survey taken by Charles Knight, a London statistician, which recorded the number of titles published in various categories: religion and sermons—10,300; history and geography—4,900; foreign language and school books—4,000; fiction—3,500; drama and poetry—3,400; children's books—2,900; medical—2,500; arts—2,460; science—2,450; biography—1,850; law—1,850; morals, manners and social instruction—1,400.

Newspaper Distribution

Between 1816 and 1828, the firm of H. & W. Smith went from being a small London newspaper seller to transporting and selling London papers throughout the provinces. At the same time, newspapers were also sent through the post by their publishers to subscribers, and the members of both houses of Parliament could send papers throughout the land via the mails without having to pay a fee for postage. The Franking Act of 1764 gave members of parliament the right to send written orders to the post office demanding the free delivery of their papers.

William Henry, of H. & W. Smith, was the first to commercially distribute newspapers on such a wide scale, sending his papers throughout the land from his premises at No. 192 Strand, London. The mail coaches left London at about 8 P.M., after having been loaded with newspapers from the Newspaper Office in Lombard Street, so that the morning papers were at least twelve hours old by the time they reached the provinces. By the mid-1820s, the new, fast stage-coaches were used by Henry to get his papers to the country at a faster pace. Always seeking ways to improve business, when George IV died, Henry chartered a special boat to carry the latest newspapers, which beat the royal messengers to Dublin with the news by twenty-four hours.

NEWSPAPER CIRCULATION

Major London Newspapers in Order of Circulation (1837–50)

The Times
Illustrated London News (from 1842)
Weekly Dispatch
News of the World (from 1843)
Morning Herald
Morning Advertiser
Morning Post
Morning Chronicle
Bell's Life in London
The Sun
Sunday Times
The Standard
Weekly Times (from 1847)
Evening Mail (evening edition of *The Times*)
Britannia (from 1839)
The Observer
Evening Chronicle
Court Journal

Newspapers and the Railroad

In the 1850s, Henry's firm, now known as Smith's, delivered the newspaper in the company's trademark red carts to the Great Western railway, which Smith's used to transport the papers. And Smith's also set up its own news agents stands in most major railway stations.

Railroads at first catered to businessmen, who rode in first class, and then offered second-class cars. In 1844, Parliament ordered every rail company to run at least one third-class train per day, for which travelers were charged a fare of one penny per mile. By 1850, first- and second-class passengers were provided with the luxury of closed carriages fitted with glass windows. Though it was impossible to read while these early trains were in motion, commuters could read while in the waiting rooms located within most stations. Smith's took advantage of this market by renting bookstalls in stations along the larger lines.

SILHOUETTES

Etienne de Silhouette (1709–1769), a French minister of finance who cut black profiles as a hobby, is credited with lending his name to the silhouette medium. These artists were originally called profile miniaturists, and their work was called profile miniatures or shades. From about 1790 on, silhouettes provided both the noble and the common with likenesses of family members and loved ones, at a much reduced cost compared to that of painted miniatures. The artists usually cut the amazingly accurate profile of a subject in just a few minutes, using paper and scissors, with some artists adding gold accents and colored paints to give their work more visual interest. The cost of a silhouette could range from a shilling to more than a guinea.

Before long, every town of any size, and especially resort and spa towns, had at least one resident silhouettist. Even Princess Elizabeth, daughter of King George III, was an amateur silhouettist. While some silhouettes were produced from a shadow thrown by a lighted candle onto a sheet of paper, others were made by machine, and the most desirable were done by hand. Materials used in the production of silhouettes included paper, wax, glass or plaster, with the more costly silhouettes being framed. Some artists affixed their labels to the back of their work; others signed them.

Among the best known silhouette artists in England was John Miers

(1756–1821), who began his career in Liverpool before opening a London studio at No. 111 Strand in 1788, at which time he was charging a guinea per silhouette. Some of his best work was done on plaster ovals, and those done on ivory found their way onto rings, lockets and bracelets. W. Phelps was also working at silhouettes from his studio in Drury Lane, where he painted his work onto plaster or buff-colored paper, adding soft shades of blue, apple green or lilac to items of clothing. William Hamlet, who was appointed profilist to Queen Charlotte and the royal family, had several studios in Bath from 1780 to 1815, and painted his silhouettes on flat or convex glass.

PHOTOGRAPHY

A decline in the quality of those silhouettes produced in the 1820s was brought about by a proliferation of unskilled artists taking up the lucrative trade. In addition, the medium was further threatened by the later advent of commercial photography. In 1854, a Parisian photographer named Andre Disderi patented a multilensed camera capable of producing eight small likenesses on one large glass negative. The resulting contact print was cut, and the portraits were trimmed and mounted on cards measuring two and a half by four inches. As this was the usual size of a visiting card, the photos were dubbed *cartes de visite,* or visiting cards. In 1859, Napoleon III had his photograph taken by this process and distributed prints among his friends, initiating the craze for collecting the cards.

The craze reached England when J.E. Mayall took *carte de visite* portraits of the royal family, published in 1861. Soon, photographers' studios opened in every town, with prices ranging from a guinea for a dozen prints in a wide variety of poses to half a guinea in provincial towns. The back of the card was used for the studio's trade plate. In 1861, 168 portrait studios existed in London, with 27 in Regent Street alone. By 1866, the number of London photographers had reached 284. Disderi himself opened two studios in London, one in Brooke Street, off Hanover Square, the other in Hedeford Lodge, Old Brompton. During the 1860s, Horatio Nelson King, a photographer with a studio in Bath, reportedly sold between sixty and seventy thousand cards in a single year.

By this time, the medium had progressed to the point where greater attention was being paid to photo backgrounds. Choices now included a painted window, through which one glimpsed a country scene, rural backcloths, classic columns and elaborately carved chairs, against which subjects posed. By the third quarter of the nineteenth century, every Victorian family owned a photograph album, a hardback book with leather covers, embossed or gilded, featuring brass clasps, which held the pages together when closed. The stiff, cardboard pages were covered in paper, which was often decorated with drawings. The earliest albums, produced in the 1860s, had spaces cut into the pages to fit *cartes de visite* only, but later these slots were alternated with those of a larger cabinet print size. Some albums featured music boxes fitted into the back cover, which played when the books were opened.

Cartes de visite that featured famous personalities of each decade were added to these family albums, with crowds gathering whenever the local photographer displayed the latest *cartes* in his shop window. Subjects included actors and society, political, clerical and military figures, with the greatest demand being for likenesses of the royal family. Within one week of the prince consort's death, not less than seventy thousand of his *cartes* were ordered from Marion and Company of Regent Street, photographic wholesalers who stocked thousands of *cartes*. *Cartes de visite* were also used as advertisements by tradesmen, who were photographed with the tools of their trades or with the items offered in their shops.

In 1879, Thomas Stevens introduced a new innovation, the silk-woven picture, which was framed in a card mount. A loom was used to weave two scenes of local interest, such as "The London and York Stagecoach" or "Dick Turpin's Ride to York." These sold for a shilling each, and new pictures were issued once a month. Later, a series of portraits was added, featuring members of the royal family, sportsmen of the day and the like. By the early twentieth century, there were silk-woven postcards, and even cards portraying famous passenger liners sold as souvenirs to passengers aboard the ships.

THE THEATER

London theaters were not open year-round, but it was estimated that twenty thousand people attended the theaters each night. Most houses were only open for six months, as the lord chancellor could grant a license for that period only—except to patent houses, of which there were only two until 1843: Drury Lane and Covent Garden. The

Haymarket was a summer house, open from April to October; the Adelphi a winter house, open from October to April.

At the beginning of Queen Victoria's reign, the most fashionable of the houses was Her Majesty's Theatre, where only Italian opera was performed. In fact, the new moral tone laid down at the beginning of Victoria's reign caused the stage to lose favor due to its so-called immoral tone, and a growing enthusiasm for music emptied the theaters and filled the opera houses and concert rooms instead. It was not until well into the 1860s, when theaters made a concerted effort to offer quality performances of interest to all, that the stage would once again become wholly respectable in the mind of society.

Members of society subscribed to an opera or theater box for the season, and on those days when levees and drawing rooms were held, the fashionable world appeared at the opera afterward in court dresses, feathers and jewels. Those who only took a box to keep up appearances often sold their unused seats (commonly called "bones," after the round, numbered bone tickets of admission) to their friends. Boxes could be rented by the night, the month or the season, and these leases could be handled through agents. Prices at the Drury Lane for boxes and stalls, of which there were two or three rows only, were 7s. each; the pit was 3s. 6d., the upper boxes 2s. and the gallery 1s. At Covent Garden, the boxes were 4s., the pit 2s., upper boxes 1s. 6d. and the gallery 1s. At the Haymarket, boxes cost 5s., the pit 3s. and the gallery 1s. 6d.

There was little luxury on display in early Victorian theaters. Except in Her Majesty's Opera House, there were no stalls, the pit reaching right up to the orchestra, and its seats being nothing better than hard wooden benches without backs. Theaters smelled strongly of beer and oranges, as between acts the fruit girls and pot boys, who ladled beer from the pots they carried into their customers' glasses, supplied the audience with those refreshments. The curtain was usually of plain green baize, and in most houses, lighting consisted only of candles and lamps. Performances generally began at 7 P.M., and at about 9 P.M., patrons were admitted to the pit and boxes at half price. Matinees were unknown until E.T. Smith began offering them at Drury Lane in 1852, when *Uncle Tom's Cabin* was playing to packed houses.

MUSIC HALLS

The music halls evolved from the singing rooms that were built onto pubs from the 1830s onward. These rooms were attached to taverns that had licenses for performing music, while establishments known as saloons offered a more professional, theatrical form of entertainment for the middle classes. The Theatre Act of 1843 separated the two by mandating that those premises licensed to present plays could not also be licensed to dispense liquor and vice versa. By the 1860s, music halls had come into their own. They contained elaborate designs and catered to all classes, with smaller halls catering to the middle and lower classes.

In addition to featured performers, there were acrobats, dancers, animal acts and jugglers. Managers wishing to emphasize the higher tone of their individual establishments sought to convince the public that their shows were not only entertaining, but educational as well. By the 1880s, music hall managers were trying even harder to rid themselves of the reputation for staging sensational programs, and they became more respectable, even fashionable. They began to attract wealthy individuals and limited joint stock companies as investors. This allowed for chains of music halls opening in larger cities throughout Britain. In 1896, the Alhambra Palace Music Hall in London's Leicester Square began showing newsreels, such as Queen Victoria's Diamond Jubilee in 1897 and short melodramas. These were filmed on the roof of the music hall.

THE BURLESQUE, EXTRAVAGANZA AND PANTOMIME

Burlesque was an immense vogue in the early Victorian era. For the most part, plays of the day were adaptations of popular novels, and burlesque was essentially a play in which the audience laughed at themselves, with those portions containing sentiment and melodrama held up to ridicule by means of exaggeration and pathos. This might have also taken the form of skits based on popular stories and favorite plays, such as the legends of Faust and Robin Hood, and even the plays of Shakespeare. Everything was ridiculed, reversed or inverted, and no one's feelings were spared.

The equally popular extravaganza was less bitter, more of a glorified whimsicality. It was usually based on a fairy legend, and a good deal of ballet dancing was worked into the plot, with the whole culminating in a grand transformation scene.

The Christmas pantomime was an old English tradition that endured, incorporating the familiar characters of clown, harlequin, pantaloon, etc. In most theaters, the pantomime followed the usual play and was not the leading performance on the program.

PANORAMAS AND DIORAMAS

Another popular amusement was the moving panorama, which featured a long continuous picture measuring thirty feet high and three or four hundred yards long, which was slowly unrolled and passed before the seated spectators, who could then see "many miles of country and foreign scenes without trouble and at little cost." There was usually a lecturer present to point out the beauties of nature or objects of interest within the scene and to help enliven the show.

Operated on a slightly different principle was the diorama, this picture being a stationary affair. The audience seats sat on a floor that was occasionally rotated, allowing the spectators to see each portion of the picture, which was in a separate room and was viewed through an aperture. This format used artistic, scenic and lighting effects, which resulted in amazingly realistic pictures depicting various parts of the world. The Egyptian Hall in London was a great venue for panoramas and dioramas.

THE CRYSTAL PALACE EXHIBITION OF 1851

. . . the giant aisles
Rich in model and design;
Harvest-toll and husbandry,
Loom and wheel and enginery,
Secrets of the sullen mine,
Steel and gold, and coal and wine,
Fabric rough or fairy-fine . . .
And shapes and hues of Art divine!
All of beauty, all of use,
That one fair planet can produce.
—TENNYSON

The Great Exhibition of the Works of Industry of All Nations, popularly known as the Crystal Palace Exhibition of 1851, was one of the most important events of the nineteenth century. During its four-month run, the exhibition changed the average Englishman's outlook on the world. Throughout the country, thousands of people who had never traveled more than a few miles from their homes came to London and mixed with such exotic visitors as Italians and Turks, Americans and people from the faraway Orient.

The concept, organization and ultimate success of the exhibition can be attributed to Albert, the prince consort, though Sir Robert Peel was also instrumental in its conception. Prince Albert's concept was to present designs relating to industry, the arts and sciences from all over the world beneath a single roof. The idea appealed to his methodical mind, and he threw himself wholeheartedly into its planning, wearing down his health in the process. Perhaps the most important outcome of the exhibition was that it roused the apathy of English manufacturers and served to lessen the Englishman's traditional suspicion of foreigners.

National exhibitions had been held in both Belgium and Paris, and, in 1849, the French Republic undertook the largest such show ever put together. No doubt these provided the seeds for Prince Albert's idea. On January 25, 1850, a meeting was held at the Mansion House, London, to discuss the project, and at its end, the lord mayor unanimously carried the resolution "That the proposal of His Royal Highness, Prince Albert, to open an Exhibition of the Works of Industry of All Nations, in the year 1851, in this metropolis, is a measure in harmony with the public feeling and entitled to the general support of the community; and it is eminently calculated to improve manufactures, and to aid in diffusing the principles of universal peace."

Lord John Russell carried another resolution, stating that "In the opinion of this meeting, the arrangements made for this Exhibition should be on a scale commensurate with the importance of the occasion; and the large fund requisite for this purpose ought to be provided by the voluntary contributions of individuals, rather than from the public revenue."

The first contributions were raised by Samuel Morton Peto, M.P., who guaranteed 50,000 pounds for the fund. After this, the prince consort, members of the court, city magnates, Lord Overstone, the Rothschilds and other influential people followed suit, until the amount raised had reached nearly 200,000 pounds. At that point, the bankers were willing to advance the remaining monies. Once the necessary funds had been raised, the question remained as to where the exhibition would be held. Much controversy arose until it was decided to hold the event in London's Hyde Park. Meantime, the building committee had advertised for plans of an appropriate building and decided upon architect Joseph Paxton's vision of an enormous structure built of iron and glass.

Paxton's plans were approved in July, and by the middle of August, fencing had been built around the site. Messrs. Fox, Henderson & Co., of Smethwick, set to work on the immense iron framework, consisting of over 3,000 columns and 1,245 iron roof girders, to be topped by 1,073,760 square feet of glass. When the structure was finished, some five hundred painters set to work, and the exhibitors' stalls were draped with red cloth or pink calico, while unbleached calico blinds prevented the glare of summer sunshine from coming through the glass roof. It was then time for the exhibitors to display their wares. The western side of the building was set aside for products from England and her colonies; the eastern portion for foreign manufactures; the center was taken over by statuary, fountains and plants. The exhibits encompassed four categories: raw materials, machinery, manufactures and fine arts.

The exhibition opened on May 1, 1851. Streams of carriages jammed the approaches to the park, and a great mass of pedestrians made their way up Piccadilly and Constitution Hill. The route was kept clear by police and Horse Guards, with the rooftops of houses being packed with onlookers. At eleven thirty in the morning, Queen Victoria and Prince Albert made their way from Buckingham Palace. When they arrived at the exhibition and entered through the north door along with the Prince of Wales and Princess Royal, the cheers of the spectators waiting within could be heard by all. The queen was greatly stirred by the reception and recorded the experience thusly in her journal: "The Park presented a wonderful spectacle, crowds streaming through it, carriages and troops passing, quite like Coronation day. . . . I never saw Hyde Park look as it did. A few drops of rain fell just as we started; but before we came near the Crystal Palace, the sun shone and gleamed upon the gigantic edifice upon which the flags of all nations were floating. The glimpse of the transept through the iron gates, the waving palms, flowers, statues, myriads of people filling the galleries and seats around, with a flourish of trumpets as we entered, gave us a sensation which I can never forget. . . .

The sight as we came to the middle, where the steps and the chair (which I did not sit on) were placed, with the beautiful Crystal Fountain just in front of it, was magical—so vast, so glorious, so touching. The tremendous cheers, the joy expressed in every face, the immensity of the building, the mixture of palms, flowers, trees, statues, fountains—the organ and my beloved husband the author of this Peace festival—all this was moving indeed.''

There were about fifteen thousand exhibitors, and the objects displayed represented every conceivable branch of human industry. Refreshments were obtainable at reasonable prices, and the exhibition authorities were required ''to supply, gratis, pure water in glasses to all visitors demanding it,'' to which *Punch* replied that, ''whoever can produce in London a glass of water fit to drink will contribute the rarest and most universally useful article in the whole Exhibition.'' Each day, parties were organized to guide the visitors around and explain the various exhibits, and every day of the week had some special draw. Monday was the great day for shopkeepers and laborers; Tuesday was the country folks' day; Wednesday and Thursday were the quietest of the shilling days, when the price of admission cost a shilling; Friday was half crown day and much favored by season ticket holders and people who wished to linger over the exhibits and examine them in detail. Saturday was half guinea day and devoted to fashion, the naves and galleries being filled with bath chairs, which enabled the queens of society to view the displays at their leisure.

George Jennings introduced public lavatories by installing them in the Crystal Palace, and over 827,000 people paid to use them, no doubt due as much to need as to curiosity. Other items on display during the exhibition included cuffs that had been hand-spun and knitted from the wool of French poodle dogs, objects made from vulcanized India rubber, a model of Heidelberg Castle fashioned from cork, farm and surgical instruments, Turkish tobacco, French perfume, Belgian chocolate, a ''furs, feathers and hair'' section featuring animal skins and ostrich feathers, a stained glass gallery, a replica medieval court, stuffed animals arranged in tableaux and the Koh-i-noor diamond, sent by India for exhibition and delivered to the Queen on April 6, 1850, as a gift.

The Crystal Palace was open for twenty-three weeks, during which over six million visitors passed through the doors, spending a half-million pounds sterling. Given the number of people who attended the exhibition, the incidents of crime were low. Only twenty-five crimes were committed, with most being limited to pickpocketing and other petty larceny. Testifying to the basic honesty of the visitors, the exhibition's lost and found department received 42 purses, 423 parcels and over 100 items of assorted jewelry. After expenses had been paid, the Great Exhibition was left with a balance of 213 pounds, which was earmarked for the promotion of industrial art. In the end, the sum was used to purchase the sites now occupied by the South Kensington Museum and the Albert Hall.

The Great Exhibition closed on October 15, and its contents were removed. The exhibition commissioners offered the building to the government, who refused the gift, and the following year it was taken south of the Thames to Sydenham, where Paxton and others reerected it. The queen opened this new Crystal Palace on June 19, 1854. The new grounds had been skillfully laid out with gardens and fountains, and the building went on to host such entertainments as fireworks, balloon ascents and concerts.

HUNTING

The gentlemen of the landed gentry often kept packs of hounds for hunting fox and stag, a pastime that could be a solitary pursuit or, most often, shared with friends and neighbors. A hunt meet was a great social event that was both hosted and underwritten by the master, or owner, of the pack. As the century wore on, and the fortunes of the aristocracy declined, subscription hunts became increasingly popular. At these meets, a fee was paid to members of a changing roster of masters who supplied their packs for hunts. The railway brought down the "London contingent," comprised of sporting solicitors, merchants, stockbrokers, etc., who had the necessary money to hire a hunter and pay his fare to the nearest railway station.

SHOOTING

Shooting was a very different sport at the beginning of the century from what it would become by Victorian times. Early on, a man might go off shooting alone, or with a friend or two, to tramp about in the woods and enjoy the pleasures of the day. With no loaders along, shots were rarely wasted, for by the time the guns were reloaded, the covey would have flown away. Lunch might have consisted of a loaf of bread and cheese, and only enough game for the kitchens would have been taken, work enough what with the tardy firing flintlock guns and the very weak powder used.

The percussion cap, which would revolutionize small arms, was patented April 11, 1807, by its inventor, the Reverend A.J. Forsyth, of Aberdeenshire. An advertisement regarding the invention appeared in the *Morning Post*, December 23, 1808, and informed sportsmen that "the inflammation is produced without the assistance of flint, and is much more rapid than in the common way. The Lock is so constructed as to render it completely impervious to water, or damp of any kind, and may, in fact, be fired under water."

Poaching

Before an 1831 change in the law, anyone caught poaching could be transported for seven years if found guilty. It was illegal for anyone to buy or sell game, which led to the professional poachers charging dearly for their catches. It was technically illegal for anyone who was not a squire or a squire's eldest son to kill game, even upon the invitation of a landowner, ensuring that hunting remained the domain of the aristocracy. Some landowners laid mantraps or spring guns, which, though intended for poachers, maimed and killed innocent walkers. These traps were banned by an 1827 act of Parliament.

BOXING

Perhaps the most popular spectator sport during the Regency period was boxing. The crowds at some boxing matches reached twenty thousand people, with the most enthusiastic supporters being the aristocracy, who presided over the matches and hired and backed the fighters. The most celebrated pugilists of the day were Tom Cribb, Savage Shelton, Randall, Belcher, Ned Turner, Tom Spring, Gully, Bill Neate and Gentleman Jackson, who taught boxing to the likes of Byron in his rooms at No. 13 Bond Street, London. Sporting gentlemen read *Bell's Weekly* which carried the boxing news, and some tavern owners hired out boxing gloves later in the century for one or two pence, should any of their patrons wish to partake in an impromptu bout.

HORSE RACING

The most important race meets were Derby Day at Epsom, The Thousand Guineas at Newmarket and the St. Leger at Doncaster. Early in the century, popular racing literature included *Baily's Racing Register, Pick's Racing Calendar, The Turf Register* and *The Sporting Magazine.*

General interest in the turf had been greatly increased by the support of the sport by George IV. During his reign and that of William IV, race courses began to admit owners who were commoners. Neither Queen Victoria nor the prince consort was a great racing enthusiast, but they did put in several royal appearances at the various races.

Derby Day, taking place in either May or June, was a sort of national holiday, with peer and commoner alike attending the races. In addition, many attractions other than racing coincided with the meet. An anonymous writer of the 1850s described it thus: "Every beer house was fronted by holiday crowds quaffing ale and inviting one to join. . . . [T]he miles of vehicles with their accompanying dust gave everyone the complexion of chimney-sweeps. Here were gipsies [sic] of the old original form, dancing booths and *tableaux vivant* booths; booths where sparring and booths where drinking might be indulged in freely, booths where terrible melodramas were given, gambling booths; roulette and three card establishments.

"Luncheon on the Derby and Oaks days was an institution that dwarfed the most ambitious displays of hampers and cold pies consumed on the tops of drags. Conceive a huge marquee with tables the entire length groaning under every delicacy, from plovers' eggs at a shilling a piece to pates and *blanc-manges* of the Gunter school of creation. Imagine vats six feet high around the entire walls distilling the best champagne in goblets filled by the most expert footmen."

The derby of 1867, won by Hermit, has a particularly tragic and romantic tale attached to it. The marquis of Hastings had won himself a reputation for wild extravagance by the 1860s. He'd begun gambling at the age of twenty-two, and in 1862 started a stable of some fifty horses, winning the Cambridgeshire, Grand Prix and Goodwood Cup over the next few years. He won and lost massive sums at the races and, when he was flush, would order cases of champagne when visiting public houses or restaurants. Perhaps his most extravagant act was his elopement in 1864 with Lady Florence Paget, an act that startled society. The lady had been engaged to Mr. Chaplin, but "the wicked

Marquis'' stole her heart and set up a daring elopement scenario. One day while out shopping, Lady Florence left her brougham at the door of a famous linen draper's shop conveniently situated between two busy streets. She entered the shop and passed straight through to the exit at the back, where the marquis's friend, Fred Granville, was waiting with a hansom cab.

During the derby of 1867, the marquis favored a horse called The Earl. However, the horse was scratched, and instead of choosing another favorite horse, the marquis simply decided to bet heavily against an entrant named Hermit—owned by his rival, Chaplin. Unfortunately for the marquis, Hermit won the derby and cost him 103,000 pounds. The marquis managed to raise the sum, but it cost him ownership of his beautiful estate, Loudoun. Wild living had already begun to affect the marquis's health, and this financial blow hit him hard, though he did not let it show. In fact, upon his deathbed, he asked a friend, ''I did not show it, did I? But it fairly broke my heart.'' The twenty-six-year-old marquis of Hastings died just five months later.

Racetrack Gambling

Gambling went hand in hand with race meets, occurring at Newmarket, Ascot, Doncaster, Epsom, Warwick, Windsor and practically every other course throughout England. During a House of Commons Select Committee on Gaming meeting in 1844, Richard Baxter gave testimony about Doncaster: ''Twenty years ago, in 1824, was my first acquaintance with the matter. I went, as a stranger, to live in Doncaster, and I found that there were forty or fifty houses, and men stationed at the doors, and passing up and down the streets, not only, by word, inviting the passers by to go into those houses, but putting into their hands cards explanatory of the game that was going on there, and, without any secrecy, or reserve, stating the name of the party at whose house the game was carried on.'' The most popular games of chance included E.O. (Even or Odd) and roulette.

Sir George Chetwynd described the gambling that went on at Doncaster in 1869: ''After dinner you would go to the subscription rooms and back horses for the Cesarewitch and Cambridgeshire. . . . [A]fter making their bets, people used to go into an inner room where hazard might be played. Hour after hour the game continued in full swing at a table crowded with punters, with green, black, red and white ivory counters.''

A day at the Ascot races, 1844

As to betting on the races themselves, betting shops stood in every town, whether a racing town or not. These were lowly places, sometimes operated alone or in conjunction with some other trade, such as tobacconist or shoemaker. Usually a partition contained a pigeonhole through which the bettor placed his money. One wall was given over to the betting lists, each race having its own slip and stating the odds for all horses. While some betting shops were operated on a more or less honest basis, others rigged the odds by touting second-rate horses as favorites in various races. Seeing that a horse was a reckoned winner, the bettor placed his money on it, only to have his choice finish out of the money. So notorious were these goings-on that on December 1, 1853, a bill was passed to suppress betting houses.

In light of this new view on racecourse gambling, the established and honest betting venues, such as Tattersall's and Goodwood, chose to make their views on racecourse gambling clear to the public. The management of Tattersall's issued a code of new rules and regulations for subscribers to their betting room. A subscription of two guineas per year was fixed, and gentlemen wishing to subscribe were to give a week's notice in writing to Tattersall's, as well as to submit character references. Nonsubscribers were admitted after paying a fee of one guinea. The room was under the sanction of the Jockey Club, and anyone defaulting on a bet was excluded not only from Tattersall's, but from other prestigious courses as well.

BIBLIOGRAPHY

Agate, James. *These Were Actors: Extracts From a Newspaper Cutting Book, 1811–1833.* North Stratford: Ayer Company Publishers, Inc., 1972.

Altick, Richard D. *The English Common Reader: A Social History of the Mass Reading Public 1800–1900.* Chicago: University of Chicago Press, 1957.

Ames, Winslow. *Prince Albert and Victorian Taste.* New York: Viking Press, 1968.

Art Journal Staff. *The Crystal Palace Exhibition; Illustrated Catalogue, London 1851.* New York: Dover Publications, 1970.

Ashton, Geoffrey. *Royal Opera House Retrospective 1732–1982.* London: Royal Opera House, 1982.

Ashton, John. *The History of Gambling in England.* New York: Franklin, 1968.

Babbage, Charles. *The Exposition of 1851.* Farnborough: Gregg International, 1969.

Bailey, L. *Gilbert and Sullivan and Their World.* London: Thames & Hudson, 1973.

Baker, Henry Barton. *History of the London Stage and Its Players 1576–1903.* North Stratford: Ayer Company Publishers, 1969.

Booth, Michael R. *Victorian Spectacular Theatre, 1850–1910.* Boston: Routledge & Kegan Paul, 1981.

Cruse, Amy. *The Victorians and Their Reading.* Boston: Houghton Mifflin, 1935.

Dalziel, Margaret. *Popular Fiction One Hundred Years Ago: An Unexplored Tract of Literary History.* London: Cohen & West, 1957.

Edward of Norwich. *The Master of Game: The Oldest English Book on Hunting.* New York: AMS Press, 1909.

Fay, C.R. *Palace of Industry 1851: A Study of the Great Exhibition and Its Fruits.* Cambridge, Mass.: Cambridge University Press, 1951.

Ford, John A. *Prizefighting: The Age of Regency Boximania.* Newton Abbot: David & Charles, 1971.

Hargreaves, John. *Sport, Power, and Culture: A Social and Historical*

Analysis of Popular Sports in Britain. New York: St. Martin's Press, 1986.

Hindle, Wilfrid. *The Morning Post, 1772–1937: Portrait of a Newspaper.* Westport, Conn.: Greenwood Press, 1974.

Howard, Diana. *London Theatres and Music Halls, 1850–1950.* Chicago: American Library Association, 1970.

Jackson, Allan S. *The Standard Theatre of Victorian England.* Rutherford, N.J.: Fairleigh Dickinson University Press, 1990.

Longrigg, Roger. *The English Squire and His Sport.* New York: St. Martin's Press, 1977.

Munsche, P.B. *Gentlemen and Poachers: The English Game Laws 1671–1831.* Cambridge, Mass: Cambridge University Press, 1981.

Peddie, R.A. *Subject Index of Books Published Before 1880.* London: Grafton & Co., 1933.

Read, Donald. *Press and People, 1790–1850: Opinion in Three English Cities.* London: E. Arnold, 1961.

Rees, Terence. *Theatre Lighting in the Age of Gas.* London: Society for Theatre Research, 1978.

Robinson, Henry Crabb. *The London Theatre 1811–1866.* Ed. Eluned Brown, London: Society for Theatre Research, 1966.

Steinmetz, Andrew. *Gaming Table: Its Votaries and Victims, in All Times and Countries, Especially in England and in France.* 2 vols. Montclair, N.J.: Patterson Smith Publishing Corp., 1969.

Taylor, George. *Players and Performances in the Victorian Theatre.* New York: St. Martin's Press, 1990.

Vamplew, Wray. *The Turf: A Social and Economic History of Horse Racing.* London: Allen Lane, 1976.

Vann, J. Don, and Rosemary Van Arsdel, eds. *Periodicals of Queen Victoria's Empire: An Exploration.* Toronto: University of Toronto Press, 1996.

Vicinus, Martha. *The Industrial Muse: A Study of Nineteenth-Century British Working-Class Literature.* New York: Barnes & Noble Books, 1974.

Wiener, Joel H. *The War of the Unstamped: The Movement to Repeal the British Newspaper Tax, 1830–1836.* Ithaca, N.Y.: Cornell University Press, 1969.

CHAPTER TWELVE

Shopping

STREET VENDORS

Most city residents conducted their daily marketing by purchasing food, supplies and services from street vendors. Each morning, the residential streets came alive with the cries of street hawkers of every description. The baker typically appeared between 8 and 9 A.M., calling out, "Hot loaves!" as he rang his bell to signal his arrival in the street. Bakers sold warm rolls at one or two a penny, and in the winter they also sold muffins and crumpets.

As common a sight as the baker was the milkmaid. Curiously enough, the delivery and sale of milk was given over entirely to women. The milkmaids' day began anywhere between 4 and 6 A.M., with milking the cows. Afterward, they delivered milk to the various houses on their routes until nearly 10 A.M. The dairy cans were then washed, and at noon, the cows were milked again. The delivery of milk was then resumed and went on till nearly 6 P.M., when the cans were washed and prepared for the next day's work.

An article of 1804 reads, "Milk is sold at fourpence per quart, or fivepence for the better sort; yet the advance of price does not insure its purity, for it is generally mixed in a great proportion with water, by the retailers before they leave the milk houses. The adulteration of milk, added to the wholesale cost, leaves an average profit of cent per cent to the vendors of this useful article. Few retail trades are exercised with equal gains.'' In 1808, it was estimated that eighty-five hundred cows were kept in and around London.

A milkmaid makes her rounds

Milkmaids who lived on farms at the outskirts of the city brought milk in daily. They walked long distances while carrying a pair of churns from a shoulder yoke. Asses' milk was thought to be much better than cow's milk for babies and invalids, and the milkmaids walked these animals to the houses of their customers, drawing the milk straight from the beast and into their customers' jugs.

On the morning of each May Day, milkmaids traditionally made their rounds in groups. They danced in the streets to music and wore flower garlands around their necks as they collected annual tips from their customers. By the 1850s, milkmaids were still selling milk from the cow in St. James's Park, London. A popular drink was syllabub, which the milkmaids prepared by drawing warm milk from the cow directly into a mug containing wine, sugar and spices. Milk sellers had to obtain permission from the home secretary in order to conduct business in the park. During the summer, there were as many as eight milk stands in the park; in winter, four.

A Variety of Vendors

Once the milkmaids and bakers had made their appearances, the streets began to teem with other vendors. Baking or boiling apples were sold by women who carried charcoal stoves in their barrows so that their customers might buy hot apples. The bandbox seller could be seen carrying his wares at the end of a pole, which he rested on his shoulder. These boxes were made in the homes of the poor and sold for sixpence to three shillings, while boxes of slightly sturdier deal, with a lock and key, sold for from three to six shillings.

The brick dust seller dispensed his product from sacks that were carried on the back of a donkey, and the dust, used in cleaning knives, sold for one penny per quart. There were also pet food vendors, who sold cat and dog food consisting of horse flesh, bullock's livers and tripe cuttings. The flesh and liver sold for two pence per pound, the tripe at one pence each.

Tradesmen, different from vendors, also plied the streets. The cry of, "Chairs to mend!" was heard in every town. Common chairs that did not have seats of wood had seats of rush, which were cut from rivers in the early autumn. The chair man carried a bolt of rushes in his arms as he went about the streets, and repairs were undertaken in the street in front of a house, with the charge for this service being from one shilling, sixpence to two shillings, sixpence.

Among the other items available for sale were sand, used for cleaning floors, live rabbits, doormats, rat traps, baskets, fish and ice, which could also be purchased from the fishmonger or from ice companies, who delivered ice to homes. They also sold ice chests, the forerunners of the refrigerator. A block of ice was wrapped in a clean cloth and placed into the wooden ice chest, which had removable shelves placed atop the ice block and onto which food could be placed and kept cold. A brass tap was fitted into these chests to allow the melted ice to drain off.

Some street sellers, like the muffin man, lasted well into the 1920s, and girls selling lavender could still be found during World War II. Street vendors sold jellied eels, pea soup and hot pies from stalls, and there were still seven hundred cow keepers in the London area in the 1880s.

Streetsellers hawk their wares

Rhyming Slang

Common to the street hawkers, and to the lower classes in general, was a form of slang that originated in the Cockney area of London. Traditionally, a Cockney is anyone who was born within the sound of Bow bells, or the bells of St. Mary-le-Bow church in Cheapside, London. However, rhyming slang could be found in other areas of England as well, especially in large cities. Flashy young men and those in sporting circles carried the practice far and wide. Originally, this type of speech was used by criminals to confound the police and the general population, and as a sort of secret language used around the rookeries (slum areas). This form of slang involved substituting common words for words or a phrase that rhymed with them. Here are a few examples:

apples and pears = stairs
trouble and strife = wife
Jimmy Skinner = dinner
Epsom races = pair of braces

To further confuse the listener, the speakers often left off the last or actual rhyming word, with the examples above being abbreviated to "apples," "trouble," "Jimmy," "Epsom." Slang even made its way into contemporary advertisements catering to the lower classes. A Whitechapel tailor ran the following advertisement during the 1850s:

> Mr. H. nabs the chance of putting his customers awake that he has been able to put his mawleys (1) on some of the right sort of stuff. One of the top manufacturers of Manchester has cut his lucky leaving behind him a valuable stock of Moleskins (2) etc. Mr. H. having some ready (3) in his kick (4), grabbed the chance, stepped home with the swag (5), and is now safe in his crib (6). He can turn out Toggery very slap (7).
>
> Translation: (1) hands (2) trousers (3) cash (4) pocket (5) loot, booty (6) shop (7) fine
>
> READY GILT—TICK BEING NO GO.
> (Cash Money—No Credit)

BUYER BEWARE

On Sundays, local bakers did a brisk trade by using their ovens to cook the dinners of the lower classes, who typically had no cooking facilities in their lodgings. While this routine may have been inconvenient, the customer could be certain of the quality of the meal, having purchased it himself. Food adulteration was a very real health risk during the nineteenth century. For instance, the best quality butter came from Epping, though a cheaper butter was produced all over the eastern counties and then salted in huge barrels in Cambridge, leading to its being known as Cambridge butter. Though cheaper than Epping butter, Cambridge butter was still edible. However, there were deceitful butter manufacturers who added candle grease to their products to increase their profit margins.

In 1848, John Mitchell published a book dealing with the falsification of foods and the chemicals used to detect those adulterants. Mitchell's findings alarmed the public, and two years later, Thomas Wakley, editor of the British medical journal *The Lancet*, set up the Analytical and Sanitary Commission to investigate the problem. They found that every loaf of London bread tested contained alum, or aluminum sulfate, an emetic and astringent that was added to the bread as a filler. Likewise, chocolate was found to have been adulterated with brick dust. These discoveries led to government standards for the production and sale of food products.

Health risks were also connected with the packaging of food. During the first decade of the nineteenth century, Frenchman Nicholas Appert devised a means of bottling food, which was successfully used during the Napoleonic Wars by the French Navy. At the same time in England, Thomas Sadington was using an almost identical method to preserve food in stout, wide-mouthed bottles after it had been put through a heating process. Sadington's method was awarded a prize by The Society of Arts in 1807.

Some decades later, Bryan Donkin invented tin-lined canisters for canning foods, and these were adopted by both the British Army and Navy. These efforts proved successful, but when private companies sought to cash in on the invention, they packed foods into larger containers, along with a quantity of air, and so encountered trouble with bacteria. Men in the armed forces became sick from these products, and in order to avoid subsequent illness, the Admiralty set up its own factory for tinned foods in 1856. It was not long afterward that tinned foods became available to the general public.

SHOPS

The bywords of nineteenth-century shopping must be *elegance* and *change*. During the Napoleonic period, it would not have been proper for a lady to have visited the shops unescorted, nor would she have found every item she might have wanted in a single store. Shopkeepers sold specialized merchandise, most often goods that they had manufactured in their own workrooms. There existed establishments that sold various sundry items, such as linens, ribbons, lace and fabrics, which were called drapers shops, while most others specialized in such things as boots, hats, gloves, fans, stays, etc. In smaller towns, such a variety of shops might have stood in the High Street, but in the larger cities, they would have been spread throughout the main streets.

Innovations in glass-making techniques and gas lighting changed the look of shop fronts. Display windows grew in size as new methods of glass manufacture allowed for larger panes, which could also be curved, or bowed. The excise duty on sheet glass was done away with in 1845, cutting its cost nearly in half. Shopkeepers took advantage of this price reduction by installing larger windows in an effort to lure customers off the sidewalks with eye-tempting displays. As shops expanded, taking over the spaces in houses on either side of them or on the floors above, new windows were fitted into the first-floor facades and used for display purposes as well.

SHOPPING ARCADES

After the victories of the Napoleonic Wars, the prince regent began a wide-scale building improvement scheme in London, headed by architect John Nash. Regent Street, Portland Place and Cavendish Square all became fashionable streets and lent a certain cachet to the pre-existing shopping streets they now crossed, such as Oxford Street and Tottenham Court Road.

Shopping arcades came into vogue around 1816. The fashion for arcades had originated in Paris, and they were soon built in Manchester, Birmingham, Leeds and Bath. Messrs. Jolly and sons opened the

MIDDLE-CLASS FINANCES

The expanding economy and industrialization led to a new class of professional men, including accountants, engineers, office workers, insurance clerks, law and bank clerks, who were all seen as belonging to the new middle class, since they were neither tradesmen nor laborers. An income of three hundred pounds per year was considered the minimum for maintaining middle-class standards of living.

Arthur L. Hayward, in his work *The Days of Dickens*, leaves us the following annual budget for a comparatively well-to-do clerk in 1844:

	£	*s.*	*d.*
House rent	25	0	0
Taxes	5	0	0
Maid of all work	7	0	0
Coal, 5 tons @ 25s.	6	5	0
Candles, 35s.; wood 5s.	2	0	0
Tea, ½ lb. a week @ 6s.	7	16	6
Sugar, lump and moist @ 2s. 7d. per week	6	14	2
Butter, 2s. a week; eggs 6d. a week	9	12	0
Meat, 16 lb. a week @ 6d. per lb.	18	6	0
Fish	2	0	0
Vegetables, potatoes @ 4 lbs. for 2d.	5	0	0
Beer, 2s. 6d. per week	6	10	0
Washing, woman once a week @ 1s. 6d. soap and her meals 55s.	6	13	0
Ironing and mangling	1	0	0
Dress, husband £11 6s.; wife £9, children £3	23	6	0
Doctor's bill	5	0	0
Church's offerings and charity	3	100	0
Odds and ends	1	8	0
Excursions and amusements	1	19	4
Savings	6	0	0

Bath Emporium at No. 12 Milsom Street in 1831, offering the inhabitants of that city a vast array of goods under a single roof. They not only sold "costume" jewelry and other trinkets, but sent their buyers to the continent to buy the finest silks and other foreign articles. Perhaps the most elegant shopping arcade of all, the Burlington Arcade, Picadilly, London, still exists today.

DEPARTMENT STORES

The fruits of the industrial revolution and the Great Exhibition of 1851 allowed the drapers shops to evolve into full-blown department stores. They began catering to all members of the family and to all of society's needs. Specialist department stores, called warehouses, opened and sold all manner of goods. There were mourning warehouses, sporting dress warehouses, waterproof clothing warehouses and tartan warehouses. After Queen Victoria purchased Balmoral, in Scotland, she used tartan fabrics on the upholstery, curtains and sofas throughout the castle. Prince Albert designed a Balmoral tartan using black, red and lavender on a green background. The earliest tartan warehouse, which opened well before the queen's purchase, was James Locke's Scotch Tartan Warehouse, No. 119 Regent Street, London. In 1839, the brothers Gardiner, who were tailors from Glasgow, opened The Scotch House in Aldgate. However, it was to the firm of Scott Addie, No. 115 Regent Street, that Queen Victoria gave the royal warrant.

While the aristocracy continued to shop in specialist stores or with tradesmen who offered them personalized shopping in their homes, omnibuses were carrying more and more shoppers into the main retail areas of every city. In the late 1830s, some shops began using price tickets, but these were considered vulgar by some and were not used in higher class establishments. Another advancement was that payment in cash became the norm, enabling retailers to extend lower prices to their customers. After the 1840s, half of London's shops opened for business after 10 A.M. on Sundays.

Store Fittings

In the 1880s, store fittings such as dress forms, arm forms for displaying gloves and bent wood counter chairs could be found in most stores. There were no tills at the various department counters, and customers had to wait as clerks took money to the office in order for change to be made. Also in the 1880s, Lambston's Cash Balls were invented. These were hollow, wooden balls that could be unscrewed. The customer's cash was placed inside, and then the clerk fit the ball onto an overhead track above the counter. The balls would arrive at the cash office, where change was made and a receipt written, and both were returned to the counter.

The larger shops still offered custom dressmaking departments, which were thought to be exclusive. These stores, and smaller tailoring establishments, began putting their labels into garments in 1869. In 1898, Harrod's Department Store became the first to install a moving staircase.

Restaurants

Shoppers from as far away as Bath, Oxford and Kent were now able to visit London by train in order to spend a day shopping in its stores. Away from home, these customers needed somewhere they could get a bite to eat, so department stores opened restaurants on their premises. These were not merely transient lunch counters, but elegant dining rooms, some of which featured live music and afternoon tea served on the best china.

Store Clerks

Shop assistants put in long days, often rising at six in the morning and working till ten at night, and most shops frowned upon married ladies acting as clerks. Clerks earned between twenty-five and forty pounds a year, and most often received food, lodging and commissions. Author H.G. Wells was a draper's assistant in Southsea in 1881. He gives an account of his experiences in his book *Experiment in Autobiography* (New York: MacMillan, 1934): "We apprentices were roused from our beds at seven. . . . We flung on old suits, tucking our nightgowns into our trousers, and were down in the shop in a quarter of an hour, to clean windows, unwrapper goods and fixtures, dust, generally before eight. At eight we raced upstairs to get first go at the wash basins, dressed for the day and at half past eight partook of a bread and butter breakfast before descending again. Then came window dressing and dressing out the shop. I had to fetch goods for the window dresser and arrange patterns or pieces of fabric on the brass line above the counter. Every day or so the costume window had to be arranged, and I had to go in the costume room and fetch those headless effigies on which costumes are displayed and carry them the length of the shop, to the window dresser, avoiding gas brackets, chairs and my fellow creatures in route. Then I had to see to the replenishing of the pin bowls and the smoothing out and stringing up of paper for small parcels. . . . Half an hour before closing time we began to put away for the last time and 'wrapper up,' provided no customer lingered in the department. And as soon as the doors were shut and the last customer gone, the assistants departed and we junior apprentices rushed from behind the counters, scattered wet sawdust out of pails over the floor and swept it up again with great zest and speed, the last rite of the day. By half past eight we were upstairs and free, supping on bread and butter, cheese and small beer. That was the ritual for every day of the week, thirteen hours of it, except that on Wednesday, Early Closing Day, the shop closed at five.'' Businesses did not close for annual holidays until the Bank Holidays Act of 1871.

MAIL ORDER

Families who lived in the country and who rarely had the opportunity to visit London or some other large city commonly appointed the proprietor of a city coaching inn to act as their agent in making purchases through the mail. Otherwise, a family might rely upon county carriers, whose wagons went on regular days from all the larger provincial towns to appointed London inns. By the 1880s, many larger stores had their own mail-order departments. In 1888, the London firm of Marshall and Snelgrove received about one thousand mail orders per day. To handle these, the store employed over one hundred clerks, accountants and examiners, who inspected all merchandise before it was shipped to the customer.

COOPERATIVES

The cooperative movement was born from a desire to stop the exploitation of the consumer by retail dealers. The movement originated in 1844, when twenty-four workmen in Rochdale opened a store in Toad Lane. The cooperative sold goods at market prices and divided profits among its members in proportion to their purchases. Shopkeepers attempted to boycott these stores but failed, and by the 1870s, cooperatives were also producing some of the goods they sold.

ADVERTISEMENTS

In 1806, the ladies' fashion magazine *La Belle Assemblee* began publishing advertisements, and in 1825, the *Lady's Magazine* became the first to run ads not only in its pages, but on the back cover as well. In 1803, a tax of three shillings, sixpence was placed upon advertisements, lowered in 1822 to one shilling, sixpence.

Out in the streets, advertising bills were affixed to many-sided columns, which sat on the bed of wagons. These horse-drawn wagons were a common sight in many cities, especially during the 1820s, when people began protesting that the wagons caused traffic jams in the already crowded streets. The use of these wagons endured despite complaints, and an account by a foreign visitor to London in 1853 provides a colorful picture of them: "Behold, rolling down from Oxford Street three immense pyramids—their outsides are painted all over with hieroglyphics and monumental letters in English. These pyramids display faithful portraits of Isis and Osiris, of cats, storks and Apis; and amidst these gods, in an inscription printed in letters a yard long, announcing that there is now on view a superb panorama of Egypt. Then comes a huge mosque, its cupola white and blue, surmounted by the Crescent and driven by a sooty-faced boy. It is a quack doctor's advertisement of a nostrum—a panacea. Vauxhall sends round a chariot drawn by cream horses and heralded by trumpets and drums; the clown of Astley's drives through the streets in all sorts of quaint costumes; even the arches of the bridges over the Thames are painted with advertisements."

Handbills were also widely used, passed out on the streets by sandwich men, who wore wooden signs on their backs and chests that bore advertising slogans or announced sales.

The practice of handing out bills was well established by the 1820s, when the *Royal Blue Book* was first published. The *Blue Book* was a detailed street guide to the occupants of every house, and also included the town and country residences of nobility and gentry. It enabled shopkeepers to target a select clientele.

Prince Puckler-Muskau wrote the following account of London advertising in general in 1827: "Every day sees some new invention. Among them may be reckoned the countless advertisements, and the manner of putting them 'in evidence.' Formerly people were content to paste them up; now they are ambulant. One man has a pasteboard hat, three times as high as other hats, on which is written in great letters, 'Boots at twelve shillings a pair, warranted.' Another carries a sort of banner, on which is represented a washerwoman and the inscription, 'Only three-pence a shirt.' Chests, like Noah's ark, entirely pasted over with bills, and of the dimensions of a small house, drawn by men and horses, slowly parade the streets, and carry more lies upon them than Munchausen ever invented."

FAIRS

Many English fairs had endured for centuries, and remained alternatives to shopping in stores until well into the nineteenth century. An eyewitness account from Hone's 1827 Year Book provides a tour of Sturbridge Fair, near Cambridge, which had been held each year since 1211: "The first booths on the north side of the road were occupied by the customary shows of wild beasts and wild men, conjurors, tumblers and rope dancers. . . . There was a large theatrical booth, occupied by a respectable company of comedians from Norwich. . . . Other show booths, occupied by giants and dwarfs. . . . extended with stunning din along this noisy line. In front of these were fruit and gingerbread stalls. On the south side of the road opposite these booths was the cheese fair. . . . Such as were fit for the London market were bought by the cheese factors from Thence; and cheese from Cheshire, Wiltshire and Gloucester by the gentry and farmers and dealers from Suffolk, Norfolk and adjoining counties.

"At the end of the show booths. . . . began the principal range of booths, called Garlickrow. This range of shops was well constructed. Each booth consisted of two rooms; the back room, separated from the shop by a boarded partition, served for a bed chamber and other domestic purposes, from which a door opened into a field. A range of booths was generally appropriated to furniture sellers, ironmongers, silversmiths, jewellers, japanners and fine cutlery dealers. Another range of silk mercers, dealers in muslin, toys and millinery. Yet another to dealers in Norwich and Yorkshire manufacturers, mercery, lace, hose, fine made shoes, boots, clogs and patterns. While dealers in fashionable wares from London, as furs, fans, toys, &c., at the end of this row stood dealers in glassware, looking glasses and small articles of mahogany furniture. The Inn, the King's Arms, I believe, was the common resort of the horse dealers. . . . The show of beautiful animals in that place (a nearby close) was perhaps unrivalled, unless in Yorkshire, the finest racers and muscular draught horses from Suffolk, and from every other country famous for breeding horses. The horse fair drew together a great concourse of gentry, farmers and dealers from all parts of neighbouring counties, and scores of valuable animals changed masters in the space of a few hours."

BIBLIOGRAPHY

Adburgham, Alison. *Shopping in Style: London From the Restoration to Edwardian Elegance.* London: Thames & Hudson, 1979.

Addison, William. *English Fairs and Markets.* London: B.T. Batsford, 1953.

Benedetta, Mary. *The Street Markets of London.* North Stratford: Ayer Company Publishers, Inc., 1972.

Bourne. H.R. Fox. *English Merchants.* London: Chatto, 1886.

Bowley, A.L. *Wages in the United Kingdom in the Nineteenth Century.* Cambridge, Mass.: Cambridge University Press, 1900.

Burnett, John. *A History of the Cost of Living.* Harmondsworth: Penguin, 1969.

Corina, Maurice. *Fine Silks and Oak Counters: Debenhams, 1778–1978.* London: Hutchinson Beham, 1978.

Davidoff, Leonore. *Family Fortunes: Men and Women of the English Middle Class, 1780–1850.* Chicago: University of Chicago Press, 1987.

Gibson-Jarvie, Robert. *The City of London: A Financial and Commercial History.* Cambridge, Mass.: Woodhead-Faulkner, 1979.

Jefferys, James B. *Retail Trading in Britain, 1850–1950.* Cambridge, Mass.: Cambridge University Press, 1954.

Lambert, Richard S. *The Universal Provider: A Study of William Whiteley and the Rise of the London Department Store.* London: G.G. Harrap and Co. Ltd., 1938.

Neal, Lawrence E. *Retailing and the Public.* London: Allen & Unwin Ltd., 1932.

Thompson, John. *Victorian London Streetlife in Historic Photographs.* New York: Dover Publications, 1994.

Thorne, Robert. *Covent Garden Market: Its History and Restoration.* East Brunswick: Nichol Publishing Co., 1980.

Wilson, R.G. *Gentlemen Merchants: The Merchant Community in Leeds, 1700–1830.* Manchester: Manchester University Press, 1970.

CHAPTER THIRTEEN

Travel

MAIL AND STAGECOACHES

t the start of the century, the only form of land transport available was the coach. The wealthy traveled in their prvately owned vehicles or by post chaise, and the very poor used wagons, carts or slow night coaches. All other passengers traveled by mail or stagecoach.

Stagecoaches were so called because they stopped at various preappointed stages in order to pick up and drop off passengers, to allow comfort stops for travelers and, most importantly, to change tired horses for fresh. It was not the most comfortable, nor the fastest, way to travel, but stagecoaches were the only way to visit those places not on the mail coach routes. Fast mail coaches were introduced in 1784, with recognized mail routes springing up across the land soon after.

Mail and stage coaches were built alike, carrying four inside passengers and up to eight outside passengers, who rode atop the coach, beside the driver or at the rear of the coach. Mailbags were piled high on the roof, and luggage was carried in large receptacles called boots at either end of the vehicle. The box seat by the coachman, which usually cost extra, was considered the most desirable and was frequently occupied by someone interested in horseflesh.

Mail coaches, which were subsidized or owned by the post office, were painted uniformly, the lower part of the carriage body being chocolate or mauve; the upper portion, fore and hind boots painted black; and the wheels and undercarriage, a vivid scarlet. The royal arms were emblazoned on the doors, the royal cipher in gold upon the fore boot and the vehicle identification number on the hind boot. The panels at each side of the window were embellished with various devices, such as the badge of the Garter, the rose, the shamrock or the thistle.

The following cities could be reached from London by mail coaches leaving from various inns.

Dover	From the Angel, St. Clements, Strand
Portsmouth, Bristol, Bath, Exeter, Liverpool, Manchester	From the Swan With Two Necks, Lads Lane
Norwich, Taunton, Yarmouth, Ipswich, Poole	From the Bell and Crown, Holborn
Chester, Holyhead	From the Golden Cross, Charing Cross
Worcester, Gloucester	From the Golden Cross and the Angel
York, Edinburgh, Glasgow	From the Bull and Mouth, Bull and Mouth Street
Shrewsbury, Leeds, Harwich	From the Spread Eagle, Gracechurch Street

Inconveniences

In truly severe weather, the suffering of the outside passengers was terrible. John Ashton left the following account of winter travel: "Falls of snow in 1814 were unprecedented in the memory of man. On one occasion it snowed incessantly for 48 hours. . . . The snow drifts were terrible all over the country. . . . On Finchley Common, in the curse of the night, it drifted to a depth of sixteen feet; on Bagshot Heath, and about Cobham and Esher, all traffic was stopped. The Kent and Essex roads were the only ones passable. From the country came worse news. The snow in the Midland Counties was very deep; indeed at

Dunchurch, a small village on the road to Birmingham, through Coventry, for a few miles round, the snow was twenty-three feet deep, and no tracks of travellers were seen for many days. The Cambridge Mail Coach was snowed up, completely covered, for eight hours, when, at last it was dragged out by fourteen waggon-horses, the poor passengers, meanwhile, being frozen to death.''

The winter of 1836 was one of the worst on record, with Christmas storms closing all coach roads for several days. On December 26, the Manchester, Holyhead, Chester and Halifax mails were all stuck in snowdrifts at Hockley Hill, near Dunstable, within a few yards of one another, and throughout the country, stories of overturned coaches and dogged heroism on the part of coachmen and guards were recounted. In one instance a guard, leaving his snowbound coach, carried out instructions by taking the mails forward on horseback. Nine miles farther on, he sent the horse back, but pushed on himself. Next morning he was found dead, a mile or two up the road, with the mail-bag still tied around his neck.

Changing Horses

Change of horses at each fresh stage was made quickly. Hostlers and stable boys were allowed a minute in which to take out the old horses and harness up a fresh team, though some could manage the job in fifty seconds. Seats on a coach had to be secured in advance at the inn from which it started or where it stopped on the road. The traveler's name was entered into a book, and half the fare was taken as a deposit. The fares by stagecoach worked out to 2½d. to 3d. a mile for outside passengers, 4d. to 5d. a mile for inside passengers. Mail coaches were dearer, averaging from 4½d. to 5d. for outsides, 8d. to 10d. for insides.

Coachman and Guard

The coachman wore beneath his coat a crimson traveling shawl, topped by a long waistcoat of a striped pattern and over that, a wide-skirted green coat, ornamented with large brass buttons. On his head he wore a wide-brimmed, low-crowned brown hat. He wore cord knee breeches, painted top boots and a copper watch chain. The responsibility for coach and passenger safety rested with the guard, who, in the case of mail coaches, had the added care of the post bags. In their red coats, with a gleaming brass horn at the ready, the guards collected

Coachman in traveling attire

fares from those who joined the coach on the road, saw that the schedule was kept to, and were entrusted with the execution of commissions.

In case of accident, the guard looked after the mails and the passengers, carrying the former by horse and arranging for a fresh coach for the latter if necessary. Guards were accustomed to making journeys up to 150 miles at a stretch, and received about ten shillings a week in wages. Inside passengers were supposed to tip the guards two shillings, sixpence, those outside two shillings, and the guard collected further tips for handling luggage or running errands.

PRIVATE COACHES

Those who had carriages of their own, or hired them, could go "post," meaning that they could have fresh horses at certain recognized stations. This form of travel, known as going post chaise, was decidedly the favored means of travel. The chaise was a light and comfortable vehicle with two or, more commonly, four wheels and was drawn by two or four horses ridden by post boys. For great haste, four horses with two postilions were used. As with a coach, the horses were changed at stages. There was room for only two passengers in a post chaise, but most carriages had a dickey, or platform, at back for a groom.

THE OMNIBUS

The horse-drawn omnibus, used for travel within major cities, was introduced to England in 1829 by George Shillibeer. Originally, these carried twelve inside passengers, three outside, but eventually carried twenty-two passengers inside, with a team of three horses. The floors were covered with straw, and the average ride cost sixpence. By 1838, omnibuses and their drivers had to be licensed. In the 1890s, there were about seventeen hundred omnibuses in London, with tickets first introduced during the same period. The first motor bus, with an omnibus body fitted atop a Cannstall-Daimler chassis, was introduced in October 1899.

THE RAILROAD

The railway from Liverpool to Manchester was opened on September 15, 1830, but rail travel did not come to the forefront until a decade later. Like any other innovation, it took some time for the notion to catch on. Northampton, for example, refused to allow the London and Birmingham Railway to build tracks anywhere near the town center, fearing that the smoke of the engines would affect the wool of grazing sheep. Needless to say, the railroad companies pressed on, and those towns that did allow the railway to enter reaped so many benefits that by the mid-1840s most of the opposition had been won over.

By 1844, a veritable railroad mania gripped the nation. Prospective companies offered the public the opportunity to buy into the new venture at ground level, and hinted at the promise of big money to be made. Capital was easily raised, prompting the government to institute a Railway Commission. One of its suggestions, which soon became law, was that every railway should arrange for at least one train to pass each way, every weekday, traveling at a speed of twelve miles per hour, to be furnished with closed third-class railway coach at a fare not to exceed a penny per mile: These were later known as Parliamentary Trains.

Railroad Speculation

It was in 1845 that railway mania hit Great Britain. As each new railroad scheme, speculation and partnership was formed, investors were sought, and the best way to reach these investors—the public—was through the newspapers. John Francis, in his *History of the English Railway*, wrote the following: "The daily press was thoroughly deluged with advertisements. . . . [I]t has been estimated that the receipts of the leading journals averaged, at one period, twelve to fourteen thousand pounds per week. The railway papers, on some occasions, contained advertisements that must have netted from seven to eight hundred pounds on each publication. The printer, the lithographer and the stationer, with the preparation of prospectuses, the execution of maps and the supply of other requisites, also made a considerable harvest.

"The advantages of competition were pointed out [to the public], with the choicest phraseology. . . . [E]verything was to pay a large dividend; everything was to yield a large profit. [One company] was formed, the directors appointed, with only the terminal points surveyed. . . . Engineers, who were examined in favour of particular lines, promised all and everything, in their evidence. . . . Many, whose money was safely invested, sold at any price, to enter the market. Servants withdrew their hoards from the savings banks. The tradesman crippled his business. The legitimate love of money became a fierce lust. The peer came from his club to his brokers; the clergyman came from his pulpit to the mart. . . . Trustees, who had no money of their own, or who had lost it, used that which was handed to them; brothers speculated with the money of sisters; sons gambled with the money of their widowed mothers . . . and it is no exaggeration to say that the funds of hundreds were surreptitiously endangered by those in whose control they were placed."

Building the Railroads

The Board of Trade announced that Sunday, November 30, was the last day on which plans of proposed railways could be accepted by them. As there was not enough skilled labor for all the surveying, plotting and drafting of plans, an influx of barely knowledgeable men applied for positions throughout the country. They were taken on by potential railroads at enormous salaries, and set to working night and day to meet the deadline. Getting the finished plans to London in time was another feat. Post horses were suddenly at a premium, and rival railroads sabotaged the trains their competitors traveled in.

While many of the plans submitted never saw fruition, enough succeeded so that a whole new field of industry was born. Tens of thousands of men joined the railroad crews in a host of new occupations. Men from the fens of Lincolnshire and Cambridgeshire were the first to be hired, but it wasn't long before men from every part of England had signed on. They were housed in rough, temporary sheds, and when payday arrived on the Lancaster-Carlisle line, a regiment of infantry and a troop of cavalry had to be present in order to stem the drinking that went on. The men, away from home and making a steady income, simply wanted to let off steam or celebrate, but the local residents invariably saw them as a threat to their peace and quiet.

Early Rail Travel

In the early days, railroad travel brought with it many of the inconveniences common to coach travel. Mishaps were possible and inconvenience the rule. Another similarity between the two modes of travel were the terms used regarding their use. The words *driver, guard, booking office* and *coach* all made their way into the new railroad vocabulary. Railroad cars at first resembled coaches, with rounded doors, small windows and luggage strapped atop the roof. First-class carriages were only moderately comfortable, fitted with black leather cushions and furnished with lap rugs for use in winter. Second-class compartments boasted only hard, wooden seats, but the third-class coaches didn't even have a roof! In fact, third class was no more than a cattle car in which the passengers stood the length of the trip. Just as in coaching days, these "outside" passengers had to dodge all the elements: dust and heat in summer, cold and snow in the winter and rain more than occasionally. The parliamentary trains mentioned earlier, which traveled long distances, were the only trains to have covered third-class carriages. The Cheap Trains Act of 1864 required all railroad companies to offer cheaper, workmen's fares in both the early morning and evening.

The police filled the positions of lineman, guard and security officer. They were in charge of all the signals and responsible for everything running smoothly. Using flags, the police sent signals up and down the lines. A white flag showed all clear, a green flag meant caution and a red flag meant stop. At night, lamps were used for signaling purposes. Mishaps were commonplace, and the following song, sung to the tune of "Rock-a-Bye Baby," shows the mood of the day:

> Rock away, passenger, in the third class,
> When your train shunts a faster will pass;
> When your train's late your chances are small—
> Crushed will be carriages, engine and all.

On Monday, June 13, 1842, Queen Victoria and Prince Albert made their first railway journey, traveling from Windsor to London on the Great Western Railway line. The trip lasted twenty-five minutes, and the Queen said of it: "I find the motion so very easy, far more so than a carriage, and cannot understand how anyone can suffer from it."

The End of an Era

Railway mania came to an end on Thursday, October 16, 1845, when the Bank of England raised its discount, which had such a disastrous effect that by Saturday people began to be alarmed. The price of stock lowered, and the confidence of the people was shaken. Advertisements were withdrawn from papers, applications for new railroad plans were ignored and stock premiums were either lowered or vanished altogether. Even established railroads had their stocks reduced in value. The nation grew alarmed as the companies they'd invested in hurriedly closed up shop, with letters directed to their addresses being returned to the post office on a daily basis.

Francis tells us: "Men who, a month before, had boasted of the large sums they'd made sent advertisements to papers denying their responsibility (in the schemes). Members of Parliament who had remained quiet under the infliction, while it was somewhat respectable, fell back upon their privileges when they saw their purses in danger. . . . It is the condition of those who are best informed that no other panic was ever so fatal to the middle class. It reached every hearth and saddened every heart. Entire families were ruined. There was scarcely an important town in England, but what beheld some wretched suicide."

WATER TRAVEL

London and other cities with major tributaries offered the services of watermen. Usually, stairs would be built that led down to the riverbank at certain points and where the watermen would be waiting to pick up passengers. Watermen were licensed by the various companies that traded on the rivers, and picked up fares in rotation, much like modern cab stands.

As a rule, fares were not exorbitant. A London waterman and his boat could be hired by the day, or half day, generally from 7s. to 10s. 6d. per day in 1810. Taking London Bridge as a center, the longest journey upriver was to Windsor, and the fare was 14s. for the whole boat, or 2s. per person. Down the river to Gravesend, the farthest point, the fare for the whole boat was 6s. or 1s. each. In addition to Gravesend, the towns of Margate and Ramsgate could also be reached, and for these long voyages, boats called hoys were used. These were one-masted and sometimes had a boom fixed to the mainsail, being rigged very much like a cutter. They are said to have taken their name from the manner in which they were hailed by passengers—"Ahoy!"

Steamboats

Larger steamboats were used for longer river trips. In London, steamboats had been going regularly downriver to Greenwich and Woolwich since the 1830s, with larger boats serving Margate, Ramsgate and Gravesend. By the 1840s, smaller steamboats traveled between London Bridge, Southwark and Westminster Bridge for four pence. Beginning in the 1850s, the railroad cut into the amount of business these boats did, and in the 1860s, the underground railroad virtually put an end to regular steamboat service.

Transatlantic Steamships

On April 8, 1836, the *Great Western*, a new and specially built steamer weighing 1,321 tons, sailed from Bristol to New York. Debate on steamship travel, and doubts about transatlantic steamship travel in general, preceded its launch. The *Savannah*, weighing only 350 tons, had crossed the ocean in 1819, but it had traveled no faster than a clipper, and the coal that fueled the journey had proved costly. The *Great Western* was experimental in design and rather squat, but the interior was the last word in elegance. A visitor who was on hand for the steamer's launch wrote the following: "Sofas, couches, handsome mahogany tables and other elegant furniture adorn the saloons; the decorations are most profuse and elaborate; while large mirrors multiply all this splendour. The sleeping apartments are so neat, so clean, so comfortable, that their improvement seems almost impossible. When I left the elegant and luxurious cabins and stood before the colossal machinery, my capacity for wonder was exhausted."

The *Great Western* proved not only luxurious, but also seaworthy, and it was given a twenty-six gun salute as it sailed into New York's Battery Harbor.

Channel Crossings

Packet boats departed for France from Dover, the nearest point to the Continent on the English coast. John Ashton provides details of the crossing: "The distance is only seven leagues, but the passage is not the less uncertain; it varies from two hours to thirty-six, when it becomes excessively fatiguing; obliged to struggle against the wind in a narrow sea, and in which it is impossible to make long tacks. . . . The cabin is so low that you cannot stand upright; it usually contains eight beds placed two by two upon one another, like drawers in a bureau. . . . The disagreeable smell of the bedding, and of the whole furniture, increase the sickness which the horizontal position would tend to alleviate. This sickness is not dangerous, but it is very severe, and sometimes persons of a delicate habit experience the effects of it for several days. However, if this passage be often painful, and always disagreeable, it is, at least, very safe. In times of peace, few days pass without packet boats crossing the Channel, and we never hear of shipwrecks. The usual price for the passage is one guinea for gentlemen, and half for servants; the hire of the whole vessel costs from five to ten guineas."

THE ENGLISH TOURIST

With the advent of the railroad, Victorians were able to reach destinations within Britain easily. Its speed allowed for day trips and weekend excursions. Spas and seaside resorts, complete with amusements, restaurants and boardinghouses, sprang up throughout the country. In addition to day trips and going on domestic holidays, Victorians began to travel the globe. Improved steamship and railway travel was a factor, as well as the rise of the tourism industry. Where a trip via ship and rail to Rome had taken twenty-three days to accomplish in 1843, it took only two and a half days to complete by 1860. Tourists could travel to America on a steamship in only five days in 1889.

The railroads broadened the horizons of vacationers and day-trippers, offering destinations and tours to suit every budget. At the start of the century, only the very wealthy could afford to visit the resorts at Bath and Brighton. By midcentury, the middle classes could visit the recreational towns of Margate and Ramsgate. Most businesses began to allow their employees annual summer holidays, or "hols," and after 1844, tourists eagerly signed on for Thomas Cook's tours.

Cook's Tours

Thomas Cook began as a publisher, offering his first excursion, a trip to Liverpool from Leicester, in 1845 for a fee of fifteen shillings first class, ten shillings second class. Three hundred and fifty travelers were along for this first tour. Very soon afterwards, he published a guidebook based on the journey, detailing every aspect of the trip. Cook continually expanded his offerings, soon offering trips to Scotland, to the Great Exhibitions in Dublin, Manchester and London and, in 1855, Paris. By 1865, Cook was able to open his first London office.

Paris had been the first Continental tour Cook offered, but this was soon followed by excursions to Switzerland, Italy, Austria and, finally, America. In addition to tours and guidebooks, Cook instituted another travel innovation—the traveler's check. In New York City in 1874, Cook distributed checks, or circular notes, in amounts of five and ten pounds against money deposited in the newly opened New York office of his company. To guard against fraud, letters of indication were issued to every check bearer, which vouched for their identities. Due to the many business connections Cook had made over the years, he was also able to arrange for his clients to be able to cash their checks at hotels, *bureaux de change* and banks.

A Lady Travel Writer

Mariana Starke was born in 1762 and lived in Exmouth, England. Between 1817 and 1819, she traveled extensively, and in 1820 wrote a book entitled *Travels on the Continent*, which was published by John Murray.

An advertisement for a London hotel from Cook's Handbook of London

This book was followed by *Information and Directions for Travellers on the Continent*, which, by 1824, was in its fifth printing. Like the later Egon Ronay, Starke rated the sites, museum collections and other points of interest she visited, though she used exclamation points as a rating system rather than stars. She offered brief historical background on each town, supplied travel distances and posting stages, recommended hotels and provided costs.

Other practical information included the fact that a four-wheeled carriage was charged four guineas to be taken across the English

Channel, with a charge of three guineas per horse and five "extra shillings for dogs." By 1836, her details of European cities had been expanded to include foreign market prices for produce, meat and the like, maps and 712 pages of pertinent information.

TIME LINE

1801 First successful test is conducted of steam carriage built by British inventor Richard Trevithick.
1803 Trevithick builds first steam railway locomotive.
1829 George Shillibeer's horse-drawn omnibus debuts in London.
1844 Great Britain's railroad boom starts.
1845 Thomas Cook operates his first tour.
1857 First steel railroad rails are laid in Great Britain.
1859 Pullman sleeper cars are put into service on railroads.
1863 London's first underground railroad, the Metropolitan Line, opens.
1874 First traveler's checks are issued by Cook

BIBLIOGRAPHY

Albert, W. *The Turnpike Road System of England 1663–1840.* London: Cambridge University Press, 1972.

Austen, Brian. *British Mail-Coach Services, 1784–1850.* New York: Garland Publishing, 1987.

Burke, Thomas. *Travel in England.* London: B.T. Batsford, 1949.

Day, John Robert. *The Story of the London Bus: London and Its Buses From the Horse Bus to the Present Day.* London: London Transport Executive, 1973.

————. *The Story of London's Underground.* London: London Transport Executive, 1979.

Freelove, William Francis. *An Assemblage of Nineteenth-Century Horses and Carriages.* Farnham: Perpetua Press, 1971.

Freeman, Michael J. *Transport in Victorian Britain.* New York: St. Martin's Press, 1988.

Priestley, Joseph. *Historical Account of the Navigable Rivers, Canals and Railways Throughout Great Britain.* New York: A.M. Kelley, 1968.

Swinglehurst, Edmund. *The Romantic Journey: The Story of Thomas Cook and Victorian Travel.* New York: Harper & Row, 1974.

CHAPTER FOURTEEN

Etiquette

When one thinks of the nineteenth century, the subject of etiquette comes rapidly to mind. One cannot help but to identify the era by its strictures, rules and codes of behavior. To be certain, social rules did apply to both ladies and gentlemen, and touched upon almost every area of daily life. The following section will illustrate just how narrow the margins for error concerning correct behavior were.

GUIDELINES FROM *THE HABITS OF GOOD SOCIETY*

Smoking

"One must never smoke, nor even ask to smoke, in the company of the fair. If they know that in a few minutes you will be running off to your cigar, the fair will do well to allow you to bring it out and smoke it there. One must never smoke, again, in the streets; that is, in daylight. The deadly crime may be committed, like burglary, after dark, but not before. One must never smoke in a room inhabited at times by the ladies; thus a well bred man who has a wife or sisters, will not offer to smoke in the dining room after dinner. One must never smoke in a public place where ladies are or might be, for instance, a flower show or promenade. One may smoke in a railway carriage in spite of bye-laws, if one has first obtained the consent of every one present; but if there be a lady there, though she give her consent, smoke not.

One must never smoke a pipe in the streets; one must never smoke at all in the coffee room of a hotel. One must never smoke, without consent, in the presence of a clergyman, and one must never offer a cigar to any ecclesiastic over the rank of curate."

Female Deportment

"As a lady enters a drawing-room, she should look for the mistress of the house, speaking to her first. Her face should wear a smile; she should not rush in head-foremost; a graceful bearing, a light step, an elegant bend to common acquaintance, a cordial pressure, not shaking, of the hand extended to her, are all requisite to a lady. Let her sink gently into a chair, and, on formal occasions, retain her upright position; neither lounge nor sit timorously on the edge of her seat. Her feet should scarcely be shown, and not crossed. She must avoid sitting stiffly, as if a ramrod were introduced within the dress behind, or stooping. Excepting a very small and costly parasol, it is not now usual to bring those articles into a room. An elegantly worked handkerchief is carried in the hand, but not displayed so much as at dinner parties. A lady should conquer a habit of breathing hard, or coming in very hot, or even looking very blue and shivery. Anything that detracts from the pleasure of society is in bad taste.

"In walking, the feet should be moderately turned out, the steps should be equal, firm and light. A lady may be known by her walk. The short, rapid steps, the shaking of the body from side to side, or the very slow gait which many ladies consider genteel, are equally to be detracted."

The Promenade

"If you are a man and you meet a lady whom you know slightly, you must wait till she bows to you. You then lift your hat quite off your head with the hand, whichever it may be, which is farther from the person you meet. . . . [N]o man may stop to speak to a lady until she stops to speak to him. The lady, in short, has the right in all cases to be friendly or distant. You raise your hat all the same, but you do not shake hands unless the lady puts out hers, which you may take as a sign of particular good will. In this case you must not stop long, but the lady has the right to prolong the interview at her pleasure. It is she who must make the move onwards. The length of this conversation must depend on the place where you meet. If in the streets, it should be very short; if in a regular promenade, it may be longer. If you are walking with a man whom your lady friend does not know, you must not stop; still less so, if she is walking with a lady or gentleman whom you do not know. If, however, a decided inclination is evinced by either to speak to the other, and you so stop, the stranger ought not to walk on, but to stop also, and it then behooves you to introduce him or her. Such an introduction is merely formal, and goes no further.

"There are some definite rules for cutting. A gentleman must never cut a lady under any circumstances. An unmarried lady should never cut a married one. A servant of whatever class—for there are servants up to royalty itself—should never cut his master; near relations should never cut one another at all; and a clergyman should never cut anybody, because it is at best an unchristian action. Perhaps it should be added that a superior should never cut his inferior in rank; he has many other ways of annihilating him. Certainly it may be laid down that people holding temporary official relations must waive their private animosities, and that two doctors, for instance, however much opposed to one another, should never introduce the cut over the bed of a patient."

Shaking Hands

"The etiquette of hand shaking is simple. A man has no right to take a lady's hand till it is offered. He has even less right to pinch or retain it. Two ladies shake hands gently and softly. A young lady gives her hand, but does not shake a gentleman's, unless she is his friend. A lady should always rise to give her hand; a gentleman, of course, never dares do so seated. On introduction in a room, a married lady generally offers her hand, a young lady not; in a ballroom, where the introduction is to dancing, not to friendship, you never shake hands; and as a general rule, an introduction is not followed by shaking hands, only by a bow."

Out and About

"When you meet a friend in the street, it must depend on the amount of familiarity whether you walk with him or not, but with a lady you must not walk unless invited either verbally or tacitly. A young and single man should never walk with a young lady in public places, unless especially asked to do so.

"In driving with ladies, a man must take the back seat of the carriage, and when it stops, jump out first and offer his hand to let them out. In your own carriage you always give the front seat to a visitor, if you are a man, but a lady leaves the back seat for a gentleman.

"In railway travelling you should not open a conversation with a lady unknown to you, until she makes some advance towards it. On the other hand, it is polite to speak to a gentleman. If, however, his answers be curt, and he evinces a desire to be quiet, do not pursue the conversation. On your part, if addressed in a railway carriage, you should always reply politely. If you have a newspaper, and others have not, you should offer it to the person nearest you. An acquaintance begun on a railway may sometimes go farther, but, as a general rule, it terminates when one of the parties leaves the carriage."

Paying Calls

"Visits of condolence or congratulation must be made about a week after the event. If you are intimate with the person on whom you call, you may ask in the first case for admission; if not, it is better only to leave a card, and make your 'kind inquiries' of the servant, who is generally primed in what manner to answer them. In visits of congratulation you should always go in, and be hearty in your congratulations. Visits of condolence are terrible inflictions on both the receiver and giver, but they may be made less so by avoiding, as much as consistent with sympathy, any allusion to the past. The receiver does well to abstain from tears. On marriage, cards are sent round to such people as you wish to keep among your acquaintance, and it is then their part to call first on the young couple, when within distance.

"Ceremonial visits must be made the day after a ball, when it will suffice to leave a card; within a day or two after a dinner party, when you ought to make the visit personally, unless the dinner was a semi-official one, such as the Lord Mayor's; and within a week of a small party, when the call should certainly be made in person. All these visits should be short, lasting from twenty minutes to half an hour at the most. It is proper when you have been some time at a visit, and another caller is announced, to rise and leave, not indeed immediately, as if you shunned the new arrival, but after a moment or two.

"I now come to a few hints about calling in general; and first as to the time thereof. In London, the limits of calling hours are fixed, namely, from three to six, but in the country people are sometimes odious enough to call in the morning before lunch. This should not be done even by intimate friends. A ceremonial call from a slight acquaintance ought to be returned the next day, or at longest within three days, unless the distance be great. In the same way, if a stranger comes to stay at the house of a friend, in the country or in a small country town, every resident ought to call on him or her, even if she be a young lady, as soon as possible after their arrival. These calls should be made in person, and returned next day.

"The card is the next point. It should be perfectly simple. A lady's card is larger than a gentleman's. The former may be glazed, the latter not. The name, with a simple 'Mr.' or 'Mrs.' before it, is sufficient, except in the case of acknowledged rank, as 'The Earl of Ducie.' The address may be put in the corner of the card. The engraving should be in simple Italian writing, not Gothic or Roman letters, and very small and without any flourishes. A young lady does not require a separate card as long as she is living with her mother; her name is engraved under her mother's. Or if there be more than one daughter presented, 'The Miss Jones Smiths.'

"[Lastly,] a lady never calls on a gentleman, unless professionally or officially. It is not only ill bred, but positively improper to do so. At the same time, there is a certain privilege in age, which makes it possible for an old bachelor like myself to receive a visit from any married lady whom I know very intimately, but such a call would certainly not be one of ceremony, and always presupposes a desire to consult me on some point or other. I should be guilty of shameful treachery, however, if I told any one that I had received such a visit, while I should certainly expect that my fair caller would let her husband know of it."

Visiting card cases were usually made of silver, ivory or papier-mâché and date from the early nineteenth century, when they were called visiting "tickets," as they'd been termed since the Georgian era. Card cases came into widespread use during the 1830s and their lids most often depicted views of castles, such as Warwick and Windsor, and were known as "castle top" cases. From the 1840s on, cases became more ornate, and lids featuring Scottish views also became popular, due to Queen Victoria's purchase of Balmoral and the novels of Sir Walter Scott. Nathaniel Mills, a manufacturer from Birmingham, was the most well-known card case maker, and the first to turn out electroplated examples.

PRESENTATION AT COURT

For the young ladies of the peerage, being presented to the queen at court marked their entry into fashionable society and the marriage market. Once she had been presented, a young woman then set out upon a whirl of balls and parties and set her mind upon finding a suitable husband from among those eligible bachelors in her own class. In addition, a woman was again presented at court before her marriage, as a formal way of informing the monarch of her change in status. Ladies of a more mature age who had not previously been presented at court could seek to be introduced to the queen, and thus to fashionable society, by securing a sponsor who would present her at court.

In *The Habits of Good Society,* there can be found the following precedents regarding court presentation: "The wives and daughters of the clergy, of military and naval officers, of physicians and barristers, can be presented. These are the aristocratic professions but the wives and daughters of general practitioners and of solicitors are not entitled to a presentation. The wives and daughters of merchants, or of men in business (excepting bankers), are not entitled to presentation. Nevertheless, though many ladies of this class were refused presentation early in this reign, it is certain that many have since been presented. No divorcee, nor lady married, after having lived with her husband or with any one else before her marriage, can be received.

"In seeking for a lady to present another lady at Court, the higher the rank and the more unexceptional the character the better. In asking this, it must be remembered that it is a favour of great delicacy to require from any one except a relation. It is necessary also for the lady who presents to be at the drawing room on the day when the presentation takes place. If a lady of rank cannot be found, the wife of a county member, or of a man high in office, or of a military man of standing, or of a barrister's wife can be resorted to. Any lady who has been presented at Court may present in her turn."

As stated above, ladies who had been divorced were forbidden from being presented at court. But Queen Victoria thought this a harsh penalty in the event that the lady was blameless in the matter. In 1889, the queen decreed that ladies who had been debarred from court through divorce were to thereafter be allowed to apply for admission, with each case then being decided based on its own merit.

After Prince Albert's death in 1861, Queen Victoria withdrew from attending public functions. Gradually, she added more appearances to her schedule, so that in 1865 she held six drawing rooms. While more drawing rooms were held in 1868, the queen herself attended only two. When holding a drawing room, the queen typically wore a black silk dress, as well as a train trimmed with crepe and net, and a cap with a long veil of white crepe lisse, ornamented with large diamonds. The number of persons who attended her courts had been limited since the death of the prince consort to a maximum of five hundred. The drawing rooms began at 3 P.M., and if they lasted more than half an hour, the queen withdrew and left the Prince of Wales to carry on. The Prince and Princess of Wales also stood in on the queen's behalf at those drawing rooms that she did not personally attend.

MARRIAGE

The Legalities

Lord Hardwicke's Marriage Act of 1753 made null and void any marriage not preceded by either the posting of banns or the securement of an official license, and that had not been carried out publicly in a church or chapel by a regular clergymen during the prescribed daylight hours. The act also prohibited marriage by persons under age twenty-one without the consent of parents; it ended contract marriages and made it mandatory that all marriages be entered into record, usually the parish register. Young people who did not have the consent of their parents to marry could always stay for a time in a crowded city and then ask the local parish clergy, who knew nothing of their backgrounds, to post banns and perform the ceremony. As these clergymen dealt with large parishes, it would have been doubtful that they would have taken the time to check all facts relating to residence and age of the marrying parties.

A marriage act of 1836 legalized the marriage services of Jews, Quakers and Roman Catholics, who previously had to submit to an Anglican ceremony in order to validate their marriages. The same act also established a civil marriage contract whereby couples were given the choice of marrying in a church or registry office, which gave rise to the phrase "married but not churched."

In the late eighteenth century, some of the aristocracy began insisting that their surnames be included as prefixes or suffixes to their sons-in-law's family names. The Cecil family changed its name to Gascoyne-Cecil when Frances Mary Gascoyne brought some of her family fortune to the Cecil family through marriage in 1820. The heiress often retained control of her separate property, which was administered by trustees.

Separate Estates

Such separate property, or estate, was held in trust for a married woman through a system called equity, which was overseen by the Chancery Court. Property could be earmarked for the "separate use" of a married woman, whether she had come into it by inheritance or through a gift from her husband or some other relative. A married woman could raise money on the property, dispose of it or leave it to whomever she wished in her will. However, sometimes restrictions were put upon the woman's rights by the person who endowed her the gift, stating that she could use the income or interest from the property however she wished, but that she could not mortgage nor dispose of it. By midcentury, only 10 percent of Englishwomen owned separate incomes. The Equity Courts did not deal with property valued at less than two hundred pounds, so any property valued at less than that amount was under the lady's personal control.

Most marriage settlements included arrangements for the provision of the wife's pin money, which was an allowance paid to her either monthly or annually, and which she could spend any way she wished. The marriage settlement also provided a jointure, or the amount of money to be settled upon her upon the death of her husband. This sum was usually proportionate to the amount she had brought into marriage. Settlements also provided sums to be received by any children of the marriage upon their father's death, and portions to be settled upon daughters at the time of their marriages. The intent of the marriage settlement was to hold the estate separate in its entirety for future generations while making provisions for the maintenance for all concerned.

Breach of Marriage Contract (Promise)

Physical infirmity was a legitimate defense against the charge, as was evidence that one of the parties had acted in an improper or immoral manner. Damages were moderate and reflected the financial standing of the persons involved, most fines ranging from one to five hundred pounds.

Prohibitions to Marriage

- A widower could not marry his deceased wife's sister.
- A widow could not marry her deceased husband's brother.
- A widower could not marry his niece by marriage.
- A widower could not marry his stepdaughter.
- A widower could not marry his aunt by marriage.
- A lunatic or idiot could not lawfully contract a marriage, except during a lucid interval.
- Insanity after marriage did not invalidate it.

While these prohibitions existed legally, clandestine marriages still took place between two people who, knowing full well their marriage would not be legal, still wanted to go through with some sort of ceremony in order to solemnize their vows. Perhaps the most infamous clandestine marriage was that between the prince regent and Maria Anne Fitzherbert. In this case, a a clergyman was bribed to look the other way in the absence of a marriage license and in light of the fact that Fitzherbert was a Catholic widow. The marriage was further invalidated by the fact that the prince regent, as an heir to the throne under the age of twenty-one, hadn't gotten the king's permission to marry.

Gretna Green

Those with means might have instead eloped to Gretna Green in Scotland to avoid such prohibitions, but this practice was not nearly as commonplace as it has been depicted in popular fiction. Lord Brougham passed a bill in 1856 that made null and void the Gretna Green marriage of English couples, unless both parties had resided in Scotland for three weeks previous to the ceremony.

Farington, October 30, 1801: "From Annan we proceeded to Gretna Green, 8 miles, and made the Inn called Gretna Hall our Headquarters. It is a very good House which a few years ago was converted into an Inn. We are now on a spot rendered very interesting by the resort of it for the purpose of marriage, by those whom the law of England would prevent from legalizing such an engagement. Having leisure before dinner I talked on the subject to one of the Landlords family, who informed me that whatever may be the supposition in England, the practice is held in great disrepute here, that the men who officiate in performing the ceremony are much despised as having no principle &c. &c. There are at present three men who offer themselves for it, Joseph Paisley, a large fat old man of 70 years of age, who has been the chief person in that capacity for 40 years past. He was a Tobacconist & never had any education or clerical function. He has on many occasions received much money, but He is drunken & improvident, & has not saved any. He formerly performed the ceremony at Gretna Green, but it is now done at Spring-field, a village abt. three quarters of a mile nearer to England. One of the other persons who acts in this capacity is David Land a labouring man who resides at Gretna Green. His business is but little compared with that of Paisley, but sometimes through the means of a Son of his who is a Chaise-driver at the Coffee House Inn, Carlisle, a party is brought to Gretna Green. The Third is Andrew Lekel. The mode of proceeding is managed by the Drivers of carriages, who on bringing a couple to Spring-field immediately send for Paisley, whose first consideration is to settle the terms on which He is to perform the ceremony. This depends in fact upon the Drivers, who judging of the condition of the parties by their manner of travelling, & appearance, signify to Paisley what He should demand. The terms vary from 50 guineas down to 10 & 5 guineas.

"When this point is settled the ceremony is immediately performed by reading the service of the Church of England before two witnesses, two persons being called into the room for that purpose. Their names are then put down, each of the parties signing and the witnesses also which completes the business, which is over in a very short time. A few years ago there were 72 weddings in one year, but the average may be estimated at from 40 to 50. A guinea is invariably paid for the room in which the ceremony is performed, and those who keep the Inn at Spring-field do not refuse that accommodation, but at Gretna Hall Inn, they think it disreputable & will not receive persons who come on that errand. The money which is recd. for performing the ceremony is not wholly the profit of the officiating man. He has only one Half of it which is agreed for, the other Half goes to the Drivers, who divide it by a settled agreement with whatever number of Drivers belong to the Inn from which they come & the Waiters &c. have also shares. There was a small ale house at Gretna Green, which before Spring-field was built 7 or 8 years ago, had the business. People of a lower order come over from the Cumberland side of the water and get married. The expence [sic] is something not more than a guinea, or half a guinea, & it is sometimes done for drink only."

Advice on Marriage from The Habits of Good Society

"A few sentences spoken in earnest, and broken by emotion, are more eloquent than pages of sentiment, both to parent and daughter. Let him, however, speak and be accepted. He is in that case instantly taken into the intimacy of his adopted relatives. Such is the notion of English honour, that the engaged couple are henceforth allowed to be frequently alone together, in walking and at home. If there be no known obstacle to their engagement, the gentleman and lady are mutually introduced to the respective relatives of each. It is for the gentleman's family to call first; for him to make the first present; and this should be done as soon as possible after the offer has been accepted. It is a sort of seal put upon the affair. This present generally consists of some personal ornament, say, a ring, and should be handsome, but not so handsome as that made for the wedding day. During the period that elapses before the marriage the betrothed man should conduct himself with peculiar deference to the lady's family and friends, even if beneath his own station.

"Upon every account, it is desirable for a young lady to have a settlement on her; and she should not, from a weak spirit of romance, oppose her friends who advise it, since it is for her husband's advantage as well as her own. By making a settlement there is always a fund which cannot be touched—a something, however small, as a provision for a wife and children; and, whether she have fortune or not, this ought to be made. An allowance for dress should also be arranged; and this should be administered in such a way that a wife should not have to ask for it at inconvenient hours, and thus irritate her husband.

"Marriage by banns is confined to the poorer classes; and a license is generally obtained by those who aspire to the habits of good society. It is within the recollection of many, even middle aged persons, that the higher classes were, some twenty years ago, married only by special license—a process costing about fifty pounds instead of five; and therefore supposed by our commercial country especially to denote good society. Special licenses have, however, become unfashionable. They were obtained chiefly on account of their enabling persons to be married at any hour, whereas the canon prescribes the afternoon; after mid-day it is illegal to celebrate a marriage. In some instances during the Crimean war, special licenses were resorted to unite couples—when the bridegroom elect had been ordered off, and felt, with his bride, that it were happier for both to belong to each other even in death. But the ordinary couples walk up to the altars of their respective parish churches.

"It is to be lamented that previously to so solemn a ceremony, the thoughts of the lady concerned must necessarily be engaged for some time upon her 'trousseau.' The 'trousseau' consists, in this country, of all the habiliments necessary for a lady's use for the first two or three years of her married life; like every other outfit there are always a number of articles introduced into it that are next to useless, and are only calculated for the vain glory of the ostentatious. A Trousseau may, in quiet life, be formed upon so low a sum as sixty or seventy pounds; it seldom costs, however, less than one hundred, and often mounts up to five hundred. The 'trousseau' being completed, and the day fixed, it becomes necessary to select the bridesmaids and the bridegroom's man, and to invite the guests.

"The bridesmaids are from two to eight in number. When a bride is young the bridesmaids should be young; but it is absurd to see a 'single woman of a certain age,' or a widow, surrounded by blooming girls. Custom decides that the bridesmaids should be spinsters, but there is no legal objection to a married woman being a bridesmaid should it be necessary. In London, for a great wedding breakfast, it is customary to send out printed cards from the parents or guardians from whose house the young lady is to be married. Early in the day, before eleven, the bride should be dressed, taking breakfast in her room. The lace (of the wedding gown) should be of the finest quality. Brussels or Honiton is the most delicate and becoming, the veil should be of the same sort of lace as the dress. A wreath of roses and orange flowers is worn round the head, not confining the veil. The silk ought to be plain; glacé, not 'moire,' if the bride be young, as the latter is too heavy; if she is no longer young, nothing is so becoming as moire silk, either white or silver grey. Widows and ladies not young are usually married in bonnets, which should be of the most elegant description, trimmed with flowers or feathers, according to the taste of the wearer.

"The gentleman's dress should differ little from his full morning costume. The days are gone by when gentlemen were married in white satin breeches and waistcoat. A dark blue frock coat—black being superstitiously considered ominous—a white waistcoat and a pair of light trousers, suffice for the happy man. The neck tie should be light and simple. The gloves must be as white as the linen. As soon as the carriages are at the door, those bridesmaids who happen to be in the house, and the other members of the family set off first. The bride goes last, with her father and mother, or with her mother alone, and the brother or relative who is to represent her father in case of death or absence. The bridegroom, his friend, or bridegroom's man, and the bridesmaids ought to be waiting in the church. It is a good thing for the bridegroom's man to distribute the different fees to the clergymen, the clerk, the pew opener, before the arrival of the bride, as it prevents confusion afterwards.

"The bridesmaids are dressed, on this occasion, so as to complete the picture with effect. When there are six or eight, it is usual for three of them to dress in one colour, and three in another. At some of the most fashionable weddings in London, the bridesmaids wear veils—these are usually of tulle or net; white tarlatan dresses, over muslin, or beautifully worked dresses are much worn, with colours introduced—pink or blue, and scarves of those colours; and white bonnets, if bonnets are worn, trimmed with flowers to correspond.

"The breakfast is arranged on one or more tables, and is provided by a confectioner when expense is not an object. When the breakfast is sent from a confectioner's, or is arranged in the house by a professional cook, the wedding cake is richly ornamented with flowers, in sugar, and a knot of orange flowers at the top. At each end of the table are tea and coffee. Soup is sometimes handed. Generally the viands are cold, consisting of poultry or game, lobster salads, chicken or fish; hams, tongues, prawns and game pies; raisins, savoury jellies, sweets of every description—all cold. Ice is afterwards handed, and, before the healths are drunk, the wedding cake is cut by the nearest gentleman and handed round. The father then proposes the health of the bride and bridegroom. The latter is expected to answer, and to propose the bridegroom's man. The bridegroom's man returns thanks, and pledges the bridesmaids, who answer through the bridegroom. All other toasts are optional, but it is 'de rigueur' that the health of the clergyman who tied the knot, if present, should be drunk.

"The bride then assumes her travelling dress. This should be good in quality, but plain like a handsome dress for morning calls. One more word about fees to servants. These form a very varying point on a marriage, and depend on the condition in life of the parties. A considerable sum is expected from a nobleman, or commoner of large fortune, but a much more modest calculation for a professional man, or a son whose father is still living, and who receives merely an allowance to enable him to marry. Presents are usual, first from the bridegroom to the bridesmaids. These generally consist of jewellery, the device of which should be unique or quaint, the article more elegant than massive. The female servants of the family, more especially servants who have lived many years in their place, also expect presents, such as gowns or shawls; or to a very valued personal attendant or housekeeper, a watch."

Precedents Set by Queen Victoria

Queen Victoria and her daughters were responsible for many of our modern-day wedding traditions. Before the nineteenth century, white wedding dresses were the exception, rather than the rule, with silver being the traditional color worn by royal brides. However, the queen chose to break with tradition on her wedding day, choosing a white gown. Here's a contemporary account of the queen's wedding attire: "The Queen wore on her head a wreath of orange blossoms and a veil of Honiton lace, with a necklace and earrings of diamonds. Her dress was of white satin, with a very deep trimming of Honiton lace. . . . The body and sleeves were richly trimmed with the same material to correspond. The train, which was of white satin, was trimmed with orange blossoms. The cost of the lace alone on the Queen's dress was one thousand pounds. The satin was manufactured in Spitalfields, and the lace at a village (Beer) near Honiton. More than two hundred persons were employed upon the latter for a period of eight months, and as the lace trade of Honiton had seriously declined, all these persons would have been destitute during the winter had it not been for the Queen's express order that the lace should be manufactured by them."

No wedding can be considered complete without the strains of "Here Comes the Bride" accompanying the bride down the aisle. This march is actually the "Bridal Chorus" from Wagner's opera *Lohengrin* and was played at the marriage of Princess Louise, Queen Victoria's granddaughter, in 1889. The more upbeat "Wedding March," composed by Mendelssohn in 1826 for a performance of Shakespeare's *A*

Midsummer Night's Dream, has accompanied newlyweds back up the aisle after the wedding ceremony ever since it was first played at the wedding of Queen Victoria's daughter Victoria.

The queen and princesses were also responsible for the traditional, showy wedding cakes we know today. The queen's own wedding cake weighed three hundred pounds and measured nine feet across. Created by the Buckingham Palace confectioner, Mr. Mawdett, it was topped by a foot-high rendering of Britannia blessing the bride and groom—whose figures had been carved from a block of ice. The cake prepared for Princess Victoria's wedding was seven feet high. While the cake at Princess Louise's wedding in 1871 was only five feet, four inches tall, it had been elaborately decorated by Her Majesty's chief confectioner, Mr. Ponder, and had taken three months to create. The base was embellished with white satin that bore the coats of arms of the bride and groom, while the cake itself held wreaths of orange blossoms and small vases containing the same flowers. Atop the cake stood doves drinking from a fountain, four statues and a temple.

BIBLIOGRAPHY

Barrett-Ducrocq, Francoise. *Love in the Time of Victoria: Sexuality, Class and Gender in Nineteenth-Century London.* London: Routledge Chapman & Hall, 1991.

Gillis, John. *For Better, For Worse: British Marriages, 1600 to Present.* New York: Oxford University Press, 1988.

Hartcup, Adeline. *Love and Marriage in the Great Country Houses.* London: Sidgwick & Jackson, 1984.

Horstman, Allen. *Victorian Divorce.* New York: St. Martin's Press, 1985.

Knight, Frances. *The Nineteenth-Century Church and English Society.* Cambridge, Mass.: Cambridge University Press, 1995.

MacColl, Gail. *To Marry an English Lord.* New York: Workman Publishing, 1989.

Montgomery, Maureen. *"Gilded Prostitution": Status, Money, and Transatlantic Marriages, 1870–1914.* London: Routledge, 1989.

Perkin, Joan. *Women and Marriage in Nineteenth-Century England.* Chicago: Lyceum Books, 1989.

Richardson, Joanna. *The Disastrous Marriage: A Study of George IV and Caroline of Brunswick.* London: Cape, 1960.

Trustram, Myna. *Women of the Regiment: Marriage and the Victorian Army.* Cambridge, Mass.: Cambridge University Press, 1984.

CHAPTER FIFTEEN

The Pleasures of Good Society

If the aristocracy was seen as being a breed apart from the general population, so was their entertainment. Country house visits, fashionable dinners and a nightly round of parties during the season ensured that only those with large fortunes, and a large measure of stamina, could indulge in such diversions. But even in diversions, there existed set precedents and rules of conduct. The fashionable nineteenth-century hostess had a wealth of etiquette books to consult, offering advice on everything from the proper sanding of ballroom floors to what time a "breakfast" should begin (not before 1 P.M.). Whether an entertainment consisted of dining, dancing or a musical program, this section will demonstrate that nineteenth-century society took its pleasures seriously.

COUNTRY HOUSE VISITING

Our authority from *The Habits of Good Society* offers the following advice concerning country house visits: "A general invitation should never be acted on. An invitation should specify the persons whom it includes, and the person invited should never presume to take with him any one not specified. If a gentleman cannot dispense with his valet, or a lady with her maid, they should write to ask leave to bring a servant; but the means of your inviter and the size of the house should be taken into consideration, and it is better taste to dispense with a servant altogether. Children and horses are still more troublesome, and should never be taken without special mention made of them. It is equally bad taste to arrive with a waggonful [sic] of luggage, as that is naturally taken as a hint that you intend to stay a long time. The length of a country visit is indeed a difficult matter to decide, but in the present day people who receive much generally specify the length in their invitation—a plan which saves a great deal of trouble and doubt. But a custom not so commendable has lately come in of limiting the visits of acquaintances to two or three days. This may be pardonable where the guest lives at no great distance, but it is preposterous to expect a person to travel from London to Aberdeen for a stay of three nights. If, however, the length be not specified, and cannot easily be discovered, a week is the limit for a country visit, except at the house of a near relation or very old friend.

"The main point in a country house is to give as little trouble as possible, to conform to the habits of your entertainers, and never to be in the way. On this principle you will retire to your own occupations soon after breakfast, unless some arrangement has been made for passing the morning otherwise. If you have nothing to do, you may be sure that your host has something to attend to in the morning. Another point of good breeding is to be punctual at meals, for a host and hostess never sit down without their guest, and dinner may be getting cold. If, however, a guest should fail in this particular, a well bred entertainer will not only take no notice of it, but attempt to set the late comer as much at his ease as possible. A host should provide amusement for his guests.

"The worst part of a country visit is the necessity of giving gratuities to the servants, for a poor man may often find his visit cost him far more than if he had stayed at home. It is a custom which ought to be put down, because a host who receives much should pay his own servants for the extra trouble given. In a great house a man servant expects gold, but a poor man should not be ashamed of offering him silver. It must depend on the length of the visit. The ladies give to the female, the gentlemen to the male servants."

Puckler-Muskau: "It requires a considerable fortune here to keep up a country-house; for custom demands many luxuries, and, according to the aspiring and imitative manners of the country, as much (in the main things) at the shopkeeper's house, as at the Duke's; a handsomely fitted-up house, with elegant furniture, plate, servants in new and handsome liveries, a profusion of dishes and foreign wines, rare and expensive dessert, and in all things an appearance of superfluity, 'plenty' as the English call it. As long as there are visitors in the house, this way of life goes on; but many a family atones for it by meager fare when alone: for which reason nobody here ventures to pay a visit in the country without being invited, and these invitations usually fix the day and hour. The acquaintances are generally numerous; and as both room and the time allotted to the reception of guests are small, one must give place to another. True hospitality this can hardly be called; it is rather the display of one's own possessions, for the purpose of dazzling as many as possible. After a family has thus kept open house for a month or two, they go for the remainder of the time they have to spend in the country, to make visits at the houses of others; but the one hospitable month costs as much as a wealthy landed proprietor spends in a whole year with us.

"Strangers have generally only one room allotted to them, usually a spacious apartment on the first floor. Englishmen seldom go into this room except to sleep, and to dress twice a-day, which even without company and in the most strictly domestic circles, is always 'de rigueur'; for all meals are commonly taken in company, and any one who wants to write does it in the library. There, also, those who wish to converse give each other 'rendezvous,' to avoid either the whole society, or particular parties, in the formation of which people are quite at liberty. Here you have an opportunity of gossiping for hours with the young ladies, who are always very literally inclined. Many a marriage is thus concocted or destroyed, between the 'corpus juris' on the one side and Bouffler's Works on the other, while fashionable novels, as a sort of intermediate link, lie on the tables in the middle.

"Ten or eleven is the hour for breakfast, at which you may appear in *neglige*. . . . The ladies do the honours of the table very agreeably. If you come down later, when the breakfast is removed, a servant brings you what you want. In many houses he is on the watch till one o'clock, or even later, to see that stragglers do not starve. That half-a-dozen newspapers must lie on the table for every one to read who likes, is, of course, understood. The men now either go out hunting or shooting, or on business; the host does the same, without troubling himself in the least degree about his guests (the truest kindness and good-breeding); and about half an hour before dinner the company meet again in the drawing-room in elegant toilette."

Greville, August 4, 1818: "I went to Oatlands [Oatlands Park, Weybridge, then home of duke of York] on Saturday. . . . On Sunday we amused ourselves with eating fruit in the garden and shooting at a mark with pistols, and playing with the monkeys. I bathed in the cold bath in the grotto, which is as clear as crystal and as cold as ice. Oatlands is the worst managed establishment in England: there are a great many servants, and nobody waits on you; a vast number of horses, and none to ride or drive."

Greville, November 4, 1829: "I arrived [at Chatsworth] just as they were going to dinner, but was not expected, and so there was no room at the table. The party was immense; 40 people sat down to dinner every day, and about 150 servants in the steward's room and servants' hall. . . . Nothing could be more agreeable from the gayety of numbers and the entire liberty which prevails; all the resources of the house—horses, carriages, keepers, etc. are placed at the disposal of the guests, and everybody does what he likes best. In the evening they acted charades or danced, and there was plenty of whist and *escarte* high and low."

Greville, Belvoir Castle, January 7, 1834: "The Duke [of Rutland] lives here for three or four months, from the end of October till the end of February or March, on and off, and the establishment is kept up with extraordinary splendor. In the morning we are roused by the strains of martial music, and the band (of his regiment of militia) marches round the terrace, awakening or quickening the guests with lively airs. All the men hunt or shoot. At dinner there is a different display of plate every day, and in the evening some play at whist or amuse themselves as they please, and some walk about the staircases and corridors to hear the band, which plays the whole evening in the hall. On the Duke's birthday there was a great feast at the Castle; 200 people dined in the servants' hall alone, without counting the other tables. We were about forty to dinner."

Frances Greville, later countess of Warwick and longtime mistress of the Prince of Wales, wrote in her memoirs, *Life's Ebb and Flow* (1929): "We began the day by breakfasting at ten o'clock. This meal consisted of many courses in silver dishes on the side table. There was enough food to last a group of well regulated digestions for the whole day. The men went out shooting after breakfast and then came the emptiness of the long morning from which I suffered silently. I can remember the groups of women sitting discussing their neighbours or writing letters at impossible little ornamental tables. . . . We were not all women. There were a few unsporting men asked—'darlings.' These men of witty and amusing conversation were always asked as extras everywhere to help to entertain the women, otherwise we should have been left high and dry. The ladies. . . . rarely took part in the shoot, not even going out to join the shooters until luncheon time. Then, dressed in tweeds and trying to look as sportsman-like as the clothes of the day allowed, we went out together to some rendezvous of the shooters. . . . After a large luncheon, finishing up with coffee and liqueurs, the women preferred to wend their way back to the house. They would spend the intervening time until the men returned for tea once more, changing their clothes. This time they got into lovely tea gowns. The tea gowns of that day were far more beautiful than the evening gowns worn for dinner. We changed our clothes four times a day at least. This kept our maids and ourselves extraordinarily busy. . . . When I think of all these gorgeous gowns round a tea table I fancy we must have looked like a group of enormous dolls. Conversation at tea was slumberous. Nobody woke up to be witty until dinner time with its accompanying good wines. The men discussed the bags of the day and the women did the admiring. With the coming of bridge in later years the hours between tea and dinner were relieved of their tedium. It used often to be sheer boredom until seven when we went off to dress for dinner."

THE FASHIONABLE DINNER

A formal style of dinner service, known as dinner *à la francaise*, had been popular in England during the eighteenth century. During a dinner served *à la francaise*, it was up to each diner to catch the footman's eye in order to be served from a dish that was set out of reach of a diner upon the table. Many diners made certain to tip the footmen before the meal, in order to ensure that they were well fed. It was considered polite to drink wine only when doing so with another person. One diner invited another to drink a glass of wine, and this invitation could not be refused, as to refuse a drink was considered rude in the extreme. Wine glasses then had rather smaller bowls than they do today so that dinner guests were not rendered unconscious by the end of the meal. As a person's wine glass was to be washed each time it was emptied, and before the butler refilled it, glasses were first rinsed in a bowl of water kept upon the butler's sideboard. Some of these bowls also had notches cut into their rims, from which glasses were hung by their stems on the outside and allowed to dry. When filled with ice and water, glasses could be hung on the inside of these bowls to be chilled.

Early in the nineteenth century, a new method of service called dinner *à la russe* became fashionable. The Russian Prince Kourakin is generally acknowledged as having been responsible for the introduction of service *à la russe* to England, and it was supposedly the Russian ambassador Count Nesselrode who had first brought it to the Imperial Court of Napoleon. The table was laid out with both plate and glass and ornamented with flowers, with dessert being the only course to be laid directly upon the table. All of the food served during the preceding courses was first brought to the sideboard. From these bowls and platters, the butler took a portion of each dish and arranged each diner's meal upon on a china plate, which was then placed in front of each guest. With each diner being served individually, the number of servants required to serve at table was increased.

It was this new method of serving dinner that brought about the necessity for menu cards. One of these cards was placed between every two diners so that guests would know what foods were to be served at the meal, thus enabling them to gauge their appetites accordingly. The menus could either be written upon porcelain menu slates or on cards that were then set into silver or porcelain menu holders. Dinner was by now being served around eight o'clock, as the fashionable hour for taking afternoon tea was five o'clock.

In 1826 *Prince Puckler-Muskau* wrote about this new mode of service thusly: "When you enter (the dining room) you find the whole of the first course on the table, as in France. After the soup is removed, and the covers are taken off, every man helps the dish before him, and offers some of it to his neighbor; if he wishes for anything else, he must ask across the table or send a servant for it; a very troublesome custom, in place of which, some of the most elegant travelled gentlemen have adopted the more convenient German fashion of sending the servants round with the dishes.

"It is not usual to take wine without drinking to another person. When you raise your glass, you look fixedly at the one with whom you are drinking, bow your head, and then drink with the greatest gravity. . . . At the conclusion of the second course comes a sort of

SAMPLE MENUS FROM ISABELLA BEETON'S *BOOK OF HOUSEHOLD MANAGEMENT*

Beeton's Game Dinner for 30 Persons (November)

FIRST COURSE

Hare Soup ∞ Soup à la Reine ∞ Pheasant Soup ∞ Puree of Grouse

SECOND COURSE

Larded Pheasants ∞ Cold Pheasant Pie ∞ Grouse
Larded Partridges ∞ Hot Raised Pie of Mixed Game

ENTREMENTS AND REMOVES

Apricot Tart ∞Vol-au-Vent of Pears ∞ Maids of Honor
Compote of Apple ∞ Charlotte Russe
Plum Pudding ∞ Dantzic Jelly

ENTREES

Salmi of Widgeon ∞ Salmi of Woodcock ∞ Lark Pudding
Fillet of Pheasant and Truffles ∞ Curried Rabbit ∞ Game Patties

THIRD COURSE

Snipes ∞ Golden Plovers ∞ Wild Duck ∞ Pintails ∞ Quails
Teal ∞ Woodcocks ∞ Snipes ∞ Widgeons

DESSERT

Preserved Cherries ∞ Filberts ∞ Dried Fruit ∞ Ginger Ice Cream
Figs ∞ Strawberry Ice Cream ∞ Pineapples ∞ Pears ∞ Apples
Grapes ∞ Lemon Water Ice ∞ Orange Water Ice

Beeton's Menu for a Dinner *à la Francaise* for 18

FIRST COURSE

Green Pea Soup ∞ Whitebait ∞ Stewed Trout ∞ Soup à la Reine

SECOND COURSE

Haunch of Venison ∞ Pigeon Pie ∞ Braised Ham
Saddle of Lamb ∞ Boiled Capon ∞ Spring Chickens

ENTREES

Lamb Cutlets ∞ Lobster Curry ∞ Chicken Patties
Scallops of Chicken

THIRD COURSE

Roast Ducks ∞ Prawns ∞ Cherry Tart ∞ Green Goose
Raspberry Cream ∞ Custards ∞ Tartlets

Beeton's Menu for Dinner *à la Russe* for 18

FIRST COURSE

Julienne Soup ∞ Vermicelli Soup

SECOND COURSE

Boiled Salmon ∞ Turbot in Lobster Sauce ∞ Filet de Soles
Red Mullet ∞ Trout ∞ Lobster Rissoles ∞ Whitebait

ENTREES

Canards a la Rouennaise ∞ Mutton Cutlets ∞ Braised Beef
Spring Chicken ∞ Roast Quarter of Lamb ∞ Tongue
Roast Saddle of Mutton ∞ Ham and Peas

THIRD COURSE

Quails ∞ Roast Ducks ∞ Mayonnaise of Chicken ∞ Green Peas
Charlotte Russe ∞ Strawberries
Compote of Cherries ∞ Neopolitan Cakes ∞ Madeira Wine

intermediate dessert of cheese, butter, salad, raw celery, and the like; after which ale, sometimes thirty or forty years old, and so strong that when thrown on the fire it blazes like spirits, is handed about. The tablecloth is then removed: under it, at the best tables, is a finer cloth, upon which the dessert is set. At inferior ones, it is placed on the bare polished table. It consists of all sorts of hot-house fruits, which are here of the finest quality, Indian and native preserves, stomachic ginger, comfitures, and the like. Clean glasses are set before every guest, and, with the dessert plates and knives and forks, small fringed napkins are laid. Three decanters are usually placed before the master of the house, generally containing claret, port and sherry, or madeira. The host pushes these in stands, or in a little silver wagon on wheels, to his neighbour on the left. Every man pours out his own wine, and if a lady sits next him, also helps her; and so on till the circuit is made, when the same process begins again. Glass jugs filled with water happily enable foreigners to temper the brandy which forms so large a component part of English wines. After the dessert is set on, all the servants leave the room: if more is wanted the bell is rung, and the butler alone brings it in. The ladies sit a quarter of an hour longer, during which time sweet wines are sometimes served, then rise from the table. The men rise at the same time, one opens the door for them, and as soon as they are gone, draw closer together. . . . Every man is, however, at liberty to follow the ladies as soon as he likes, a liberty of which Count B. and I very quickly availed ourselves. We had the singular satisfaction of learning that this was in accordance with the latest mode, as much drinking is now 'unfashionable.'

The hallmark of these formal nineteenth-century dinners was the presentation of numerous food courses. As Captain Gronow related: "The menu of a grand dinner was thus composed: Mulligatawny or turtle soups were the first dishes placed before you; a little lower, the eye met with the familiar salmon at one end of the table, and the turbot, surrounded by smelts, at the other. The first course was sure to be followed by a saddle of mutton or a piece of roast beef; and then you could take your oath that fowls, tongue, and ham would as assuredly succeed as darkness after 5 days.

"Whilst these never-ending *pieces de resistance* were occupying the table, what were called French dishes (removes) were, for custom's sake, added to the solid abundance. . . . A prime difficulty to overcome was the placing on your fork, and finally in your mouth, some half-dozen different eatables which occupied your plate at the same time. For example, your plate would contain, say, a slice of turkey, a piece of stuffing, a sausage, pickles, a slice of tongue, cauliflower and potatoes. . . . The dessert, if for a dozen people, would cost at least as many pounds. The wines were chiefly port, sherry, and hock; claret and even Burgundy, being then designated 'poor, thin, washy stuff.' A perpetual thirst seemed to come over people, both men and women, as soon as they had tasted their soup; as from that moment everybody was taking wine with everybody else till the close of the dinner; and such wine as produced that class of cordiality which frequently wanders into stupefaction. How all this sort of eating and drinking ended was obvious, from the prevalence of gout, and the necessity of every one making the pillbox their constant bedroom companion.

"There was another custom in my young days which has luckily fallen into disuse. If one dined at any of the great houses in London, it was considered absolutely necessary to give a guinea to the butler on leaving the house."

An itemized list of the tremendous amount of supplies laid in by country house hosts in order to entertain their guests is preserved in *The History of Belvoir Castle*, written by the Reverend Irvin Eller in 1839: "Consumption of Wine and Ale, Wax lights, &c. from December, 1839, to April, 1840, or about eighteen weeks: Wine, 200 dozen; Ale, 70 Hogsheads; Wax lights, 2,330; Sperm-oil, 630 gallons. Dined at his Grace's table, 1,997 persons; in the steward's room, 2,421; in the servant's hall, nursery, and kitchen departments, including comers and goers, 11,312 persons. Of loaves of bread there were consumed 3,333; of meat, 22,963 lbs., exclusive of game. The quantity of game killed by his Grace and friends, and consumed at Belvoir Castle alone, was 2,589 head."

Conspicuous consumption was not confined to private homes alone. The menus for many public and official dinners have been recorded and present an amazing array of selections. Farington, February 26, 1804: "Mr. J. J. Angerstein's (City merchant and art collector) I dined at. We dined at 6 o'Clock. The dinner consisted of 2 courses viz: a fine Turbot at the top, a Sirloin of Beef at the bottom & vermicelli Soup in the middle, with small dishes making a figure of 9 dishes. The remove roast ducks at the top & a very fine roast Poulet at the bottom, macaroni, tartlets &c. &c. afterwards Parmesan & other cheese & Caviere [sic] with toast. Champagne & Madeira were served round during dinner. Mr. Angerstein gave us the Bulletin of the King's Health (George III) today, which expresses that a speedy recovery is not expected. From that it was concluded that a Regency would be formed."

Ashton, January 1, 1811: "General Grosvenor, Mayor of Chester, gave a dinner to his friends, and two hundred sat down. Here is the bill of fare: Sixteen tureens of turtle, eight boiled turkeys, three hams, four dishes of a la mode beef, five pigeon pies, three saddles of mutton, thirteen plum puddings, six dishes of murinade [sic] pork, eight

French pies, four roasted turkeys, eight dishes of rabbits, three legs of mutton, four geese, two fillets of veal, ten dishes of chickens, four dishes of veal surprise, three beef-steak pies, three dishes of sweet breads, six hares, six venison pasties, eight dishes of ducks, six oyster patties, six dishes of mutton casserole, six dishes of pig, six lemon puddings, eight dishes of haricoted mutton, four neat's tongues, three dishes of collared veal, and a round of beef.

Removes—Ten haunches of venison, ten necks of venison.

Sweets—Thirty salvers of whips and jellies, twenty moulds of jelly, forty moulds of *blanc mange*, tarts, cheese cakes, mince pies, puffs, &c., &c."

Dinner Service

At about ten minutes before dinner was to be served, a footman would have rung the dinner bell to alert the guests before carrying everything that might be wanted at dinner up from the kitchens and pantry. During the meal, the footman stood behind his master's or mistress's chair until after the soup and fish courses had been served. The butler then rang the dining room bell in order to alert the cook to have the removes, or side dishes, ready for the table. Should anyone's glass be empty at any point during the meal, the footman placed the glasses upon a tray and brought them to the butler for refilling.

Once the first course had been eaten, the butler gave the cook notice that the second course was wanted. An under footman would have been sent down to the kitchens for the next courses and would have brought them upstairs, placing them on a stand in the warming cupboard, located just outside of the dining room. While he was doing this, the butler, footmen and maids replaced the dirty plates, silver and glasses with new. After placing the second course before each diner, the butler removed the covers from the guests' plates, handing them to the footman, who took them away.

After the third course, and before the dessert was brought out, everything would have been removed from the table, including the tablecloth. The butler then placed the wines upon the table and an under butler or maid would have laid a plate and silverware at each place. Once the dessert had been served, the footman would have gone directly to the drawing room to stoke the fire and sweep the hearth. This was done in order to ready the room for the ladies, who removed themselves to the room to drink tea, while the gentlemen stayed behind in the dining room drinking port.

Planning the Dinner Party

From *The Habits of Good Society*: [The Hostess's] first duty is to send out her invitations in due time and proper form. With regard to the time, it is necessary, during the height of the London season, to send an invitation three weeks before the dinner party; but, in the quiet season of the year, or in the country, it is neither essential to do so, nor usual. These invitations should be properly sent by a servant, and not by the post, unless the distance be great."

And about dinner service: "Women wait more quietly but a butler who can care well and rapidly is indispensable. If, however, you have men servants, they should not be too many. A party of ten can be perfectly well served by two men and a butler, and, if there are more than these, they only get in the way of one another, or stand pompously by staring while you eat. Your servants should be well trained and instructed, and should obey every order given by the butler. A master or mistress should never speak to them at dinner, and they must be themselves as silent as trappists. They should wear light shoes that cannot creak, and if they have a napkin instead of gloves, you must see that their hands are perfectly clean. They should have their 'beats' like policemen, one beginning at a guest on his master's right and ending with the lady of the house, the other with the guest on his mistress's right ending with the master."

COUNTRY BALLS

From *Manners and Tone of Good Society* (London, 1879; written by "A Member of the Aristocracy"): "Nowhere is 'class' more brought into prominence than at a 'Country Ball,' where there is a recognized though unwritten law, which every one obeys, to infringe which would be a breach of etiquette, and argue a want of knowledge of the social code observed at Country balls, where each class has its own set, and where a member of the one set, would be foolish were he or she to attempt to invade another or higher set. Thus, a couple belonging to say the professional set, or strangers in the town attending the ball, would not take their places in a quadrille at the top of the ball-room—

which is always appropriated by the aristocratic element, head stewards, and titled patronesses—under risk of being mortified by some act of avoidance on the part of those whose set they had so indiscreetly invaded. The *vis-a-vis* under such circumstances would either silently walk away, or a gentleman would remark superciliously to the offending couple—'We have a *vis-a-vis,* thank you'—or make some such cutting speech. At some public balls a cord is drawn across the ball-room to render the upper end unassailable, but this extreme exclusiveness is not often resorted to, 'clique' and 'class' being thoroughly maintained without its aid.

"As contrast, we may look at the most exclusive dances of the upper classes, chief amongst them being those held at Almack's Assembly Rooms in London. During the Regency period, society was exclusive. One either belonged to it or did not; there was no middle ground, no circles which overlapped. If you did not go to Almack's you might yet be considered a very interesting, praiseworthy, well bred creature; but you could not claim to be in society. Therefore, everyone who aspired to status desired to be seen at Almack's. However, Almack's was even more exclusive, at times, than Court. Riff raff might go to Court; but they could not get to Almack's, whose portals were guarded by six turbanned ladies who comprised the Lady Patronesses, or the Committee. Dancing here began at eleven to the strains of Weippert's and Collinet's orchestra. The favourite dances being the Valse, or waltz, the Galop and the Quadrille, with particular favourites of this sort being *L'Eclair* and *La Tete de Bronze.* Favourite waltz's [sic] included those by Strauss by the thirties, as well as *Le Remede contre le Sommeil.*"

By the 1770s every English town of any size boasted an assembly room, which usually confined its schedule of concerts and dances to the summer months, until Brighton began a new trend with a winter season in the 1820s. Only at Bath did the season run for eight months. Summer seasons coincided with local race meets or hunts. Larger assemblies always had a master of ceremonies, who set the tone both in fashion and social conduct. Some assemblies had a committee of local ladies who served as governesses or patronesses. Light refreshments were served, with large sit-down suppers being held only to mark some important event, such as the king's birthday or a national celebration.

Assemblies provided the opportunity for social advancement and were the perfect venue for matchmaking. Likewise, visitors to the town were introduced into local society and careers could be furthered by fortuitous introduction. Assemblies in seaside or resort towns were naturally less select as far as the company they admitted.

Some assembly rooms were financed by subscription, with each important family in the town taking out shares in the building. These might also be known as subscription rooms. The grandest of these buildings contained marble floors, neoclassical columns, a gallery, huge chandeliers and many touches reminiscent of the Adam brothers. As select society built larger houses, they began to host an increased number of private balls and dances, and the assembly rooms lost their cachet after the 1840s, though many continued to offer entertainments until the 1870s.

The Habits of Good Society: "Public balls are not much frequented by people of good society, except in watering places and country towns. Even there a young lady should not be seen at more than two or three in the year. County balls, race balls and hunt balls are generally better than common subscription balls. Charity balls are an abominable anomaly. At public balls there are generally either three or four stewards on duty, or a professional master of ceremonies. These gentlemen, having made all the arrangements, order the dances, and have power to change them if desirable. They also undertake to present young men to ladies, but it must be understood that such an introduction is only available for one dance. It is better taste to ask the steward to introduce you simply to a partner, than to point out any lady in particular. He will probably then ask you if you have a choice, and if not, you may be certain he will take you to an established wallflower. Public balls are scarcely enjoyable unless you have your own party."

Farington, August 11, 1804: "I passed the morning in writing and reading and walking. In the evening we went to Ramsgate to the Assembly room, where Madame Bianchi sang several songs to a Piano forte & Meyer (Philip James) played on the Harp. At half past 9 the music was over. 7s. 6d. was paid by each person for admittance. A Ball then commenced. At Eleven we came away."

The lower classes attended public dances, such as those held at Enon Chapel, Clement's Lane, London, where two penny hops were regularly held and attracted patrons of both sexes and all ages. These dancers were most often accompanied by a fiddler, and a free-flowing quantity of liquor was consumed by all. The dances began at half past eight and ran until well after midnight. Between 1823 and 1842, Enon Chapel was an active church and twelve hundred souls were buried in its crypt. The church closed in 1842, when it was turned into a dance hall. The dance hall then used the advertising slogan "Enon Chapel—Dancing on the Dead." The chapel was purchased in 1848 by a surgeon who removed the bodies to the Norwood Cemetery. Popular dances at the Enon Chapel included jigs, country dances and the polka, which arrived in England in 1844.

Hosting a Ball

To host a truly successful ball could be the making of a member of the social elite. Weeks, sometimes months, of planning went into everything from invitations to decorations. Often, many balls were held on a single evening and a person might receive anywhere from two to six invitations for the same night. A gauge of one's standing might be the arrival time of guests. With so many balls to choose from, the less desirable were attended in quick succession early on, with the most socially significant and promising of the evening saved for last. Therefore, the later one's guests arrived, and stayed, at a ball, the more successful the host or hostess.

The Habits of Good Society: "In London, and during the season, if a ball is given as a formality, and the rooms are not large, it is better to give up the hope of comfortable dancing, and have the *renommee* of a crush. All the gentlemen who failed to get into the drawing-room, and all the young ladies whose dresses were hopelessly wrecked, will execrate, but still remember you, and it is something to be remembered in London, whether well or ill. So that when you have called your guests together as close as sheep in a fold, allowed them to take an hour to climb the stairs, and half an hour to get down again, given them a supper from Gunter's, with champagne of the quality which induced impudent Brummell to ask for 'some more of that cider; very good cider that,' you have done the notorious if not the agreeable thing.

"Your best plan, therefore, is to invite only one third more than your rooms will hold, for you may be sure that more than that number will disappoint you. The invitations should be sent out three weeks beforehand, and you need not expect answers, except from those who have an excuse for not accepting. The requisites for an agreeable ball are good ventilation, good arrangement, a good floor, good music, a good supper, and good company. Any sacrifice should be made to secure a refreshment room, if not a supper room, on the same floor as the ball-room, nothing being more trying to ladies' dresses than the crush down and up the stairs. A cloak room down stairs for the ladies, with one or two maids to assist them; a tea and coffee room, with at least two servants; and a hat room for gentlemen, are indispensable. If the ball is a large one, numbered tickets should be given for the cloaks and hats.

"Up stairs the colour and lighting of the rooms is essential. The ball-room especially should be that which has the lightest paper; and if there be dark curtains, particularly red ones, they must be taken down and replaced by light ones. The best colour for a ball-room is very pale yellow. Chandeliers are dangerous, and throw a downward shadow; at any rate, wax should always be replaced by globe lamps. A polished floor, whatever the wood, is always the best thing to dance on, and if you want to give a ball, and not only a crush, you should hire a man who, with a brush under one foot, and a slipper on the other, will dance over the floor for four or five hours, till you can almost see your face in it. Above all, take care that there is not bees' wax enough to blacken the ladies' shoes. Four musicians are enough for a private ball. If the room is not large, do away with the horn; the flageolet is less noisy, and marks the time quite as well. A piano and violin form the mainstay of the band; but if the room be large, a larger band may be introduced with great advantage. The dances should be arranged beforehand, and, for large balls, you should have printed a number of double cards, containing on the one side a list of the dances; on the other, blank spaces to be filled up by the names of partners. A small pencil should be attached to each card, which should be given to each guest in the cloak room. Every ball opens with a quadrille, followed by a waltz. The number of the dances varies generally from eighteen to twenty-four, supper making a break after the fourteenth dance. Let us suppose you have twenty-one dances; then seven of these should be quadrilles, three of which may be lancers. There should next be seven waltzes, four galops, a polka, a polka-mazurka and some other dance.

"The refreshments may be simple, comprising tea, lemonade, that detestable concoction called negus, iced sherbet, ices, wafers, cakes and bonbons. The Supper (quite separate from refreshments) hour in London is generally midnight, after which it goes on till the end of the ball. At a ball no one sits down to supper; at a small dance the ladies sit and the gentlemen stand behind them."

DANCING

Dances changed very little during the nineteenth century, with country dances, the quadrille, polka and waltz being the mainstays. The quadrille, once a somewhat rolicking dance, had become by the Regency period more sedate, the steps being merely walked through by the dancers. The waltz, when it first arrived in England from Germany in 1813, was frowned upon. Despite popular belief, it was not the "wickedness" of the quick steps that alarmed society, but the many quick turns and spins involved. It was thought that they would bring on dizziness and prove too much on the delicate female participants. When Queen Victoria gained the throne in 1837, she was hearty enough to dance the waltz, or valse, at most of her own balls, thus giving the steps her personal stamp of approval.

The Quadrille

The Habits of Good Society: "In the present day the art is much simplified, and if you can walk through a quadrille, and perform a polka, waltz, or galop, you may often dance a whole evening through. Of course, if you can add to these the Lancers, Schottische, and Polka Mazurka, you will have more variety. . . . The quadrille is pronounced to be essentially a conversational dance, but inasmuch as the figures are perpetually calling you away from your partner, the first necessity for dancing a quadrille is to be supplied with a fund of small talk. . . . The next point is to carry yourself upright. Steps, as the *chasser* of the quadrille is called, belong to a past age, and even ladies are now content to walk through a quadrille. To be graceful, however, a lady should hold her skirt out a little. Dancing masters find it convenient to introduce new figures, and the fashion of *La Trenise* and the *Grande Ronde* is repeatedly changing. It is therefore useful to know every way in which a figure may be danced, and to take your cue from the others.

"I do not attempt to deny that the quadrille, as now walked, is ridiculous; the figures, which might be graceful if performed in a lively manner, have entirely lost their spirit, and are become a burlesque of dancing; but, at the same time, it is a most valuable dance. Old and young, stout and thin, good dancers and bad, lazy and active, stupid and clever, married and single, can all join in it, and have not only an excuse and opportunity for *tete-a-tete* conversation, which is decidedly the easiest, but find encouragement in the music, and in some cases convenient breaks in the necessity of dancing."

From *The Quadrille and Cotillion Panorama*, by Thomas Wilson, London, 1818: "This fashionable species of Dancing is entirely of French origin, and only differs from the well-known Dance, the Cotillion, by leaving out the changes; being much shorter, and frequently composed of Figures that require but four Persons to their performance; as may be seen by the first set of French Quadrilles that were publicly danced in this country, viz. *Le Pantalon*, *L'Ete*, *La Poule*, and *La Trenise* neither of which require more than four persons in their performance."

Listed here are the steps used in quadrilles: *sissonne ballotté*, *chassé*, *coupé ballotte*, *jeté*, *balancé*, *assemblé*, *Rigadoon*, *glissade*, *emboîté*, *pas de basque*.

Formation of the Quadrille is as follows: Previous to each figure, there are eight bars of music to be played, during which it is customary for the gentleman to bow, first to his partner and then to the lady on his left, and the lady, at the same time, to curtsy to her partner and afterward to the gentleman on her right.

The Waltz

The Habits of Good Society: "The position is the most important point [in dancing the waltz]. The lady and gentleman before starting should stand exactly opposite to one another, quite upright, and not, as is so common in England, painfully close to one another. If the man's hand be placed where it should be, at the centre of the lady's waist, and not all round it, he will have as firm a hold and not be obliged to stoop, or bend to his right. . . . It is the gentleman's duty to steer, and in crowded rooms nothing is more trying. He must keep his eyes open and turn them in every direction, if he would not risk a collision and the chance of a fall, or what is as bad, the infliction of a wound on his partner's arm. The consequences of violent dancing may be really serious. Not only do delicate girls bring on thereby a violent palpitation of the heart, and their partners appear in a most disagreeable condition of solution, but dangerous falls ensue from it."

TERMS USED BY THE CALLER IN COUNTRY DANCES

Brisé—to cast round, or turn around another person, or by one's self.
Dance address: to perform a set step, as the ballotté or *pas et basque.*
Olevettes—to *interchassé,* as in a reel of three, with three persons on one side of the choir, and employ as much time in doing it, as in right and left.
Moulinet—to cross right hands with contrary partners, and pass round half of a circle and cross left hands, and pass back again to your places.

The Polka or Galop

Performance of the polka or galop from *The Ball Room Dancing Annual,* London, 1844: "The Polka is a *danse a deux,* commencing at pleasure, couples following each other adopting any of the figures, but returning occasionally to the first. In dancing La Polka, there should be no stamping of the heels or toe; this may be tolerated at a Bohemian *auberge,* it is inadmissible into the salons of London or Paris. The Polka should be played not quite so fast as the Galop.

"Before commencing the figure, there is a short introduction, consisting of four bars, danced thus: leading your partner to her place in the circle, placing yourself *vis-a-vis* you then take the lady's left hand in your right, making the first step four times; first forward, then backward, forward again, then backward, taking care to gain ground in the forward steps, then commence with the first figure."

OTHER ENTERTAINMENTS

The aristocracy had no shortage of diversions. In addition to evening entertainments and weekend visits, other popular gatherings included receptions, musicales, breakfasts and the simple drinking of tea. Every occasion was a cause for issuing invitations, purchasing and wearing the appropriate dress and, most importantly, making further social contacts.

The Habits of Good Society: "Town parties consist of conversations, private concerts, private theatricals, tea parties and matinees. The first, which also go by the names of Receptions and 'At Homes,' have for principal object conversation only, so that in the selection of guests youth and beauty are less considered than talent, distinction and fashion. The invitations should be sent out from a week to a fortnight beforehand. Tea must be served in a separate room, to which the guests are first conducted, and ices handed at short intervals throughout the evening. The hour for meeting is between nine and ten, and the party breaks up before one in the morning. The lady and gentleman of the house both receive guests, somewhere near the door. Two or three rooms must be thrown open, curiosities, good engravings, handsome books, rare miniatures, old china, photographs, stereoscopes, and so forth, laid out gracefully on the tables, and a liberal supply of ottomans and sofas placed about in convenient positions. In the larger receptions gentlemen should not sit down, and, above all, not linger close to the door but come forward and talk sense—not ball-room chit chat—to such people as they happen to know. Introductions are not here the order of the day, as they must be in balls, but the lady of the house will take care to introduce gentlemen to such ladies as seem to have none to talk to.

"Private concerts and amateur theatricals ought to be very good to be successful. Professionals alone should be engaged for the former, none but real amateurs for the latter. Both ought to be, but rarely are, followed by a supper, since they are generally very fatiguing, if not positively trying. In any case, refreshments and ices should be handed between the songs and acts. Private concerts are often given in the 'morning,' that is, from two to six P.M., in the evening their hours are from eight to eleven. The rooms should be arranged in the same manner as for a reception, the guests should be seated, and as music is the avowed object, a general silence preserved while it lasts.

"The tea party is a much more social affair, and may vary in the number of guests from ten to thirty. The lighting is by ordinary lamps and candles; two rooms suffice, and tea should be either handed or set out on a side table in one of them. The guests should be chiefly of one set, and known to one another. The ladies all sit down, and so may the gentlemen if they like, which they are, poor things, almost forbidden to do at receptions. The entertainment consists mostly of music and singing, by ladies and gentlemen present, but sometimes a few round games are got up.

"The 'matinee' requires three things to make it successful, good grounds, a good band, and good weather. Money can command the first two, but, as we have no check over the clerk of the weather, 'matinees' are as well left alone in towns, where people will dress exorbitantly for everything of this kind. The company should be very numerous, comprising all the best dressed people you know, for dress is everything on these occasions. In addition to a good brass band, you would do well to obtain the services of a glee club to sing in the open air between instrumental pieces. You invite your guests for one o'clock, they arrive at two, and disperse in time to dress for dinner. They content themselves with walking about, listening to the music, taking refreshments, or if you give it them, a lunch, in the large marquee, which, of course, you have erected on the lawn."

Breakfasts

Breakfasts were popular entertainments during the early part of the century. Why these should have been called breakfasts remains a mystery, for they very rarely began before one o'clock in the afternoon. On July 6, 1807, Lady Sarah wrote from Spencer House, London, about a breakfast her family had given and to which were invited eight hundred guests: "Very few people arrived before three, but when they did come it was the prettiest sight I ever saw, I think. The numbers of people dressed in brilliant colours, wandering out under trees and on the lawn and in the portico, the sound of the different bands of music, the extreme beauty of the place, which had put on its best looks, the profusion of roses and pinks in every part of the house and about it, and the sincere pleasure one saw in every countenance, made it quite a delightful thing. Every creature was, I believe, equally delighted with it; nobody left us till six or seven o'clock, and all were not gone till nine. . . . While we were watching the country dances on the west side of the house, the Duke of Cambridge and Lady Charlotte Campbell and two more people began waltzing on the other, to the great admiration of everybody."

Farington, August 22, 1804: "At one o'Clock went in the Chaise with Miss Glover to Dandelion (a village to the south of Westgate-on-Sea) to a public Breakfast. . . . There was much company, who breakfasted in boxes, & at long tables on one side of a space of ground like a bowling green. A stage for dancing was also laid and a small band of music in the circular orchestra. Several young people and Children danced under the direction of Mr. Le Bas, Master of the Ceremonies at Margate & Ramsgate. . . . There was much fashionable company. The dance was made up of a very mixed party, many Citizens Children being of the number, & it was agreeable to see the different ranks partaking of the amusement."

BIBLIOGRAPHY

Aldrich, Elizabeth. *From the Ballroom to Hell: Grace and Folly in Nineteenth-Century Dance.* Evanston, Ill.: Northwestern University Press, 1991.

Escott, Thomas H.S. *Society in the Country House.* London: T. Fisher Unwin, 1907.

Freeman, John. *Victorian Entertaining.* Philadelphia: Running Press, 1989.

Girouard, Mark. *Life in the English Country House: A Social and Architectural History.* New York: Viking Penguin, 1980.

————. *A Country House Companion.* New Haven: Yale University Press, 1987.

————. *The Victorian Country House.* New Haven: Yale University Press, 1985.

Horn, Pamela. *Ladies of the Manor: Wives and Daughters in Country-House Society, 1830–1918.* Gloucestershire: Alan Sutton Publishing, 1989.

Keller, Kate Van Winkle. *The Playford Ball: 103 Early English Country Dances, 1651–1820.* Chicago: Chicago Review, 1990.

Lowe, Joseph. *A New Most Excellent Dancing Master.* Stuyvesant, N.Y.: Pendragon Press, 1992.

Margetson, Stella. *Victorian High Society.* New York: Holmes & Meier, 1980.

Roberts, Robert. *Roberts' Guide for Butlers and Household Staff.* Bedford: Applewood Books, 1988.

Vince, John. *The Country House: How It Worked.* London: John Murray, Ltd., 1991.

CHAPTER SIXTEEN

Mourning

Family values were a mainstay of the nineteenth century, and these are evidenced best in the mourning practices of the period. While the dead were revered in prior centuries, it was during the Victorian period especially that funerals and remembrance of departed loved ones became a near obsession. Mourning warehouses, large shops that sold everything needed for funerals and mourning, sprang into being and catered to the needs of the newly bereaved. Large, showy funerals became the norm, and mourners followed prescribed rules for the length of mourning various relatives and members of the royal court. Widows, more than anyone else, held to strict patterns of mourning, going through three distinct stages, including full or deep mourning, half mourning and, finally, slight mourning. The degree of black worn and the absence of such things as jewelry and dress decoration lessened with each of these stages. However, considering the mortality rate during the period, it is not surprising that many men and women spent most of the year wearing one degree or another of mourning dress, and that many complained of the inconvenience. Still, with Queen Victoria's penchant for the strict adherence to mourning rituals, nineteenth-century society continued to follow her lead.

MOURNING DRESS

During the first year of mourning, widows were to conduct themselves as veritable social outcasts, forced to refuse all invitations, the only visits permitted being to close relatives or church services, including weddings and christenings. Further, once the initial mourning period had ended, a lady might very well be plunged right back into deepest black by the death of another relative or by state or court mourning. It is important to bear in mind how much impact the ritual of mourning had on fashions during this period. In addition, a wife always wore mourning attire for her husband's relatives, exactly as she did for her own. A lady also wore mourning dress when an in-law of her married child died, donning black for six weeks, without crepe. It was further customary when a man had married for a second time after the death of his first wife that the new wife wear slight mourning fashions for three months upon the death of a parent of the first wife.

APPROPRIATE MOURNING ATTIRE, CIRCA 1875

Parent or Child	Twelve months, six in paramatta with crepe trim, three months in black, three in half mourning
Sibling	Six months, three in crepe, three in black
Aunt or Uncle	Three months in black
First Cousin	Six weeks in black

In 1876, a widow's dress might have been made of paramatta, entirely covered in crepe to within an inch or so of the waist. For the first nine months of mourning, the waist had no tucks, after which two tucks could be taken in the crepe. The bodice was entirely covered with crepe, deep lawn cuffs and collar and a cap à la Mary Stuart. A mantle of paramatta with crepe was worn, the bonnet made entirely of crepe, with a widow's cap inside and a veil with a deep hem. This dress was worn for a year and a day, when the widow "slighted" her mourning and adopted instead a dress of black silk, heavily trimmed with crepe, for an additional six months, after which the crepe was lessened and jet jewelry (see "Mourning Jewelry," p. 214) was permitted. After eighteen months of mourning, crepe was omitted altogether, and after two years, the usual fashionable colors of dress might be worn, although it was considered far better taste to wear half mourning for at least six months more, with many widows never again wearing any color save black.

Mourning costume (Ackermann's Costume Plates)

For both men and women, the mourning dress was to be made from dull, matte black cloth, usually broadcloth, crepe or paramatta. Because the mourning period consisted of three distinct stages, each calling for new dress allowances as mourning lessened, it was quite costly to outfit all immediate family members, not to mention servants, as the following list of items considered essential for a widow in 1881 illustrates.

- 1 best dress of paramatta covered entirely with crepe
- 1 dress, either a costume of Cyprus crepe, or an old black dress covered in rainproof crepe
- 1 paramatta mantle lined with silk, deeply trimmed with crepe

- 1 warmer jacket of cloth lined and trimmed with crepe
- 1 bonnet of best silk crepe, with long veil
- 1 bonnet of rainproof crepe, with crepe veil
- 12 collars and cuffs of muslin or lawn, with deep hems
- 1 black-stuff petticoat
- 4 pairs black hose, either silk, cashmere or spun silk
- 12 handkerchiefs with black borders, cambric, for ordinary use
- 12 of finer cambric for better occasions
- muff of paramatta trimmed with crepe
- Summer parasol of silk, deeply trimmed with crepe, but no lace or fringe for the first year

Note: Furs are not admissible in a widow's first mourning wardrobe, though very dark sealskin and astrakhan can be worn when the dress is changed.

Mourning costs could be defrayed by dying existing clothing black, a centuries-old practice. One could take the clothes to a professional dyer, or attempt dying it herself by using Indian logwood. It was not only the private citizen who resorted to hastily dying existing items upon a sudden death. In 1901, the London firm of Dickens & Jones was busy filling its shop windows with white household linen of every description when Queen Victoria died. A report of their dilemma: "The day Queen Victoria died was the eve of the White Sales. By the next morning, everything was turned to black. Everything that could be dyed was used to meet the colossal demand."

By 1892, half-mourning costumes might have been of woollen velvet, with violet grounds striped by thick lines of gray, white or black. By this time, there had been a general stand made against the use of so much crepe by the ladies of London, and it was the princess of Wales herself who dealt crepe the coup de grâce by dispensing with it entirely during her mourning for the duke of Clarence.

MOURNING JEWELRY

The jewelry worn by bereaved family members directly coincided with the depth of mourning. In deepest mourning, a dull finish was expected; some opted to dispense with jewelry altogether. From the early 1700s onward, jewelry was designed to be taken apart and worn in various ways, such as being mounted on a black background for mourning. During half mourning, diamonds, amethysts and pearls could be worn, with pearls being the most favored. They were made into large, teardrop earrings, crosses and rope necklaces. Jet jewelry has been associated with mourning for some time, though it was not mass-produced before the early nineteenth century. Jet is made from the fossilized driftwood of the monkey puzzle tree and is also found in the form of slate. In its natural state, it is dull in appearance, but, once polished takes on a brilliant sheen. In England, jet was mined in the town of Whitby.

The wearing of jet by widows became de rigueur after Queen Victoria wore it upon the death of Prince Albert in 1861 and continued to wear it until her own death in 1901. By the second half of the nineteenth century, ebonite, bulcanite and early forms of plastic were used in mourning jewelry, as was a black, cut glass called French jet. Jewelry made from the hair of the deceased was popular from 1790 to 1840, and this, too, was incorporated into mourning jewelry, being given settings of black or white enamel, jet and gold, and often embellished with the words "In Memorium." By 1884, diamond ornaments set into black enamel were allowed, even in deepest mourning. At Queen Victoria's death in 1901, The Parisian Diamond Company of New Bond Street advertised pearls and diamonds for mourning, with pieces including hair combs, choker necklaces, bracelets and ropes of pearls.

Special mourning stationery and seals, black sealing wax and visiting cards edged in black were to be used only when mourning crepe was worn, meaning that these would not be used by grieving aunts, uncles and like relations. The black edges on writing paper and envelopes gradually thinned as the degree of mourning lessened. The handkerchiefs used by widows were white, bordered in black, the width of which was narrowed during the final stages of mourning. Handkerchiefs used by Queen Victoria were of white lawn, decorated with black and white tears and the initials V.R. (Victoria Regina).

CHILDREN'S AND SERVANTS' MOURNING

The same rituals that applied to the funerals of adults also applied to those of children. The exceptions were that all accessories of dress and the coffin were white. Undertakers' mutes, feathermen and coachmen wore white shoulder sashes, carried white wands and wore white crepe hat weepers. Weepers were long scarves, about three yards long, that represented the mourning cloaks of previous centuries. Black horses were outfitted with white ostrich plumes and white saddle fittings. Male mourners wore white gloves, with white crepe weepers, and were often given white neck scarves. Parents mourned the death of a child for a period of one year. In a Harrod's catalog of 1900, a child's funeral was advertised as costing from two pounds, ten shillings, according to "age and appointments."

It was a common practice for children to attend family funerals. They were put into mourning clothes and made to observe the same periods of mourning as their parents. Upon the death of a parent, mourning lasted twelve months, the first six in dull black with heavy crepe, the next three months wearing black silk without crepe and the final three months in half-mourning colors. Even babies were clad in white robes that were trimmed with both black embroidery and ribbon.

Young ladies who became brides while still in mourning wore black or gray on their wedding days. By the Victorian period, wedding guests who were in mourning were allowed to dispense with black for the day and wear half-mourning attire of gray or purple instead. A widow attending the wedding of her child was permitted to wear a dress of some deep red shade, rather than black or half mourning.

By the latter nineteenth century, simple black dresses with bonnets, collars and cuffs of crepe were worn by female servants in the employ of a bereaved family, and during half mourning, the trimmings were white. Male servants wore black suits, sans shiny buttons, suitable ties and armbands, with white weeper cuffs. All servants were given two sets of mourning clothes, one to work in, the other to be worn on Sundays and reception days, with this second black uniform made of better quality fabric. For at least eight years after the death of Prince Albert, royal servants continued to wear black crepe armbands upon the instruction of Queen Victoria.

THE BUSINESS OF MOURNING

By the early 1800s, ladies' magazines regularly featured fashion plates depicting proper funeral attire, along with articles detailing proper etiquette for the occasion, with court and aristocratic mourning dress and behavior setting the standard. It was common practice for linen drapers shops to offer a mourning department, and many larger drapers shops also conducted an undertaker's business. One of the first categories of clothing to be mass-produced was mourning clothes. The deep bands of mourning crepe, crepe collars and cuffs were supplied by milliners, as were widows' caps. These were being mass-produced by 1842, but mourning dresses remained the bane of dressmakers, who had to fit, cut, sew and complete them on extremely short notice. Before the opening of mourning warehouses, full mourning dress could not be donned for eight days after a death took place, as it took that long, at least, to make up the required clothing.

A man named Gabriel Douce had a shop in New Round Court circa 1762 from where he sold "all sorts of silk stuffs, Norwich crepes, camletts, and all sorts of black silks for hoods and scarves at reasonable prices," but the supply of funeral garments on a large scale did not occur until the nineteenth century. Firms began to specialize in funeral wear, with one of the best known being Jay's Mourning Warehouse, at Nos. 247, 248 and 249 Regent Street, London, founded by William Chickall Jay in 1841. The workroom there maintained a staff of several hundred people, and the warehouse was able to make up a quantity of stock mourning clothes, constructing dresses ahead of time and leaving only the bodice to be fitted to the individual customer later.

To gain some insight into exactly what Jay's offered, and on what scale, we can refer to Henry Mayhew's personal observations, taken from his 1865 work, *The Shops and Companies of London*: "After gazing for some time at the tastefully arranged window, and inspecting the variety of mourning garb there exhibited, let us walk inside. Here we are once more struck with the total 'unshoppiness' of the place. . . . We wander into another department, and here we see a wonderful assemblage of caps, which seem to range in density from the frosted spider-web to the petrified 'trifle.' We observed one widow's cap which was a marvel: this wonder was under a glass-case; for it was as light in texture as thistle-down, with long streamers like fairies' wings. . . . Boxes taken from their shelves reveal collars of white crepe, of black crepe, of tulle and of muslin, collars dotted with black and edged in black."

Other mourning warehouses soon opened, including Pugh's in 1849 at No. 173 Regent Street, the premises that were formerly the Argyll Rooms. The savvy Pugh brothers advertised their wares in the death columns of the city's newspapers and issued a book entitled *Mourning Etiquette*, available free of charge to the recently bereaved. The firm that was the greatest competition to Jay's was Peter Robinson's, which opened as a Court and General mourning warehouse at Nos. 256, 258, 260 and 262 Regent Street. In order to distinguish this specialized branch from Robinson's main shop, at No. 103 Oxford Street, the Mourning Warehouse became commonly known as "Black Peter Robinson's." By the late nineteenth century, Harrod's, too, was supplying funerals and all the necessary trappings of mourning.

Because etiquette decreed that widows and daughters of the newly deceased not be seen out of doors before the funeral, these mourning warehouses had employees who visited the ladies in their homes. Black Peter Robinson's kept a brougham ready harnessed in order that it might set off for a customer's house at a moment's notice. The coachman was dressed in black from head to foot, with crepe hat and armbands, his whip decorated with flying black bows. Two lady fitters, also black clad, rode inside the coach, their pattern books in hand. When put into storage, mourning dresses were placed in boxes that were lined with papers registered by Wellington Williams, which depicted appropriate mourning motifs, such as hearses, tombstones and angels.

Undertakers supplied all the accoutrements necessary for mourning, including the dispatch of two mutes, who were immediately posted outside the front door of a family's home when notified of a death. Dressed in black coats, sashes and top hats with weepers, they were chosen especially for their glum expressions, and also walked in funeral processions, carrying draped wands symbolizing the family's grief. The mutes were followed by the undertaker's feathermen, one to four men who carried large, black ostrich plumes, an eighteenth-century custom. Horses were also provided, sometimes being dyed black and given glossy, false tails, and they wore black velvet caparisons with black harnesses trimmed in silver. Black plumes were mounted between their ears, with black rosettes worn on the forehead. Sometimes the funeral procession traveled considerable distances, in which case stops were made along the way for refreshment of both man and beast, the bereaved family being billed for the costs.

A.R. Bennet's description of the undertaker's business, from his work *London and Londoners in the 1850s and 1860s,* provides us with a contemporary account of the nineteenth-century mourning ritual: "As soon as a death occurred in a house, the entire household, including the servants, went into deepest mourning. The house blinds were drawn, the clocks stopped and the mirrors covered to prevent the decedent's spirit from becoming trapped inside them. Whilst it was considered unwise to ever lock the door of a room containing a corpse, in

MOURNING FABRICS

(Date fabric was first used)

Alamode	Lightweight silk (17c)
Albert Crepe	Fine-quality black silk crepe (19c)
Alpaca	Fine, soft wool (19c)
Barathea	Silk and worsted fabric (19c)
Barpour	Twilled wool and silk mix used for trimmings on Victorian mourning clothes (19c)
Black Chambray	Almost trasparent black silk warp and cotton (18c)
Black Taffety	Crisp silk with a fine rib (18c)
Bombazet	Plain, twilled cotton and worsted mix, chiefly used for the cheaper mourning clothes of servants (18c)
Bombazine	Medium-weight black silk and wool blend (18c)
Broadcloth	Plain, heavy wool with napped finish (17c)
Coburg	Wool and cotton twilled fabric (19c)
Crepe	Lightweight, semitransparent black silk; imported to Britain since before 1690; often crimped into three-dimensional patterns (17c)
Crepe de Chine	Lightweight silk or silk and worsted fabric (19c)
Foulard Silk	Thin, lightweight silk with a twilled finish, popular with Edwardians (19c)
Grosgrain	Heavily corded black silk (19c)
Gray Tabby	Medium-weight silk with a fine rib (18c)
Holland	Fine, white linen lawn (17c)
Italian Lustering	Fine, crisp white silk (18c)
Looking Glass Silk	Glacé silk with a shiny surface (19c)
Mantua	Medium-weight silk (17c)
Merino	Fine-quality wool fabric (19c)
Muslin	Finely woven, lightweight cotton (17c)

Norwich Crepe	Silk warp and woollen weft fabric (17c)
Serge	Twilled worsted, later a twilled woven silk, with a cheaper version available in cotton (17c)
Stormont Cotton	Medium-weight cotton, printed in tiny, repeat designs on gray or mauve (18c)
Tabby	Fine silk-like taffeta with a watered finish (17c)
Twilled Sarcenet	Very lightweight, finely ribbed black silk (18c)

case the spirit became trapped inside, the body was never to be left alone between the time of death and burial and was watched over at all times. Candles were kept burning near the corpse and a plate of salt was sometimes placed on its chest to both delay corruption and ward off evil. It was considered the height of bad manners for any visitor to the house not to at least view the body, no matter how casual the acquaintance. In order to allow the body to lie in peace and the family to remain undisturbed in their grief, a thick layer of straw was laid on the street and sidewalk outside the house to muffle the sound of traffic, as was also done when a person who lived in the house was seriously ill."

When a peer or other worthy died while in residence at his country estate, his funeral was preceded by the lying in state of the body. Tenants, neighbors, tradesmen and others filed past the coffin, sometimes by the hundreds, and at the funeral, once the coffin was placed into the grave, the family's upper servants symbolically broke their staffs of office and threw them down upon the coffin. Before the casket lid was lowered, coins were placed over the eyes or in the hand of the deceased. An ancient custom, the coins were meant as payment to the ferryman of the river of death. Due to the presence of grave robbers, some families hired the services of a watcher, who remained by the grave to deter thefts of both the body and its possessions.

BURIAL

Although the practice of cremation had been in existence among certain races and religions for centuries, it was not used in England until 1874, when Queen Victoria's surgeon, Sir Henry Thompson, published his book *Cremation: The Treatment of the Body After Death.* Because of the overcrowded conditions of London cemeteries, cremations became a viable option, with Thompson organizing The Cremation Society of England. Embalming had also been successfully performed for centuries, its modern use brought about in the 1600s by English physiologist and discoverer of the circulatory system, William Harvey. Even so, embalming was not much used for another hundred years, and even then was not a common practice.

In rural communities, the ringing of a "passing bell" in the parish church signaled that someone lay on his or her deathbed. The bell tolled six times for a woman, nine for a man, followed by a peal for each year of the dying person's life. When the body was later brought to the grave for burial, an additional toll, the death knell, was sounded to inform the parish that the deceased had been safely laid to rest. If the deceased had committed suicide, the body was required by law to be buried at a crossroads until 1823, with a stake driven through the heart to prevent the ghost from walking. Until 1870, all of a suicide's personal possessions were forfeited to the crown, and until 1832, the law required that the body be buried only at night, between the hours of nine and midnight, with no service being said over the body.

The wealthy ensured that their graves would remain untouched by robbers and kept in repair by bequeathing an annual distribution of alms at or near the actual site of the grave. A form of charity as well, the distributions were intended to be regular reenactments of the lavish alms dispersals customary at aristocratic burials. Additionally, a "month's mind" could be held one month after burial, at which further alms were distributed, with a feast held afterward. It was believed that with so much charity being distributed, and with so much traffic round the gravesite, thieves would be loathe to attempt to rob the site.

The final, and perhaps most lasting, tribute placed upon an aristocratic grave was the tombstone. The most fashionable place to secure such an item, until well into the Edwardian period, was located in Regent Street, at the corner of Air Street. Augustus Sala comments on a visit to the shop in his 1859 work, *Twice Round the Clock*: "Then there was the funeral monument shop, with the mural tablets, the obelisks, the broken columns, the extinguished torches, and the draped urns in the window, and some with the inscriptions into the bargain, all ready engraved in black and white, puzzling us as to whether the tender husbands, devoted wives, and affectionate sons, to whom they referred, were buried in that grisly shop—it had a pleasant, fascinating terror about it, like an undertaker's, too.''

Funerals were of great importance to the working classes, who saw the lack of proper funerals with all the trimmings for their loved ones as a social stigma. In order to provide such a service, workers regularly contributed a sum each week to an insurance fund that paid for funeral expenses. There were also assurance companies who specialized in life insurance for adults and children and whose premiums were used for funeral expenses. The Prudential, founded in 1854, was the most successful of these companies, and by the 1870s had over a million subscribers.

The Victorians kept mourning mementos of all sorts. Especially popular were the postcards issued to commemorate the passing of royalty. The three examples here were issued upon the death of King Edward VII and include (1) a photo of the late king in death, taken by command of his wife, Queen Alexandra; (2) a photo of the king's body lying in state at Westminster Hall; and (3) a memorial card bearing the king's likeness and issued by Raphael Tuck and Sons, one of the largest postcard firms of the day.

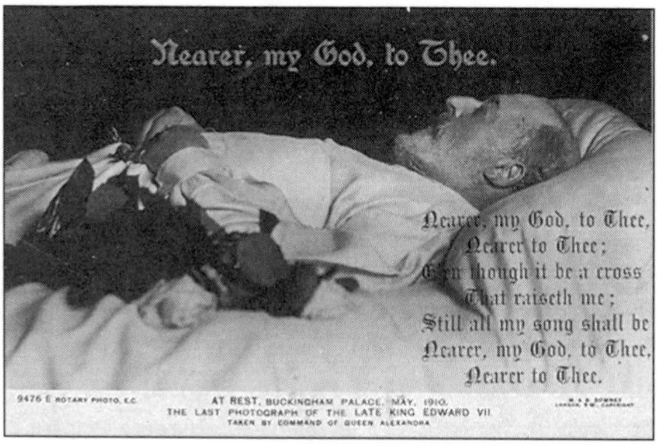

COURT MOURNING

Court mourning dress was worn by those persons with direct court connections. While commoners also donned mourning attire upon the death of a member of the royal family, their mourning was termed "general." The duration of court and national mourning varied according to the nearness of the deceased to the sovereign, both in geographical sense and relationship. When the queen of Hanover, Queen

Victoria's aunt, died in 1841, mourning lasted only twenty-one days, with the degree being lessened after the first two weeks.

When the court was in mourning, ladies attending a state ball were advised to consult the official notice relating to mourning dress, which appeared in *The Gazette*. Gentlemen wore crepe on the left arm, in addition to the display of mourning evident in their dress. Should a gentleman have forgotten his armband, one was supplied to him at the cloak room within the palace. It was also imperative that this armband be worn at all state concerts or levees.

By the 1880s, the length of mourning was twelve weeks for a monarch, six weeks for the death of the child of the sovereign, three weeks for a monarch's sibling, two weeks for a nephew, niece, uncle or aunt and ten days for the first cousins of the royal family. Rules for court mourning dress provided that all clothing should be black. Bombazine dresses were trimmed with black crepe, crepe fans were carried and no jewelry was worn. Second mourning consisted of black silk dresses trimmed in fringed or plain linen, white gloves, black or white shoes and the wearing of fans, tippets, white necklaces and earrings was permissible.

For men, first court mourning fashion consisted of black woollen suits with black buttons, plain muslin or lawn cravats in black, black wool stockings, shammy shoes, gloves, a crepe hatband and special black swords and shoe buckles. For second mourning, a gentleman could add fringed linen to his various articles of clothing. The color purple was only to be used at royal funerals, while softer shades of mauve have been the official color for half mourning at court since the eighteenth century. State funerals, those for dignitaries other than royalty, were also quite elaborate and dignified affairs. To this day, the largest state funeral ever held in England was that of the duke of Wellington in 1852, with a million and a half mourners attending the ceremony, and commemorative souvenirs of all types being produced for the occasion. Wellington's body lay in state at Chelsea Army Hospital November 10–17. So great were the crowds filing past that two persons were killed in the crush. The centuries-old tradition of the dead man's riderless horse following his coffin was observed, with Wellington's charger walking behind the funeral car, the duke's riding boots (made by the royal bootmaker, Hoby) having been placed, reversed, in the stirrups.

The following passage from Lady Sarah provides some idea of the extent to which the public entered into national mourning. Spencer House, November 8, 1810: "It will be a dismal sight next week, for the death of Princess Amelia [daughter of George III] has put everybody in the deepest mourning. When I say everybody, I mean it literally. All tradespeople, workpeople, servants out of livery, every creature who can scrape up money to buy a black rag, will mourn. All the shops are full of black. In short, it is quite an odd look it gives London."

BIBLIOGRAPHY

Bland, Olivia. *The Royal Way of Death.* London: Constable, 1986.

Culbertson, Judi. *Permanent Londoners: An Illustrated Guide to the Cemeteries of London.* Post Mills, Vt.: Chelsea Green Publishing Co., 1990.

Cunnington, Phyllis. *Costume for Burials, Marriages and Deaths.* London: A. & C. Black, 1972.

Gittings, C. *Death, Burial, and the Individual in Early Modern England.* London: Croom Helm, 1984.

Jerrold, Clare. *The Widowhood of Queen Victoria.* London: E. Nash, 1916.

May, Trevor. *The Victorian Undertaker.* Princes Risborough: Shire Books, 1996.

Morley, John. *Death, Heaven and the Victorians.* London: Studio Vista, 1971.

Puckle, Bertram. *Funeral Customs: Their Origin and Development.* Detroit: Omnigraphics, 1990.

Stern, Marvin. *Thorns and Briars: Bonding, Love and Death 1764–1970.* New York: Foundation of Thanatology, 1991.

Taylor, Lou. *Mourning Dress: A Costume and Social History.* London: Allen & Unwin, 1983.

Walker, George A. *Gatherings From Graveyards, Particularly Those of London: With a Concise History of the Modes of Interment Among Different Nations From the Earliest Periods.* North Stratford: Ayer Company Publishers, 1977.

APPENDIX

Bibliography

Ackroyd, Peter. *Dickens' London: An Imaginative Vision.* London: Headline, 1987.

Alexander, Sally. *Women's Work in Nineteenth-Century London: A Study of the Years 1820–50.* London: Journeyman Press, 1983.

Allen, Eleanor. *Victorian Children.* Chester Springs, Penn.: Dufour, 1979.

Altick, Richard D. *The Shows of London: A Panoramic History of Exhibitions 1600–1862.* Cambridge, Mass.: Harvard University Press, 1978.

Anderson, Patricia. *The Printed Image and the Transformation of Popular Culture, 1790–1860.* Oxford: Clarendon Press, 1994.

Armitage, Gilbert. *The History of the Bow Street Runners, 1729–1829.* London: Wishart, 1932.

Ashton, John. *The Dawn of the Nineteenth Century in England.* Detroit: Gale Research, 1968.

———. *Social England Under the Regency.* Vol. 1. Boston: Charles River Books, 1976.

———. *When William IV Was King.* Detroit: Singing Tree Press, 1968.

Ashworth, William. *An Economic History of England, 1870–1939.* London: Methuen, 1960.

Aspinall, A., ed. *The Correspondence of George, Prince of Wales, 1770–1812.* 8 vols. London: Cassell, 1963.

———. *The Letters of King George IV, 1812–1830.* 3 vols. Cambridge: The University Press, 1938.

———. *Letters of the Princess Charlotte, 1811–1817.* London: Home & Van Thel, 1949.

Barker, T.C. *A History of London Transport.* London: Allen & Unwin, 1975.

Barrell, John. *The Dark Side of the Landscape: The Rural Poor in English Painting 1730–1840.* Cambridge: Cambridge University Press, 1980.

Bayly, C.A., ed. *The Raj: India and the British, 1600–1947.* London: National Portrait Gallery Publications, 1990.

Beeton, Isabella. *A Victorian Alphabet of Everyday Recipes.* Boston: Bullfinch Press Book, 1993.

Bell, Aldon D. *London in the Age of Dickens.* Norman: University of Oklahoma Press, 1967.

Bellringer, Alan, ed. *The Victorian Age in Prose.* Atlantic Highlands: Humanities Press International, Inc., 1988.

Benson, E.F. *As We Were: A Victorian Peep Show.* North Pomfret: Trafalgar Square, 1986.

Birley, Derek. *Land of Sport and Glory: Sport and British Society, 1887–1910.* Manchester: Manchester University Press, 1995.

Blunt, Wilfrid. *The Ark in the Park: The Zoo in the Nineteenth Century.* London: Hamilton, 1976.

Borer, Mary C. *The British Hotel Through the Ages.* Guildford: Lutterworth Press, 1972.

———. *An Illustrated Guide to London, 1800.* New York: St. Martin's Press, 1988.

Bosanquet, Helen Dendy. *Social Work in London, 1869–1912.* London: John Murray, Ltd., 1914.

Boulton, William. *The Amusements of Old London.* North Stratford: Ayer Company Publishers, Inc., 1969.

Bourke, Algernon. *The History of White's.* 2 vols. London: Waterlow & Sons, 1892.

Briggs, Asa, and Archie Miles. *A Victorian Portrait: Victorian Life and Values as Seen Through the Work of Studio Photographers.* New York: Harper & Row, 1989.

Bushaway, B. *By Rite: Custom, Ceremony and Community in England, 1700–1880.* London: Junction Books, 1983.

Caine, Barbara. *Victorian Feminists.* Oxford: Oxford University Press, 1993.

Calloway, Stephen. *The Victorian Catalogue of Household Furnishings.* London: Studio Editions, 1994.

Cannadine, David. *Lords and Landlords: The Aristrocracy and the Towns, 1774–1967.* Leicester: Leicester University Press, 1980.

———. *The Pleasures of the Past.* New York: W.W. Norton, 1989.

Chancellor, E. Beresford. *The Annals of Fleet Street.* New York: Frederick A. Stokes Co., 1913.

———. *Life in Regency and Early Victorian Times: An Account of the Days of Brummell and D'Orsay, 1800–1850.* London: B.T. Batsford, 1926.

———. *Lives of the Rakes.* Vol. 6. London: New York, 1925.

———. *Memorials of St. James's Street; Together With, The Annals of Almack's.* London: Grant Richards, Ltd., 1922.

———. *The Pleasure Haunts of London During Four Centuries.* London: Constable, 1925.

Charlesworth, George. *A History of British Motorways.* London: T. Telford, 1984.

Chesney, Kellow. *The Victorian Underworld.* Harmondsworth, England: Penguin, 1979.

Clark, A.A. *Police Uniform and Equipment, 1840 to Present.* Aylesbury, England: Shire Publications, 1991.

Colson, Percy. *White's, 1693–1950.* London: Heinemann, 1951.

Coolidge, John. *Gustave Dore's London.* Dublin, N.H.: William Bauhan, 1994.

Coote, Stephen. *William Morris: His Life and Work.* New York: Smithmark Publishers, 1995.

Corey, Melinda, ed. *The Encyclopedia of the Victorian World.* New York: Henry Holt & Co., 1996.

Cunningham, Colin. *Building for the Victorians.* Cambridge: Cambridge University Press, 1985.

Cunnington, Phyllis. *Handbook of English Costume in the Nineteenth Century.* London: Faber & Faber, 1970.

Curl, James Steven. *Book of Victorian Churches.* London: B.T. Batsford, 1995.

Curtin, Michael. *Propriety and Position: A Study of Victorian Manners.* New York: Garland Publishing, 1987.

Davidoff, Leonore. *The Best Circles: Society, Etiquette and the Season.* Totowa, N.J.: Rowman & Littlefield, 1973.

Delgado, Alan. *Victorian Entertainment.* New York: American Heritage Press, 1971.

Denvir, Bernard. *The Early Nineteenth Century: Art, Design, and Society, 1789–1852.* London: Longmans, 1984.

Dimond, Frances. *Crown and Camera: The Royal Family and Photography, 1842–1910.* Harmondsworth, England: Viking, 1987.

Doyle, John. *The Seven Years of William IV.* London: Avalon Press, 1952.

Duff, David. *Victoria Travels: Journeys of Queen Victoria Between 1830 and 1900.* London: Frederick Muller, 1970.

Dyos, H.J. *The Victorian City: Images and Realities.* 2 vols. London: Routledge & Kegan Paul, 1973.

Eckardt, Wolf von. *Oscar Wilde's London: A Scrapbook of Vices and Virtues, 1880–1900.* Garden City, N.Y.: Anchor Press. 1987.

Eeles, Henry S. *Brooks's, 1764–1964.* London: Country Life Ltd., 1964.

Elmes, James. *Metropolitan Improvements; or, London in the Nineteenth Century.* New York: B. Blom, 1968.

Erskine, Beatrice, ed. *Twenty Years at Court.* New York: Charles Scribner's Sons, 1916.

Esher, Reginald Baliol Brett, ed. *The Girlhood of Queen Victoria: A Selection From Her Majesty's Diaries Between the Years 1832 and 1840.* 2 vols. London: John Murray Ltd., 1912.

———. *The Letters of Queen Victoria: A Selection From Her Majesty's Correspondence Between the Years 1837 and 1861.* 3 vols. London: John Murray Ltd., 1907.

Farwell, Byron. *Eminent Victorian Soldiers: Seekers of Glory.* New York: W.W. Norton, 1985.

Ford, C. *A Hundred Years Ago: Britain in the 1880s in Words and Photographs.* London: Bloomsbury Books, 1994.

Fraser, Hilary. *Beauty and Belief: Aesthetics and Religion in Victorian Literature.* Cambridge: Cambridge University Press, 1986.

Fulford, Roger, ed. *Dearest Child: Letters Between Queen Victoria and the Princess Royal, 1858–1861.* New York: Holt, Rinehart & Winston, 1964.

———. *Dearest Mama: Letters Between Queen Victoria and the Crown Princess of Prussia, 1861–1864.* New York: Holt, Rinehart & Winston, 1969.

———. *Your Dear Letter: Private Correspondence Queen Victoria and the Crown Princess of Prussia, 1865–1871.* New York: Holt, Rinehart & Winston, 1971.

Gatrell, V.A.C. *The Hanging Tree: Execution and the English People 1770–1868.* Oxford: Oxford University Press, 1994.

Gourvish, T.R. and Alan O'Day. *Later Victorian Britain: 1867–1900.* New York: St. Martin's Press, 1988.

Green, D.R. *People of the Rookery: A Pauper Community in Victorian London.* London: King's College, 1986.

Harries-Jenkins, Gwyn. *The Army in Victorian Society.* Hull: University of Hull Press, 1993.

Harris, Michael, ed. *The Press in English Society from the Seventeenth to Nineteenth Centuries.* Rutherford: Fairleigh Dickinson University Press, 1986.

Harrison, Brian. *Drink and the Victorians: The Temperance Question in England 1815–1872.* Staffordshire: Keele University Press, 1994.

Harvey, A.D. *Britain in the Early Nineteenth Century.* New York: St. Martin's Press, 1978.

Hellerstein, Erna Olafson, ed. *Victorian Women: A Documentary Account of Women's Lives in Nineteenth-Century England, France, and the United States.* Stanford, Calif.: Stanford University Press, 1981.

Hembry, Phyllis. *The English Spa, 1560–1815: A Social History.* Rutherford: Fairleigh Dickinson University Press, 1990.

Herstein, Sheila. *A Mid-Victorian Feminist: Barbara Leigh Smith Bodichon.* New Haven: Yale University Press, 1986.

Hibbert, Christopher, ed. *Captain Gronow: His Reminiscences of Regency and Victorian Life 1810–60.* London: Kyle Cathie Ltd., 1991.

Hibbert, Christopher. *The Horizon Book of Daily Life in Victorian England.* New York: American Heritage Publishing Co., 1975.

Hitchcock, Henry Russell. *Early Victorian Architecture in Britain.* 2 vols. New York: Da Capo Press, 1972.

Holloway, S. *London's Noble Fire Brigades, 1833–1904.* London: Cassell, 1973.

Hughes, Mary V. *A London Child of the 1870s.* Oxford: Oxford University Press, 1970.

———. *A London Girl of the 1880s.* Oxford: Oxford University Press, 1978.

———. *A London Home in the 1890s.* Oxford: Oxford University Press, 1978.

Jones, Gareth Stedman. *Outcast London: A Study in the Relationships Between Classes in Victorian Society.* Oxford: Clarendon Press, 1971.

Jordan, John O., ed. *Literature in the Marketplace: Nineteenth-Century British Publishing and Reading Practices.* Cambridge: Cambridge University Press, 1995.

Keating, P.J. *The Working Classes in Victorian Fiction.* London: Routledge & Kegan Paul, 1971.

Lamington, Alexander Dundas, Cochrane Baillie and Ross Wishart. *In the Days of the Dandies.* Edinburgh: Blackwood, 1890.

Lejeune, Anthony. *The Gentlemen's Clubs of London.* New York: Dorset Press, 1979.

Lewis, Judith. *In the Family Way: Childbearing in the British Aristocracy, 1760–1860.* New Brunswick, N.J.: Rutgers University Press, 1986.

Low, Donald A. *Thieves' Kitchen: The Regency Underworld.* London: Dent, 1982.

Marcus, Steven. *The Other Victorians: A Study of Sexuality and Pornography in Mid-Nineteenth-Century England.* New York: Norton, W.W. 1985.

Margetson, Stella. *Leisure and Pleasure in the Nineteenth Century.* New York: Coward-McCann, 1969.

Mason, Michael. *The Making of Victorian Sexuality.* Oxford: Oxford University Press, 1994.

Mathias, Peter. *The First Industrial Nation: An Economic History of Britain, 1700–1914.* London: Methuen, 1969.

May, Trevor. *The Victorian Schoolroom.* Princes Risborough: Shire Publications, 1995.

McKendrick, Neil. *The Birth of a Consumer Society.* Bloomington: Indiana University Press, 1982.

McLaren, Angus. *Birth Control in Nineteenth-Century England.* New York: Holmes & Meier, 1978.

Miles, Alice Catherine. *Every Girl's Duty: The Diary of a Victorian Debutante.* London: Deutsch, 1992.

Miller, Wilbur R. *Cops and Bobbies: Police Authority in New York and London, 1830–1870.* Chicago: University of Chicago Press, 1977.

Mitchell, Sally. *Victorian Britain: An Encyclopedia.* New York: Garland Publishing, 1988.

Murphy, Sophia. *The Duchess of Devonshire's Ball.* London: Sidgwick & Jackson, 1984.

Murray, David L. *Regency: A Quadruple Portrait.* London: Hodder & Stoughton, 1936.

Musgrave, Clifford. *Regency Furniture, 1800–1830.* London: Faber, 1970.

Olsen, Donald J. *Town Planning in London: The Eighteenth and Nineteenth Centuries.* New Haven: Yale University Press, 1982.

Oppenheim, Janet. *The Other World: Spiritualism and Psychical Research in England, 1850–1914.* Cambridge: Cambridge University Press, 1988.

Orbach, Julian. *Victorian Architecture in Britain.* New York: W.W. Norton, 1988.

Owen, Alex. *The Darkened Room: Women, Power and Spiritualism in Late Victorian England.* Philadelphia: University of Pennsylvania Press, 1990.

Owen, David. *The Government of Victorian London, 1855–1889.* Cambridge, Mass.: Belknap Press, 1982.

———. *The Parish of St. James Westminster Part Two: North of Piccadilly.* 2 vols. London: University of London, 1963.

Payne, P.L. *British Entrepreneurship in the Nineteenth Century.* Houndsmill, England: Macmillan Education, 1988.

Peck and Snyder. *Nineteenth Century Games and Sporting Goods.* Princeton, N.J.: Pyne Press, 1971.

Perugini, Mark Edward. *Victorian Days and Ways.* London: Hutchinson, 1946.

Peterson, M. Jeanne. *Family, Love, and Work in the Lives of Victorian Gentlewomen.* Bloomington: Indiana University Press, 1989.

Philips, David. *Crime and Authority in Victorian England: The Black Country 1835–1860.* London: Croom Helm, 1977.

Phillips, K.C. *Language and Class in Victorian England.* Oxford: Basil Blackwell, 1986.

Phillips, Walter C. *Dickens, Reade, and Collins: Sensation Novelists.* New York: Russell & Russell, 1962.

Plint, Thomas. *Crime in England: Its Relation, Character, and Extent, as Developed from 1801 to 1848.* New York: Arno Press, 1974.

Porter, Bernard. *The Origins of the Vigilant State: The London Metropolitan Police Special Branch Before the First World War.* Woodbridge: Boydell & Brewer, 1991.

Pratt, Edwin A. *A History of Inland Transport and Communication in England.* New York: A.M. Kelley, 1970.

Quennell, Peter, ed. *Mayhew's London Underworld.* North Pomfret: Trafalgar Square, 1987.

Reed, John. *Victorian Conventions.* Athens: Ohio University Press, 1985.

Reid, John C. *Bucks and Bruisers: Pierce Egan and Regency England.* London: Routledge & Kegan Paul, 1971.

Reid, Stuart J. *The Life and Times of Sydney Smith.* London: S. Low, Marston & Co., 1896.

Royle, Edward. *Modern Britain: A Social History, 1750–1985.* London: Routledge Chapman & Hall, 1988.

Rumbelow, Donald. *The Complete Jack the Ripper.* London: W.H. Allen, 1975.

———. *I Spy Blue: The Police and Crime in the City of London From Elizabeth I to Victoria.* London: Macmillan, 1970.

Schwartz, L.D. *London in the Age of Industrialization: Entrepreneurs, Labour Force and Living Conditions, 1700–1850.* Cambridge: Cambridge University Press, 1992.

Seaborne, Michael. *Photographer's London, 1839–1994.* London: Museum of London, 1995.

Seaman, L.C.B. *Life in Victorian London.* London: B.T. Batsford, 1973.

Shepherd, J. *A Social Atlas of London.* Oxford: Clarendon Press, 1974.

Shepherd, Thomas. *London and Its Environs in the Nineteenth Century.* New York: B. Blom, 1968.

Sheppard, Francis. *London 1808–1870: The Infernal Wen.* London: Secker & Warburg, 1971.

Shonfield, Zuzanna. *The Precariously Privileged: A Professional Family in Victorian London.* Oxford: Oxford University Press, 1987.

Simo, Melanie. *London and the Landscape: From Country Seat to Metropolis, 1783–1843.* New Haven: Yale University Press, 1988.

Sitwell, Edith. *Victoria of England.* London: Faber & Faber, 1936.

Skelley, Alan. *The Victorian Army at Home: The Recruitment and Terms and Conditions of the British Regular, 1859–1899.* London: Croom Helm, 1977.

Smith, Phillip T. *Policing Victorian London: Political Policing, Public Order, and the London Metropolitan Police.* Westport, Conn.: Greenwood Press, 1985.

Smitherman, P.H. *Military Uniforms of the British Army 1660–1790.* London: Hugh Evelyn, 1965.

Steedman, C. *Policing the Victorian Community: The Formation of English Provincial Police Forces, 1856–80.* London: Routledge & Kegan Paul, 1984.

Storch, Robert, ed. *Popular Culture and Custom in Nineteenth-Century England.* New York: St. Martin's Press, 1982.

Thompson, F.M.L. *English Landed Society in the Nineteenth Century.* London: Routledge & Kegan Paul, 1963.

———. *The Rise of Respectable Society: A Social History of Victorian Britain 1830–1900.* London: Fontana, 1988.

Toller, Jane. *The Regency and Victorian Crafts.* London: Ward Lock, 1969.

Walton, John K. *The English Seaside Resort: A Social History, 1750–1914.* New York: St. Martin's Press, 1983.

———. *Leisure in Britain, 1780–1939.* New York: St. Martin's Press, 1988.

Watson, Ernest B. *Sheridan to Robertson: A Study of the Nineteenth Century London Stages.* North Stratford: Ayer Company Publishers, Inc., 1963.

Weightman, Gavin. *Bright Lights, Big City: London Entertained, 1830–1950.* London: Collins & Brown, 1992.

White, R.J. *Life in Regency England.* New York: G. Putnam's Sons, 1963.

Wilkes, J. *The London Police in the Nineteenth Century.* Cambridge: Cambridge University Press, 1977.

Wilson, C. Anne. *Food and Drink in Britain: From the Stone Age to the Nineteenth Century.* Chicago: Academy Chicago Publishers, 1991.

Wohl, Anthony. *Endangered Lives: Public Health in Victorian Britain.* Cambridge: Harvard University Press, 1983.

———. *The Eternal Slum: Housing and Social Policy in Victorian London.* New York: Holmes & Meier, 1980.

Wood, Christopher. *Victorian Panorama: Paintings of Victorian Life.* London: Faber & Faber, 1991.

Worsley, Giles. *Architectural Drawings of the Regency Period, 1790–1837.* London: A. Deutsch, 1991.

Yelling, James A. *Slums and Slum Clearance in Victorian London.* London: Allen & Unwin, 1986.

Young, G.M. *Early Victorian England, 1830–1865.* 2 vols. London: Oxford University Press, 1934.

———. *Victorian England: Portrait of an Age.* New York: Oxford University Press, 1964.

Youngson, A.J. *The Scientific Revolution in Victorian Medicine.* London: Croom Helm, 1979.

Museums Featuring Regency or Victorian Subjects

The following list is by no means meant to be complete, but is intended as a representation of what forms of research concerning nineteenth-century daily life can be conducted through museums, their holdings and so forth.

Abbey House Museum—Exhibits include nineteenth- to twentieth-century costume, toys, dolls, domestic appliances. Also included are reconstructions of street scenes of the late eighteenth and nineteenth centuries representing such trades as chemist, haberdasher, hairdresser, saddler, tobacconist and printer. Abbey Road, Kirkstall, Leeds, West Yorkshire LS5 3EH. Tel: 0532 755821

Apsley House—Home of the first duke of Wellington, the museum displays collections of paintings, plate, furniture, porcelain and personal items related to the duke. 149 Piccadilly, London WIV 9FA. Tel: 499 5676

Arundel Toy Museum—Housed in an early 1800 cottage, the collection includes period dolls, dollhouses, soldiers, bears, games, etc. 23 High Street, Arundel, West Sussex BN18 9AD. Tel: 0903 883101 882908

Ashford Local History Museum—Exhibits reflect social and domestic life of the past 150 years. Topics include daily life, transport, crafts, business. Ashford Central Library, Church Road, Ashford, Kent. Tel: 0233 20649

Bath Postal Museum—Housed in what was the town's main post office during the first half of the nineteenth century, displays include history of letter writing, methods of carrying mail and emphasis on work of Ralph Allen and John Palmer. 8 Broad Street, Bath, Avon BA1 5LJ. Tel: 0225 60333

Biggar Gasworks Museum—Opened in 1839, the works ceased operation in 1973. The museum illustrates the complete process at a typical gasworks in the nineteenth century, as well as gas appliances. Gasworks Road, Biggar Ayshire Scotland. Tel: 0899 21050

Blandford Forum Museum—Good collections of domestic equipment, militaria and Victorian/Edwardian costume are found here. It also has a Rural Bygones Room. The Old Coach House, Bere's Yard, Market Place, Blandford Forum, Dorset DT11 7HU

Bressingham Steam Museum—Housed here is one of the most comprehensive collections of steam engines in the world, with locomotives, road and industrial engines. Bressingham, Diss, Norfolk IP22 2AB. Tel: 037988 386

British Commercial Vehicle Museum—The museum covers the history of vehicles from horse-drawn period to present day. King Street, Leyland, Preston, Lancashire PR5 1LE. Tel: 0772 451011

British Dental Association Museum—The collection includes instruments, equipment and documentary history of the art and science of dentistry. 64 Wimpole Street, London W1M 8AL. Tel: 935 0875

British in India Museum—This museum focuses on life and achievements of the British in India, with collections of photographs, uniforms, coins, documents, paintings. Sun Street, Colne, Lancashire BB8 0JJ. Tel: 0282 63129

British Telecom Museum—The history of telecommunications is illustrated with over 150 telephones on display, including Bell's Gallows telephone of 1875, and working switchboards. 35 Speedwell Street, Oxford OX1 1RH. Tel: 0865 246601

Brontë Parsonage Museum—It is decorated in early nineteenth-century style, with a large collection of manuscripts, drawings, books and other personal possessions of the family on display. Haworth, Keighley, West Yorkshire BD22 8DR. Tel: 0535 42323

Carlyle's House—Thomas Carlyle and his wife occupied the house during nearly fifty years of the nineteenth century. Collections include furniture, personal items, portraits, manuscripts and items of everyday life. 24 Cheyne Row, Chelsea, London SW3. Tel: 352 7087

Castle Cary Museum—Housed in the Market House (1856), emphasis is upon nineteenth- to twentieth-century domestic equipment, trades, industries, documents, photographs and local social life. The Market House, Castle Cary, Somerset BA7 7AL. Tel: 0963 50277

Cater Museum—Though housed in an eighteenth-century building, principal exhibits include collection of nineteenth-century photographs, mid-Victorian furnishings and model fire engines. 74 High Street, Billericay, Essax CM12 9BS. Tel: 02774 22023

Churchill Gardens Museum—The museum building is a Regency house with Victorian additions, including a coach house. Displays include costume, furniture, paintings and period rooms: Victorian nursery, butler's pantry and parlor. Venns Lane, Hereford, Hereford and Worcester. Tel: 0432 268121

Clipper Ship Cutty Sark—The *Cutty Sark* is a nineteenth-century tea clipper that can be explored in its entirety by visitors. King William Walk, Greenwich, London SE10 9HT. Tel: 858 3445

Court Dress Collection—Housed in a series of restored nineteenth-century rooms, the collection dates from 1750 and includes court dress and uniforms. Kensington Palace, London W8 4PX. Tel: 937 9561

Dickens House Museum—Charles Dickens lived in the house from 1837–1839, and collections include letters, manuscripts, furnishings, pictures and personal items relating to the author. 48 Doughty Street, London WC1N 2LF. Tel: 405 2127

Disraeli Museum—The house was purchased by Benjamin Disraeli in 1848 and contains Disraeli's furnishings, paintings and much of his personal library. Hughenden Manor, High Wycombe, Buckinghamshire HP14 4LA. Tel: 0494 32580

Duke of Cornwall's Light Infantry Museum—Friendly staff are ready to answer questions about the history of the regiment and the amazing display of Napoleonic uniforms, weapons, maps, soldiers' personal items, etc. The Keep, Victoria Barracks, Bodmin, Cornwall PL31 1EG. Tel: 0208 2810

East Midlands Gas Museum—The collection is housed in an 1878 gasworks gatehouse and includes archival material illustrating the history of the production and distribution of gas in the East Midlands area, as well as a collection of domestic lighting, heating and cooking equipment. Emgas Service Centre, Aylestone Road, Leicester, Leicestershire LE2 7HQ. Tel: 0533 549414 ext. 2192

Flambards Victorian Village—The village is actually a full-scale reproduction of a Victorian street, complete with shops and their goods, fashions and carriages. Culdrose Manor, Helston, Cornwall TR13 0GA. Tel: 0326 57340

Florence Nightingale Museum—The location is Claydon House, once home to Lady Verney, Nightingale's sister, whom Nightingale often visited. In addition to objects associated with the nurse and the Crimean War, the house contains many fine examples of Victorian furnishings. Claydon House, Middle Claydon, nr Aylesbury, Bucks MK18 2EY. Tel: 029673 349 693

Fox Talbot Museum of Photography—The collection illustrates pioneering photographic achievements of William Henry Fox Talbot and the history of photography in general. Lacock, nr Chippenham, Wiltshire SN15 2LG. Tel: 024973 459

Gallery of English Costume—One of the most comprehensive collections in the country, it is supplemented by a research library (with very helpful curators) and eighteenth- and nineteenth-century magazines, etiquette books, fashion plates and photographs. Platt Hall, Platt Fields, Rusholm, Manchester M14 5LL. Tel: 061 224 5217

Gladstone Court Museum—This is a reconstruction of Victorian Street, including shops, equipment, costume, transport, also period advertisements. Biggar Museum Trust, Moat Park, Biggar, Ayshire ML12 6DT Scotland. Tel: 0899 21050

Great Barn Museum of Wiltshire Folk Life—Depicted here are the rural life and agriculture of Wiltshire during the nineteenth century, with exhibits including shops, crafts, domestic life, transport. Avebury, nr Marlborough, Wiltshire SN8 1RF. Tel: 06723 555

Greater Manchester Police Museum—Housed in the former police station built in 1879, displays include original cells, uniforms, equipment and photographs that tell the story of policing since 1819. Newton Street, Manchester M1 1ES. Tel: 061 855 3290

Gunnersby Park Museum—Once the home of the Rothschild's banking family, displays include nineteenth-century kitchens, items of domestic life, tools, costumes and textiles, toys and dolls and two of the family carriages. Gunnersby Park, London W3 8LQ. Tel: 992 1612

Gustav Holst Birthplace Museum—Holst was a pianist and composer whose life and work are illustrated within the Regency house. Also displayed are a late Regency sitting room, Victorian bedroom, working Victorian kitchen, scullery, laundry and basement servants' rooms. 4 Clarence Road, Cheltnham, Gloucestershire GL52 2AY. Tel: 0242 524846

HMS Victory/ Royal Naval Museum—The *Victory* was Admiral Lord Nelson's flagship at the Battle of Trafalgar (1805) and can now be boarded by visitors. The nearby Naval Museum covers the history of the navy from Tudor times, but is especially strong in the development of the navy during the Victorian period. HM Naval Base, Portsmouth, Hampshire PO1 3PZ. Tel: 0705 826682

Hoar Cross Hall—The hall is a seventy-room mansion built during the nineteenth century to replace the previous structure. Contains William Morris wall coverings, Victorian furniture, paintings, sewing machines and costumes. Hoar Cross, nr Burton-upon-Trent, Staffordshire DE13 8QS. Tel: 028375 224

Hornsbury Mill—Mill dates from 1870. Displays include complete milling machinery and equipment, agricultural tools, domestic items and clothing. Chard, Somerset TA20 3AQ. Tel: 04606 3317

House of Pipes—Exhibited in re-created Victorian shopping arcade, items include pipes, snuff boxes, matches, lighters, cigarette holders, trade tokens and more. Bramber, Steyning, West Sussex BN4 3WE. Tel: 0903 812122

Imperial War Museum—Housed in the former Bethlem Royal Hospital, or Bedlam (1815), collections illustrate all areas of military affairs with uniforms, documents, medals and photographs. Lambeth Road, London SE1 6HZ. Tel: 735 8922

Jane Austen's House—Austen's mother moved here with her daughters in 1809, and the house includes many family items, including a large number of letters and documents. Chawton, Hampshire GU34 1SD. Tel: 0420 83262

Keats House—The poet lived here from 1818-1820, and the interiors remain as they were during his residence, with the collection including books, letters, portraits and personal items. Wentworth Place, Keats Grove, Hampstead, London NW3 2RR. Tel: 435 2062

Lanhydrock—Most of the original seventeenth-century house burned in 1881 and was then rebuilt in late Victorian splendor. Kitchen quarters are complete period furnishings. Bodmin, Cornwall PL30 5AD. Tel: 0208 3320

Leeds Industrial Museum—The mill dates from 1806 and was at one time the world's largest woolen mill. Displays focus upon textile, clothing and optics trades, reconstructions of early sweatshops, workrooms and showrooms. Armley Mills, Canal Road, Leeds, West Yorkshire LS12 2QF. Tel: 0532 637861

Lilliput Museum of Antique Dolls and Toys—Dolls from the eighteenth and nineteenth centuries are exhibited, including examples from Madame Augusta Montanari of London, active in the 1860s. High Street, Brading, Isle of Wight PO36 0DJ. Tel: 0983 407231

Linley Sambourne House—Edward Linley Sambourne, *Punch* cartoonist, built the house in 1871, and the interiors remain unchanged. Items include original furnishings, William Morris wallpaper, photographs and family possessions. 18 Stafford Terrace, Kensington, London W8 7BH.

Medina Camera Museum—The more than sixty cameras exhibited comprise both still and moving types dating from the 1880s. Golden Hill Fort, Freshwater, Isle of Wight. Tel: 0983 753380

Mellerstain House—One of the finest examples of Robert Adam's architecture, the house contains plasterwork, period library, furniture, needlework and art collection. Mellerstain, Gordon, Berwickshire TD3 6LG. Tel: 057381 225

Merseyside Maritime Museum—The museum is located at the dockside and includes such buildings as the Albert Dock warehouse (1846) and the piermaster's house (1852). Collections also illustrate the history of the Port of Liverpool and the story of the seven million emigrants who left from Liverpool between 1830 and 1930. Pier Head, Liverpool, Merseyside L3 1DN. Tel: 051 709 155

Metropolitan Police Thames Division Museum—The River Police were founded in 1798, and the museum illustrates their history with documents, uniforms, crime relics and a wide range of equipment. Wapping Police Station, 98 Wapping High Street, London E1 9NE. Tel: 488 5391

Mounted Branch Museum—The history of the force—from its inception as London's Bow Street Patrol to present day—is outlined here. Metropolitan Police Mounted Branch, Imber Court, East Molesey, Surrey KT8 0BT. Tel: 541 1212

Museum of Costume—Many examples of male, female and children's period clothing, including royal examples, are displayed in room settings covering over a century of history. A Fashion Research Centre and library are affiliated and located at 4 The Circus, within walking distance. Staff are sometimes willing to point you in the right direction when you know what it is you're looking for. Assembly Rooms, Bennett Street, Bath, Avon BA1 2QH. Tel: 0225 461111

Museum of the Duke of Wellington's Regiment—Displays include weapons, uniforms, equipment, medals and personal memorabilia and items of the first duke of Wellington. Bankfield Museum, Akroyd Road, Halifax, West Yorkshire HX3 6HG. Tel: 0422 54823

Museum of the Staffordshire Regiment (The Prince of Wales's)—Exhibits cover the history of the regiment from its origins in 1705 and include items relating to the Sikh Wars, the Crimea, Indian Mutiny, Zulu Wars and South Africa. Regimental Headquarters, Whittington Barracks, Lichfield, Staffordshire WS14 9PY. Tel: 0543 433333 ext. 229

National Army Museum—The museum houses an extraordinary collection of uniforms covering five centuries and containing twenty thousand items. There is also a Weapons and Portrait Gallery. Royal Hospital Road, Chelsea, London SW3 4HT. Tel: 730 0717

National Maritime Museum—Exhibits cover ship design, ships' logs and furnishings, telescopes, maps, weapons, uniforms and personal items, such as the coat in which Lord Nelson died. Romney Road, Greenwich, London SE10 9NF. Tel: 858 4422

National Railway Museum—The museum tells the story of the railway in Britain with a large collection of locomotives, including Queen Victoria's state railway carriage, models, photos, film, signal boxes and other equipment. Leeman Road, York YO2 4XJ. Tel: 0904 21261

Newstead Abbey—The house, once a monastary, was purchased in 1540 and owned by the Byron family until 1817, when poet Lord Byron was forced to sell in order to meet his debts. Collections include Byron's manuscripts, letters, portraits, furnishings, Crimean War relics and architectural plans. Linby, Nottinghamshire NG15 8GE. Tel: 0623 793557

Osborne House—Built by Queen Victoria and Prince Albert in 1845 as a private royal residence, all rooms are virtually the same as when the family lived here. It contains excellent examples of Victorian design and furnishings. East Cowes, Isle of Wight. Tel: 0983 200022

Pighouse Collection—Housed in former piggery of Corr House, displays include twenty-seven hundred acquisitions made over 150 years, including Victorian dresses, bills, household items, needlework, etc. Corr House, Cornafean, County Cavan, Ireland. Tel: 049 37248

Police Museum—The museum covers law enforcement in Bath over 150 years. Bath Police Station, Manvers Street, Bath, Avon BA1 1JN Tel: 0225 63451 ext. 272

Queen Alexandra's Royal Army Nursing Corps Museum—Illustrated here is the history of army nursing from Crimean War to present. Archival photos and documents and Florence Nightingale's carriage are displayed. Regimental Headquarters, QARANC, Royal Pavilion, Farnborough Road, Aldershot, Hampshire GU11 1PZ. Tel: 0252 24431 ext. 301/315

Robert Opie Collection—This is one of the most comprehensive collections of old advertising memorabilia, including packaging, signs, trade and display cards, posters, boxes and bottles. Albert Warehouse, Gloucester Docks, Gloucester, Gloucestershire GL1 2EH. Tel: 0452 302309

Royal Borough Collection—The exhibits emphasize the connections between Windsor and the royal family, conditions in Victorian Windsor, local shops and trades and social life of the town. Windsor and Eton Central Station, Windsor, Berkshire SL4 1PJ. Tel: 0753 857837

Royal Corps of Transport Regimental Museum—Displays tell the history of transport in the British Army from the eighteenth century onward. Vehicles, uniforms, photographs, documents, weapons are on hand. Buller Barracks, Aldershot, Hampshire GU11 2BX. Tel: 0252 24431 ext. 2417

Royal Crown Derby Museum—Displays are of derby pottery and glass from the seventeenth century onward, with a strong collection of nineteenth-century examples. 194 Omaston Road, Derby, Derbyshire DE3 8JZ. Tel: 0332 47051

Royal Pavilion—Designed by John Nash and built between 1815 and 1822 for George IV, it contains Regency furnishings, decor, silver and kitchens. Brighton, East Sussex BN1 1UE. Tel: 0273 603005

Royal Pump Room Museum—The Pump Room was built in 1842 and has a sulphur well in its basement. Exhibits include pottery, costumes and Victoriana. Royal Parade, Harrogate, North Yorkshire. Tel: 0423 503340

Royal Welch Fusiliers Regimental Museum—With origins in 1689, the regiment played prominent parts in the Napoleonic Wars, the Crimean War, the Indian Mutiny and the Boer War. Caernarfon Castle, Caernarfon, Gwynedd LL57 2AY Wales. Tel: 0286 3362

Sandringham House Museum—The original eighteenth-century house was completely rebuilt in 1870 for Queen Victoria's son Edward, Prince of Wales. Collections include original furnishings, paintings and personal items relating to the royal family. Sandringham, nr King's Lynn, Norfolk PE35 6EN. Tel: 0553 772675

Spode Museum—While the firm was founded in 1770, much is focused upon the bone china introduced by the company circa 1800 and the company's parian porcelain, which debuted in 1842 and was a favorite decorative ware during the Victorian period. Church Street, Stoke-on-Trent, Staffordshire ST4 1BX. Tel: 0782 46011

S.S. Great Britain—The ship was built in Bristol and launched in 1843 as the world's first oceangoing, propeller-driven iron ship, now fully restored. Great Western Dock, Gas Ferry Road, Bristol, Avon BS1 5TY. Tel: 0272 20680

Standen—The house was built in 1894 for James Beale, solicitor and friend of William Morris, and so contains many fine examples of furniture made by Morris & Co. East Grinstead, West Sussex RH19 4NE. Tel: 0342 23029

Town Docks Museum—Housed in the former Dock Office (1870), the fine Victorian interiors have been preserved. Displays relate to whaling, local fishing industries and shipbuilding. Queen Victoria Square, Kingston-upon-Hull, North Humberside HU1 3DX. Tel: 0482 222737

Transport Museum—Vehicles include buses, trams, trolleybuses and 1882 horse tram. Mallard Road, Bournemouth, Dorset BH8 9PN.

Transport Museum—Nineteenth-century vehicles, including a horse-drawn fire engine, 1880 tram and farm wagons are on display. The Old Fire Station, Bearland, Gloucester, Gloucestershire (by appointment only)

The Tyrwhitt-Drake Museum of Carriages—Most carriages on display are nineteenth-century examples, including Queen Victoria's dress landau built in 1870. Mill Street, Maidstone, Kent ME15 6YE.

Victoria and Albert Museum—The museum encompasses many centuries and areas of interest but is especially strong in Victorian interior design, art, pottery and glass and costume. Cromwell Road, South Kensington, London SW7 2RL. Tel: 938 8500

William Morris Gallery—The nineteenth-century designer's work is documented with wallpapers, textiles, carpets, furniture, glass and ceramics. Water House, Lloyd Park, Forest Road, Walthamstow, London E17 4PP. Tel: 527 5544 ext. 4390

Windsor Castle—While the castle has medieval origins and the collections encompass centuries of history, there are many items and rooms related to George IV, William IV and, of course, Queen Victoria. Windsor, Berkshire. Tel: 07535 68286

Yorkshire Carriage Museum—Displays are of work and pleasure vehicles from town coaches to bread vans, from the coaching and driving age. Aysgarth Falls, Aysgarth, Leyburn, North Yorkshire DL8 3SR. Tel: 09693 652

Nineteenth-Century Societies

Beau Monde—Regency special interest chapter of the Romance Writers of America, newsletter, annual conference. P.O. Box 3313, Burbank, CA 91508-3313; website: **http://www.members.aol.com/regencyrdr/beaumonde.htm**

Georgian Society—Regency dancing. Website: **http://www.thuntek.net/mandala/artists/georgian**

Jane Austen Society of North America—Scholars and enthusiasts study Jane Austen via regional groups, annual conference, publications. Contact Barbara Larkin, 2907 Northland Dr., Columbia, MO 65202; website: **http://www.pemberley.com/janeinfo/janausoc.html**

Napoleonic Association—5 Thingwall Dr., Irby, Wirral, Merseyside L61 3XN England; website: **http://www.napoleon.org/**

Napoleonic Society of America—Members celebrate and research life and times of Napoleon; newsletter, meetings, tours, research center. 1115 Ponce de León Blvd., Clearwater, FL 34616; (813) 586-1779

Society of London Ladies The Society newsletter, *Belle Letters*, is published by Kristine Hughes and celebrates the Georgian, Regency and Victorian periods; bimonthly newsletter, meetings. Website: **http://www.members.aol.com/LONDON20/index.html**
E-mail: **London20@aol.com**

Victorian Society in America—Monthly newsletter, local chapters, annual meetings, tours. East Washington Square, Philadelphia, PA 19106; (215) 627-4252; website: **http://www.burrows.com/vict.html**

Victorian Society—The Society is concerned with preserving Victorian architecture. Sites in Britain, newsletter, lectures. 1 Priory Gardens, London W4 1TT

INDEX